☟ **W9-BZG-801**

COMMUNAL SOCIETIES IN AMERICA
AN AMS REPRINT SERIES

HEAVEN ON EARTH

AMS PRESS
NEW YORK

THE DESERET ALPHABET

HEAVEN ON EARTH
A Planned Mormon Society

BY
WILLIAM J. McNIFF
Miami University

The Mississippi Valley Press
Oxford, Ohio
1940

Library of Congress Cataloging in Publication Data

McNiff, William John.
    Heaven on earth.

    (Communal societies in America)
    1. Mormons and Mormonism.   I.   Title.
BX8635.M332   1974   289.3   72-8632
ISBN 0-404-11007-X

Reprinted from the edition of 1940, Oxford, Ohio
First AMS edition published in 1974
Manufactured in the United States of America

AMS PRESS INC.
NEW YORK, N.Y.   10003

TO

L. D. S.

PREFACE

In its highest reaches, Mormon theology desired to bring about a heaven on this earth, and this present book portrays efforts of the Mormon leaders to achieve their Zion. In the development of their culture Mormon leaders made particular efforts to develop a distinctive Latter Day Saint attitude towards education, the drama, and music. Economic enterprises such as community coöperatives and funds to assist emigrants were part of the ecclesiastical campaign for a better order here below.

Church publications, such as the *Deseret News, The Millennial Star,* and *The Journal of Discourses,* illustrate both the theory and practice of Mormonism in planning and meeting the practical difficulties of a saintly commonwealth; free use has been made of these church sources for this volume. Much information on the Utah of 1847 to 1877 has been gained from works and articles written by both residents in the Territory of that period and by the many travellers who found it worth their while to publish their thoughts about the New Jerusalem being fashioned by the followers of Joseph Smith and Brigham Young.

In this narrative, the analysis of the attempt of the Mormon leaders is concluded in the year 1877. There are several reasons for this date. By 1877, the year of Brigham Young's death, the ideals of Mormonism had been firmly implanted in the Church doctrines. The teachings and deeds of both Joseph Smith and Brigham Young still are influential, even though the Mormon environment has changed greatly since 1877. Another reason for taking the year 1877 as a convenient stopping place lies in the fact that outside forces were effectively working upon Mormon society by that time. The railroad had come to Utah in 1869; by 1877 those forces and people who now found it comparatively éasy to reach Utah had had ample time and resources to effect a planned Zion. What previously had been a problem of Mormon leadership and Mormon ideals now had the added problem of absorbing outside interests to Mormonism or else Mormonism itself would be absorbed by those outside interests. This struggle still goes on.

That the beliefs and practices have both received their full share of scholarly attention is attested by the numerous collections of books and articles on Mormonism in the United States. I am especially indebted for the many courtesies extended to me by the librarians in charge of the Berrain collection at the New York Public Library and of the collection at Columbia University. I wish to express my graditude for the many kindnesses on the part of the librarians at Widener Library, Harvard University; at the Divinity School at the University of Chicago; and at the Salt Lake City Free Public Library.

Professor Lewis D. Stilwell, of Dartmouth College, first stimulated my interest in Mormon cultural life. Further enthusiasm was engendered by Dr. Frederick Merk, of Harvard University, and Dr. A. C. Cole, of Western Reserve University. I owe a deep debt of gratitude to Dr. Philip D. Jordan, of Miami University, for his unfailing patience, careful criticisms, and helpful suggestions. To Dr. E. J. Howard and Mr. E. W. King of the Miami University faculty, and to President H. C. Dale, of the University of Idaho, I wish to express my appreciation for assistance. I am indebted to Miss Betty Biller and to Mr. Don Hatcher for assistance in preparing the manuscript. For mistakes and errors, as well as interpretations, I alone am responsible.

Oxford, Ohio   W. J. McN.
February 1, 1940.

CONTENTS

CHAPTER I

AMERICA THE BEAUTIFUL

MORMONISM

WHATEVER ELSE the early ninteenth century lacked, it did not fail to have individuals who were most eager to point out the way to a better life. For planners of Utopias, the land on the frontier offered limitless possibilities for that type of human mind which enjoys planning a heaven on earth. America the beautiful, with its spacious skies and amber waves of grain, had more to it than the flag-waving shibboleth of mere land-grabbing. Emerson was a sympathetic understander of this aspect of American life. In a letter to Carlyle he wrote: "We are all a little wild here with numberless projects of social reform. Not a reading man but has a draft of a New Community in his waistcoat pocket."[1] The sage of Concord once attended a meeting of the Friends of Universal Progress in Boston during 1840, which he said was made up of "madmen, madwomen, men with beards, dunkers, muggletonians, come-outers, groaners, Agrarians, Seventh-day Baptists, Quakers, Abolitionists, Calvinists, Unitarians, and philosophers."[2] There were few of these groups which did not have a panacea for the illnesses afflicting mankind.

Some of the groups proposed abolishing the status quo immediately and sweepingly in such revered institutions as government and religion. Others preferred to abolish specific evils such as negro slavery or war. Coöperation —as witness Brook Farm—was in the air. For those whose digestive systems needed care, Sylvester Graham was advocating a saner diet than the majority of Americans practiced. For those who were not willing to live by bread alone, there were such frontier preachers as Alexander Campbell, who founded "The Disciples of Christ" about 1812, and William Miller, who was preaching "Second Adventism" at Low Hampton, New York, about twenty years later.

The inhabitants near Rochester, New York, seemed especially adept at giving their emotions public expression and group organization. It has been pointed out that if one took Rochester as a centre and used a line fifty miles in length as a radius, one could draw a circle that would include much of the territory in which the excitement of this period took place. This circle would include Batavia, the scene of the Morgan abduction in 1826, an episode which gave rise to much of the Anti-Masonic feeling of the time. It would also include the town of Acadia, where the Fox sisters heard mysterious rappings and first demonstrated the possibilities of modern spiritualism. This is the region in which Fourier's schemes of social planning caused great excitement. In addition, it is also on the edge of the "burnt-district", an area dear to evangelists seeking crowded and amenable revival meetings.

Into this highly charged region came a family of Smiths from Vermont. Among the children was Joseph, the fourth child of a family of seven sons and three daughters. This boy, according to his own account, was confused by the theological discussions carried on by the frontier preachers. It must be remembered that each frontier sect claimed that it had the answer to the problems which agitated men's souls. For those victims who disagreed, the preachers gleefully predicted the vivid torments of hell fire and brimstone. Ecclesiastical punches were not pulled in Christian deference for a doubter's sensitiveness. The blows were aimed at a convert for an immediate knock-out blow. Joseph Smith was caught in this seething cauldron of ecclesiastic claims and denials.

Wherein Joseph Smith differed from many another human being whose reason and emotion were worked upon at revival meetings lies in his attempt to solve the theological puzzle. For thousands of people, Joseph Smith did solve the puzzle. For many others he added a piece which never would fit. In fact, for some of his critics he made an entirely new puzzle out of an old problem, when he contended that he was the prophet of a new religion, Mormonism.

There is difficulty in determining what sort of person Joseph Smith was as a youth. Opponents of Mormonism assert that the prophet's parents were illiterate and superstitious. It is even contended that a strain of epilepsy ran through the family.[3] Joseph Smith himself, the doubters of Mormonism say, was the village ne'er-do-well, was addicted to searching for gold by the light of the moon, and was willing, for pay, to find underground water by means of a forked hazel-stick.

Mormons vehemently deny these charges generally and specifically. The Smiths were undoubtedly poor, but on the American frontier the mark of poverty was no disgrace. In spite of the Smiths' poverty, it was the treachery of a supposed friend which forced them to lose their possessions. The Mormons admit Joseph Smith searched for precious metals. But this searching was done only as the agent of another man. Although compelled by need to take this man's wages, Joseph, according to Mormon writers, had tried to convince his employer of the worthlessness of gold and silver mines in western New York and Pennsylvania.[4]

Whatever his faults and advantages, Joseph Smith seems to have had personal magnetism. He was also intensely devoted to whatever he undertook. Joseph's story of his religious life runs somewhat as follows: in 1820, he was stirred by a religious revival and thereupon took his religious doubts greatly to heart and considered them carefully. Then followed a period of emotional turmoil. In September, 1823, an angel of the Lord, Moroni, appeared to Joseph and told the eighteen-year-old lad that the Lord had an important work for him to do. Through him God's power and kingdom were to be restored to earth. The angel described to Joseph a place where were hidden gold plates on which he would find the story of the lost tribes of Israel. Two peep-stones—Urim and Thummim—were to help Joseph read the gold plates.

Joseph, according to his own story, soon found the spot described by the angel. It was then, and still is, known as Cumorah Hill; it is situated about twenty-five miles southwest of Rochester, New York. As Joseph was preparing to carry off his treasure, the angel, Moroni, reappeared and told the boy that he must wait another four years before taking the plates. Joseph waited and, in four year's time, came and received the plates. As soon as a scribe could be procured, Joseph began the work of translating the hieroglyphics from "Reformed Egyptian" into western New York vernacular. Several scribes were employed before Oliver Cowdery, a teacher, appeared and satisfactorily filled the position. The prophet sat behind a screen and read what he saw to the copyist seated on the opposite side of the partition. No profane eye was to see these plates. Doubters began to question; therefore Joseph, in time, received a revelation giving him permission to have witnesses. The testimonials of these witness may be seen prefixed to every copy of the Book of Mormon. What Joseph read to Oliver Cowdery makes up the contents of the Book of Mormon.

In 1829, this book was sent on its way into the world in an edition of five thousand copies. A year later the Church of Jesus Christ of Latter Day Saints was organized at Fayetteville, Seneca County, New York. The later careers of the six charter members of the church illustrate the strenuous conditions surrounding Mormons in the early days of their faith. Two were murdered in jail, two apostatized, one became an anti-Brighamite (as those were known who refused to follow Brigham Young as leader of the Mormon Church after Joseph Smith's death), and one died of over-exertion.

Palmyra, another town in western New York, soon gained recognition as a Mormon centre. But those who were actively hostile to the new faith were strong enough to drive out from their midst those whom they considered religious zealots. A new settlement of the believers was made at Kirtland, Ohio, soon followed by a second at Independence, Missouri. In none of these places could the Mormons and their Gentile (as all non-Mormons became known to the followers of Joseph Smith) neighbors remain at peace with one another for any length of time. In the Ohio settlement a bank controlled by Joseph Smith collapsed in the panic of 1837. After this the prophet deemed it wise to move to the Missouri settlements. Many of the faithful soon followed their leader.

Certain inhabitants of Missouri, however, were even more hostile to Mormonism than the people of New York and Ohio had been. The frontiersmen of Missouri were not inclined to treat those leniently whom they regarded as religious fanatics. They accused the Mormons of "blasphemy, pretensions of healing the sick, casting out devils, interfering with negro slaves, and declaring that the coun-

try was theirs by revelation."[5] Finally, the Mormons were
accused of that unpardonable sin in democracy— of vot-
ing in a compact mass under the dictatorship of their leaders. All of these factors led to the use of force by the Missourians. The Mormons, on the other hand, declared that
their prosperity as a group and their neutral stand on the
slavery question aroused the ire of their neighbors. By
1839, the Missourians had forced the Mormons from their
state. To the Mormons the days spent in Missouri are bitter memories of bloodshed, of hate, and of injustice.

A temporary resting place—for that is all it proved to
be—was eventually found by the Mormons at Commerce,
on the Illinois bank of the Mississippi River. Here the
Mormons were assured of an hospitable reception, for their
suffering in Missouri had aroused sympathy for them in
many districts. New York speculators also were willing to
rid themselves of the area about Commerce, obviously in-
fected with malarial fevers and seemingly immune to
financial booming. The politicians were willing to grant
favors in order to gain Mormon votes in a closely contested
state. And finally Joseph Smith had a revelation on the
subject.

The Mormons bought the land and by hard work in time
made the locality fit for human habitation. Within a short
period the city of Commerce became Nauvoo, an appellation
which, according to its new founder, meant "beauty and
rest"; Nauvoo soon boasted a population of 15,000. From
foreign lands converts arrived who added variety to the
native strain of Mormonism. From the Illinois legislature
was obtained a charter which made the city virtually in-
dependent of state control. Printing presses were soon
busy sending forth copies of the Book of Mormon and other
religious publications of the sect. A temple was in process
of construction, a university was planned, and Nauvoo had

all the earmarks of a booming Western town; but with this difference, there was an overwhelming sense of religious enthusiasm present in all of its affairs. Joseph Smith was grand chaplain of the Masonic lodge, treasurer of the bank, ex-officio judge of the municipal court, mayor of Nauvoo, registrar of municipal deeds, lieutenant-general of the Nauvoo legion, editor of the Mormon publication, *Times and Seasons,* president, apostle, and prophet of the Mormon Church, and, finally, a candidate for the presidency of the United States.

With rumors of polygamy in the air and direct evidence of the Mormons' aspiration to political power before their eyes, the Gentiles about Nauvoo became aggressively anti-Mormon. The aggression broke out into physical hostility in June, 1844. In its columns the Nauvoo *Expositor* attacked Joseph Smith. The office of the *Expositor,* in return, was attacked and the type destroyed. The owners of the press procured warrants in the neighboring town of Carthage against the Mormon leaders. The anti-Mormons asserted that a conviction of Joseph Smith would be impossible in Nauvoo. In fact, they insisted that no Mormon could be convicted in the Mormon stronghold, nor could any Gentile obtain a fair trial. Therefore, the owners of the press had obtained warrants in the more congenial (to them) atmosphere of Carthage. A local civil war seemed impending in southern Illinois. Governor T. Ford, of Illinois, arrived at Carthage and sent a posse to secure the men named in the warrant. At first Joseph and his companions thought it best to go into hiding. Eventually, however, the Mormon leader decided to go to Carthage. Joseph prophesied truly when he said they were going "like lambs to the slaughter." A mob broke into the jail where the Mormon Prophet was committed and brutally murdered him and his brother, Hyrum, on July 27, 1844.

The era of the prophet and seer was now over. The Carthage mob did more than kill a man when they murdered Joseph Smith. After July 27, 1844, the Mormon religion had an ever greater hold upon its adherents than it had possessed while Joseph Smith had been alive. The supreme sacrifice of its leader placed a halo of martyrdom about the founder of Mormonism. The murder also widened the gap between those without and those within the folds of the new religion. The sense of having been unjustly treated gave further solidarity to the Mormon group. The immediate result of Joseph Smith's death was the rise of Brigham Young to a position of preëminence among the amazed and bewildered inhabitants of Nauvoo.

The next great force in developing Mormonism was Brigham Young, who like Smith was a Vermonter transplanted to western New York. He joined the Mormon Church in 1832, when thirty-one years of age. From the first, his ability was recognized. Mormon tradition tells that at the first meeting of the Prophet and Brigham Young, the former prophesied that Young would one day lead the Church.[6] Brigham Young's earliest outstanding success came in the building up of a missionary centre for Mormonism at Liverpool, England. Young was in the eastern United States on a missionary trip when the word of Joseph Smith's death reached him. He immediately returned to Nauvoo, where another prominent Mormon of the period, Sidney Rigdon, was putting before the Mormons at that place a claim to be the inheritor of Joseph's power of revelation and also to the presidency of the Church. Young opposed the plans of Rigdon, holding that Joseph Smith's powers were inherited by the council of twelve, of which Brigham Young was head. The Mormons gave the council of twelve a vote of confidence and the question of the presidency was left to a future time. Young, as the leading member of the council of twelve, thereby became the actual head of the Mormon Church. In a few days Rigdon and his followers were excommunicated or, as the Mormons say, cut-off from the Church, and Brigham had a group which would follow his lead.

From the moment of Young's accession a decisiveness and sureness asserted itself in the Mormon higher councils. It became apparent that soon there would be a severe struggle with the Gentiles; therefore the Mormons began preparations for another move westward. By day and night, it is said, the ring of the anvils and the sawing of wood could be heard in Nauvoo. Horses were shod, and twelve thousand wagons were prepared for a journey of a length unknown even to the leaders. Necessities of all sorts, for only necessities could be taken, were loaded on-to the wagons. Even with departure an absolute certainty, Brigham Young ordained that the temple be completed— a wise move, for thus was one of Joseph Smith's prophetic utterances fulfilled. As soon as the temple was dedicated, the sacred vessels were packed for removal. Land was sold to anyone who could buy; and on February 4, 1846, the great exodus, the Mormon "Via Dolorosa," began.

Across the prairies the stern impassioned pilgrim feet started, small children crying with the bitter cold as their parents faced a numb future. By June, sixteen thousand people were on the march; but another homeless winter (1846-47) of uncertainty had to be endured amidst the greatest hardships. At the camp of Winter Quarters a fever broke out, and over six hundred bodies were buried there. While on the way west, the Mormons first heard of the war going on between the United States and Mexico. A Federal officer was sent to recruit a battalion among these exiles, and without difficulty a band of over five hundred men was enlisted. An opinion is held that these men signed merely for pay, for money was sorely needed among the Mormons. But credit must be given to these men who marched as an expeditionary force the two thousand and eighty miles to California, via the Santa Fé and Old Spanish trails. It is hardly conceivable that men would leave their families in such a predicament for a few months' pay.[7]

Reports of Salt Lake Valley and other valleys of the mountain region had been brought by the Rocky Mountain fur traders and trappers to the comparatively well-settled East. It is fairly certain that Brigham Young had read Fremont's *Journal* describing the Salt Lake region and had talked with Father De Smet, a Jesuit priest who had explored the district.[8] The Mormon leaders were looking for a place far from the centres of Gentile civilization. In 1847, a scouting expedition of 145 men, under Brigham Young, started westward in order to find a new haven for their oppressed group.

The scouting party was followed by other bands at regular intervals. Brigham Young maintained strict order; disobedience in any serious matter was followed by excommunication. The men were organized into military units of "hundreds," "fifties," and "tens." Military obedience was exacted by the bishops, elders, and deacons of the Church who commanded these units. The Mormons were in earnest and were willing to sacrifice much to escape the Gentiles. And Brigham Young, with all the power at his command, was determined that the group should carry out its religious beliefs with unobstructed freedom. Thus, one sees the American pioneer submerging his individuality in that of the Mormon group. Here also is evident the power of a religious enthusiasm both to bind men of a certain belief closer to each other, and, at the same time, alienate them from all other men.

The first group of Mormons entered Great Salt Lake Valley on July 24, 1847. To Brigham Young this was "the place," and work was started. The ground was so dry it was necessary to irrigate before a plow could take a firm hold. Large-scale irrigation was a new method of cultivation to the American pioneer; yet by means of it the Mormons made "the desert bloom as the rose." The Salt Lake Valley is four thousand feet above the level of the sea. On the east rises the Wasatch range of mountains, in the canyons of which the pioneers cut their lumber. From its streams, sparkling in the clear desert air, came the life-giving water which the Mormons turned onto their lands. Once the water was brought to this region, where the annual average rainfall is only thirteen inches, the land became fertile.

The majority of settlements in Utah were made, not by individuals, but by groups. In each new colony the first question that had to be settled was the amount of water available. The land was then parcelled out in order to obtain the most efficient use of this water supply to the community. Thus in Salt Lake City the maximum amount of land allowed to an able-bodied individual was twenty acres. After they had investigated the available water supply, the early settlers of Springville also decided to limit the holdings in their settlement to twenty acres.

The necessity of employing irrigation in order to win a food supply from the hitherto barren land had important effects upon the life of the settlers. Nature was not lavish with her gifts. There were no great areas of underbrush to be cleared or forests to be girdled before the plow could be used. Here fertility had to be wooed and carefully led to the soil, not driven away by fire and axe. Painstaking caution was a prime requisite for the Utah farmer. He could estimate early in the summer the amount of water available for the following year; and, to a certain extent, after the winter's snowfall the question of rainfall was eliminated from the farmer's mind.

The need for irrigation canals strengthened another factor in Mormon life. All members arriving in Utah had a common capital—their own labor. Few had much more. The need of water on this sun-baked soil was evident. There was only one way to bring water to the soil, and that was by coöperation. Under the control of the Church the men worked together and pooled their resources. A system of interdependence upon one another, and upon the church as a director of temporal affairs, grew up alongside of irrigation in Utah.

The early settlers frequently had the Indians in mind when they built their first cabins near enough to one another to do duty as forts in the event of hostilities. There was also the practical fact that a greater utilization of the water supply could be obtained by having the irrigated fields contiguous to each other on the outskirts of the town and by having the inhabitants of the town near one another in a small area. Waste ditches and draining difficulties could be concentrated and the labor necessary to bring the water into the town could be done most efficiently in a centralized area. This organization of community life which seemed most practicable had the added incentive of being socially desirable. Under these arrangements the settler could be near the bishop's home and the meeting house. Within this area the community dances, the spelling bees, and the religious meetings were held. And here the Church and its officers were near the people —a factor of importance, as the Church was interested in the temporal well-being of its members.

Utah, itself, was likely to intensify the desire for human companionship. The desert, with its lack of life, made the Mormons gather closely about the evening camp fire.

These Latter Day Saints were not to be hermits or ascetics living solitary lives in the deserts and mountains of Utah. The huge mountains overshadowing such towns as Provo, San Pete, or Manti made man, with his adobe houses, seem small and insignificant—and consequently drew the inhabitants near to one another. Undoubtedly, there were some who felt suffocated by the smoke from a neighbor's cabin, miles away; but the total effect of a Mormon's surroundings, both geographic and ecclesiastical, drew him into the village settlement.

It seemed at first that the Mormon leaders might have a place in which their religious ideas might be tried out on this earth. Here was the chance to attain a millennium on earth. But the Mormons were never quite able to achieve an absolute isolation on this practical earth. In addition to their inherited cultural background of Gentile customs, the Mormons always continued to be in contact with the Gentile world. Gentiles appeared in Great Salt Lake City soon after its founding; after a few years the name became Salt Lake City, and from this point on that designation will be used. In 1849, many Gentiles made Salt Lake City a stopping-place on their way to California. In 1869, the railroad connected Utah with the outside world. The desired isolation or insulation had never quite been achieved. In 1847, roughly speaking, Utah (as far as white inhabitants, at least, were concerned) was a region controlled by the Mormons. Thirty years later this relationship had changed. After 1869 Gentile influences in the management of Utah affairs have to be taken into account. Before that period they were subordinated to prevailing Mormon management. And, eight years after the coming of the railroad to Utah, another blow fell, which many thought would end Mormonism.

On August 20, 1877, Brigham Young died. His practical

ability and leadership had been the most important factor within Mormon councils since the martyrdom of Joseph Smith. The death of Brigham Young did not end Mormonism, but one is safe in saying that with his death and with the coming of the railroad to Utah in 1869 one phase in the development of Utah as a Mormon commonweath was brought to a close. After 1877 the successors of Brigham Young in the councils of the Mormon Church found that his hand had definitely directed the Church's attitude in esslesiastical, economic, and cultural matters. By 1877 the mould had been set. The Church did not adopt inflexible rules, but Joseph Smith and Brigham Young had given the Mormon Church basic principles and practices which have been followed since their time.

CHAPTER II

MAY GOD THY GOLD REFINE

ECONOMIC COOPERATION

FROM JULY, 1847, when the first pioneers emerged upon the sun-baked plains of the Salt Lake Valley, until the railroad came in 1869, the problem of obtaining the necessary food, clothing, and shelter was of primary importance. Therefore, the handling of the economic problems, in so far as the Church authorities attempted to handle this problem, was a fundamental problem of Mormonism in early Utah.[1] Experiments under Church auspices ranged from the setting up of individuals as farmers to attempts at founding coöperative stores and directing communal villages. The Church took upon itself the problem of bringing converts, especially from Europe, to Utah. It colonized, it manufactured, it transported converts and paved the way for pilgrims' feet, picturing a new heaven on earth; and, all in all, it prospered as an institution.

As with so much of Mormon life one finds the material and the spiritual intertwined, working together and influencing one another. Thus any understanding of the Church's attitude towards economic affairs necessitates a knowledge of the Mormon ecclesiastical organization and of Mormon leadership.

The actions and thought of the Mormon ecclesiastical hierarchy strongly affect the temporal lives of their followers as well as acting as guides in religious affairs. As head of the Mormon ecclesiastical hierarchy, Joseph Smith led his people in and out of New York, Ohio, Missouri, and Illinois. As head of the Mormon priesthood in Utah and throughout the world Brigham Young succeeded to a position which gave him immense power over his fellows. In the early days no member of the priesthood received any salary or wages for doing church tasks, and there were few Mormon men who did not occupy an office of some sort in the Church. The Mormons believed that one was more likely to become interested in an institution to which he gave time, effort, and personal thought.

The ecclesiastical leadership gave the direction and planned the campaigns. The mass of followers provided the disciplined troops. The likeness of the Mormon Church to an army has not gone unnoticed by observers. One commentator, writing in 1903, compared the Mormon Church of that day to what many considered the most efficient machine then devised by human ingenuity—the army of Kaiser Wilhelm II.[2] But if the Kaiser in shining armor was seeking his place in this world, the Mormon leaders in their sombre civilian attire were attempting to bring this world and the hereafter closer to one another.

The Mormon ecclesiastical organization has changed but slightly in practice since the days of Brigham Young. A description of the Mormon hierarchy is necessary in order to give one a complete and clear picture of how the Mormon Church works. The Church in action depends for its work upon a hierarchy of priests consisting of two divisions. Almost all male Mormons are members of one or the other of these divisions, and some may be members of both at the same time. The Melchisedek, or higher priesthood, consists of the apostles, patriarchs, high priests, seventies, and elders. The members of this division administer all the spiritual affairs of the Church. The Aaronic priesthood, the subordinate branch, is composed of the bishops, priests, deacons, and teachers. The members of this division administer the temporal affairs of the Church. Members of the higher order of priesthood can perform the functions of the lower, but the lower priesthood cannot perform the functions of the higher order.

The head of the entire Church is concentrated in a council known as the first presidency of the high priesthood. This council consists of a president and two counsellors— a body which governs all the affairs of the Church, both temporal and spiritual. In all meetings this body is given precedence. The first president, or chairman of this council, is considered the inheritor of Joseph Smith's power of prophecy—he is the prophet of God, seer, receiver of revelations, and translator.

Second in authority to the members of the first presidency are twelve apostles. Upon the death of the president, authority passes to this body. The president of the twelve, chosen in the first instance by reason of seniority of ordination, usually becomes president of the Church. The office of the twelve is to teach and preach throughout the world, regulating the affairs of the Church everywhere under the direction of the first presidency. It was as head of this group that Brigham Young led the Mormons in the days following the death of Joseph Smith.

The seventies are groups of various councils of seventy men, known as quorums. Each council of seventy has seven presidents, chosen out of the seventy. One of the first council of seventy presides over all the councils of seventies. The members of the seventies are the elders chosen for missionary work. At the April session of the semi-annual conferences in Salt Lake City, the elected officers of the Church are chosen by the officials in office and the appointments of others announced, including those as-

signed to missions. A show of hands by the delegates to
the conference ratifies the choice of officials, but the choice
of the officials is tantamount to an election. The leader
of a mission, if several missionaries go together to the
same place, also assumes the title of president. He, likewise,
has two counsellors, and the same procedure as that of
the parent organizations in Salt Lake City is followed, if
the number of missionaries assigned to a specified field,
such as England, warrants it.

The last office in the hierarchy is that of teacher. It is
through this office that the upper offices are apprised of
the needs and desires of the rank and file. It is the office
which assists the upper officers in making Mormonism
vital and effective to its adherents. If the Mormon organization may be likened to an army, the office of teacher is
similar to that of the top sergeant. The duty of the teacher
is to visit, to meet, and to assist every member of the
Church in his district. Once a month these lay guardians
of the Church meet and compare notes: matters of dispute
between Mormons may be arbitrated at these meetings;
Mormons who need employment can be put into communication with co-religionists who need employees; families
which can afford to furnish some of their members as missionaries are listed; the conditions of the families of those
who are on missions is also noted, particularly if assistance
is needed.

Every young Mormon is expected to give at least two
years of his life to the missionary work. Training in public
speaking and extemporaneous discussion and lessons explaining the Church's doctrines are provided as necessary
equipment for missionary work. Then, at his own expense
and without remuneration of any sort, literally obeying the
Scriptural injunction to travel "without purse or scrip,"
the Mormon missionary goes forth to remote areas of the

world. One may go to a pleasant southern Pacific island,
another to the slums of an industrialized city of England,
while a third may be sent to a lonely, snow-covered valley
of the Scandinavian peninsula. Not having his expenses
paid, the Mormon missionary is forced to work his way as
he goes. In this manner he becomes acquainted with men
in factories, upon farms, and in the holds of ships, for it
is among the working people that the Mormons gain most
of their male converts.

This method of procedure demands much sacrifice on
the part of the missionaries. Some assert that it is a system
open to great abuse by those in high office, who can, by
sending them abroad as missionaries rid themselves of
rebellious spirits. The working of the system does, of
course, depend to a great extent upon the integrity of the
upper officers; yet no faithful Mormon fails to respond
when summoned.[3]

As a result of the almost complete participation of the
male members of the Church in missionary work, the Mormons as a class are widely travelled. This travel has benefits of its own. Bishop Talbot, an Episcopalian whose diocese included many Mormons, somewhat enviously wrote
of this phase of Mormonism:

> Think what it means to send every year throughout our country
> and the various countries of Europe these young missionaries
> numbering some times over two thousand . . .[4]

And think of the influence upon these two thousand
young people. In regard to the religious influence, there is
either the strengthening or the entire repudiation of a
man's faith when he is called upon to make sacrifices for
that faith and to defend it before hostile groups.

From the period of its founding, the Mormon Church
had adopted an active missionary spirit. To bring converts

to Zion proved to be one of the greatest tasks faced by the Church leaders. The effort of the Church in this direction is one of the best illustrations of the Mormon hierarchy at work in the sphere of economic coöperation. In 1837, Heber C. Kimball, one of the ecclesiastical leaders, wrote that:

The prophet Joseph came to me while I was seated on the front stand above the sacrament table on the Melchisedek side of the Temple in Kirtland, and whispering to me said, Brother Heber, the spirit of the Lord has whispered to me, Let my servant Heber go to England and proclaim my gospel and open the door of salvation to that nation.[5]

In conformity with this revelation, Heber C. Kimball and Orson Hyde, accompanied by Willard Richards and four elders of the Church, went to England to take charge of a mission there. This band of evangelists reached Liverpool on July 27, 1837, and immediately began preaching. Their forums were held in the streets, in the squares of market towns, in dingy hired halls, in the back alleys of cities—anywhere that a group could be inveigled into listening. Some of these missionaries were even invited to speak in chapels belonging to the non-conforming sects.

The audiences were as varied as the meeting places. Many who had no interest in theological subtleties or had lost any desire for eternal salvation might stop to listen when the Mormon preacher began enlarging upon the economic prospects of life beyond the Atlantic. To some provocative souls the chance was a good one for a religious argument. How the words must have been tossed back and forth as the Mormons invaded the Presbyterian strongholds of Scotland! As usual, opposition made the missionaries more energetic. To many English workers, however, the Mormon preacher offered real and substantial prospects. There could be little argument on that score. Here was a

chance to achieve a heaven upon earth where "God shed
his grace on thee." By April 8, 1838, the Church was reported to have had a membership of over two thousand
people in England. Three-quarters of this number were
credited to the work of the untutored, but magnetic, Heber
C. Kimball.

But it was in 1840 that the frontal attack on unsaved
England began. In this drive one finds the sure hand of
Brigham Young; the arrival of that energetic and practical
person, on April 6 of that year, explains much. Conferences of elders were held regularly during his sojourn
there. According to Young's own words, he

. . . baptized between seven and eight thousand souls, printed
five thousand books of Mormon, three thousand hymn books,
twenty-five hundred volumes of the *Millenial Star,* and fifty
thousand tracts, immigrated to Zion one thousand souls, establishing a permanent shipping agency which will be a great blessing to the Saints . . .[6]

And before he left England, Brigham Young gave direc-
tions that copies of the Book of Mormon be especially prepared and bound for presentation to her Majesty, Queen
Victoria. To Queen Victoria this presentation might not
have meant much; among the Mormons it was at least a
fact to be advertised and exploited.

The greatest number of converts was gained in England.
Scotland, Wales, and Ireland also had missionaries assigned
to them; of these three countries, Wales proved to be the
most responsive to the new doctrine, Ireland the least.[7]
Mormon missionaries, on their own time and money,
reached the countries of Europe, South America, South
Africa, Australia, India, and the islands of the Pacific.[8]
Perhaps their greatest success outside of the English field
was in the Scandinavian countries.[9]

By April, 1841, the Mormon Church in England claimed

six thousand followers;[10] twelve years later the number had grown to thirty thousand.[11] In the fifteen years preceding 1855 twenty-two thousand Mormons took ship for the United States.[12] Between 1850 and 1856 the emigration to Salt Lake City appears to have reached its culminating point. "Elders were exhorted to thunder the word of the Almighty to the Saints to arise and come to Zion. The brethren were commanded to shake from their feet the dust of Babylon and hasten to the Holy City." "Every Saint who does not come home," according to the *Sixtieth General Epistle of the Twelve,* "will be afflicted by the Devil."[13] And the Saints came, frequently bringing their household utensils and tools with them, and casting off as many as possible of their old lares and penates.

As a means of expediting immigration and assisting the needy Saints in Europe to reach the city of their hopes, the Perpetual Emigration Fund Company was organized at Salt Lake City on October 6, 1849. The sum of five thousand dollars was raised at Salt Lake City that same year.[14] On March 29, 1850, Elder Richards, of the Twelve Apostles, introduced the subject of the fund to the British mission, which immediately favored it.

The presidency of the entire Church had charge of the money, but the European administration of these funds was vested in the head of the British mission. Every member of the Church was expected to contribute. One donation of four hundred dollars was given by a single individual. By July, 1854, the British Isles had contributed £7,113 to the fund.[15]

Those desirous of emigrating could deposit money with the Church officers until a small part of the total expense was accumulated; then at the volition of the president of the British Church, the remainder could be advanced to the prospective emigrant as a loan. The Saint whose passage was thus defrayed could work out his debt in the shops of the tithing office in Utah. There the worker was supplied with food from the Deseret (Church) Store; he received half the value of his labor, the other half going to pay his indebtedness.[16] Upon arrival in Utah others were given work by their friends, if they were fortunate enough to have any; or else the Church found work for them among the settlers. The passage money was repaid—with interest; and, therefore, the fund could be used again and again and was perpetual.

This fund was used in an ingenious manner to assist emigration. The Perpetual Emigration Fund was the Mormon solution of a problem which confronted those who desired to emigrate but who were restrained by a lack of money. After the Perpetual Emigration Fund was well organized, part of the fund was used to help the emigrants cross the plains. Volunteers also were called for in Utah, and some men paid their tithes by providing teams, personal services, and food to the expedition that left Salt Lake each spring to meet the newcomers.[17]

Applications for passage to the United States were received by the Mormon agent in England. When a sufficient number of converts was prepared to emigrate, the agent chartered a vessel. The passengers were then notified by printed circulars containing instructions on the method of procedure, the date of departure from Liverpool, the price of passage, and the amount of provisions allowed. From inland points to the port of embarkation the Mormons travelled in groups as much as possible in order to secure reduced rates and to assist one another.

During this period some interesting sidelights on Mormon emigration were given by Englishmen. According to Dickens, a select committee of the House of Commons in 1854, investigating conditions on emigrant ships, called the Mormon agent and passenger broker as one of the witnesses. This committee came to the conclusion that no ships under the provisions of the "passengers' act" then enforced could be depended upon for comfort and security to the same degree as those under Mormon administration. Dickens quoted from their report: "The Mormon ship is a family under strong and accepted discipline with every provision for comfort, decorum, and internal peace."[18] Henry Mayhew, a London journalist, while engaged upon his work, *Labour and the Poor*, in the summer of 1850 was attracted by the small stream of Mormon emigration. As a consequence, he published in 1851 one of the early objective histories of Mormonism.[19]

The average emigrant travelling under his own auspices did not have so easy a path to the United States as did those travelling under Mormon protection. It was during the period of 1840-60 that the business of transporting emigrants of all classes from Great Britain to the United States was rotten with greed and dishonesty. Soon after their landing the emigrants frequently lost their savings and their Utopian illusions concerning the new world. At the points of departure and arrival, sharks and speculators were waiting to seize the savings of the unsuspecting emigrant. Over-crowding, poor rations, and inhumane treatment were the lot of the bewildered traveller in the steerage, although conditions slowly changed for the better as steam displaced the old sailing vessels.[20]

In comparison the Mormons had few of these troubles. They travelled in a group, kept their own order, and had an officer of their own as commander. Before leaving port the president of the mission appointed a president of the ship and two counsellors. The ship's president acted in a capacity similar to that of a colonel embarking with his regiment. A clerk was appointed to note all that happened on the voyage. The Morman emigrants were divided into groups (known as wards), with one member placed in charge of each. The leaders determined the order and time for each ward to see to its cooking. Everything on board was prearranged as far as it was possible to do so.[21]

Experiments were made to find the port of arrival best for Mormon purposes. At first New Orleans was the favorite city, the passage price from Liverpool varying from £3, 12s, 6d, to £4. From New Orleans to Salt Lake City the cost was £20.[22] Before the Civil War the cost of the entire journey via this route was reduced to £10 because of increased effectiveness in methods.[23] After 1861, the system of transportation became even more efficient. The Mormon agent at Liverpool saw the emigrant on board a steamship of the Guion Line, and another agent met the ship upon its arrival at New York, which by this time had become the favored port. The officer on board who was in charge knew before he left Liverpool the exact amount of fare that each family had to pay for the remainder of the journey; he collected this sum, and the agent at New York knew where to make the best exchange without unnecessary delay. Special trains were hired over the Pennsylvania, Pittsburgh, and Fort Wayne Railroad, to Chicago. Telegrams were sent ahead to Chicago so that food would be ready upon arrival of the trains. After a brief rest the travellers continued their journey over the Chicago and Northwestern Railroad to Omaha. Before 1869 they went from Omaha on to their Zion by wagon. After that date the trip was completed in the comparative luxury of Union Pacific coaches.

At each transfer point there was an agent to look after the comfort of the immigrants and furnish them with the necessary supplies. For the journey across the plains a carrying company was organized which transported pas-

sengers and luggage as well as freight. This did away with
the necessity of purchasing oxen and carts at the congested
points on the upper Mississippi, where crowds of immigrants were desirous of setting out for California and Oregon. "In this service and in the retailing of oxen, wagons,
and food to the bewildered farmers there was abundant
opportunity for maltreatment and speculation; but the representatives of the Church seem, as a rule, to have performed their duties with commendable zeal."[24]

Thus the way of the pilgrim to a new and better land
was prepared for the traveller by the Mormon hierarchy.
The comparative heaven of Utah was pictured to possible
converts in lonely Scandinavian hamlets and teeming English factory towns. The missionary planted the seeds of
thought. Then the Church's resources gave the financial
support necessary to bring the converts to Utah. The Mormon hierarchy helped pave the way to Zion with economic and personal assistance as well as with good intentions.

The newly arrived immigrant needed help when he
reached Utah as much as he did while on his way there.
Here again the Church organization took control of the
newcomers. As the possibilities of Utah unfolded to the
eyes of the leaders, the Mormons decided to preëmpt spaces
for their own use. With Mormons occupying the habitable
valleys, troublesome Gentiles could be warded off; in addition, the Mormons expected their own growing population would need all the space possible within a few generations. Therefore, a plan of controlled colonization was
evolved.

This plan shows the Church leaders and their followers
working together in enterprises where mutual helpfulness
was especially desirable. A call would come similar to a
mission call asking people to go on a mission to settle new
regions.[25] The settlers would meet at an appointed ren-

dezvous with their heavy prairie wagons loaded with
household goods, seeds, and farm implements. Usually a
whole family went together. The young boys on horseback
took charge of the livestock, the mothers did their sewing
on the way and cared for the babies. Quite often newly
arrived immigrants were sent out in a group led by old-
timers experienced in the wiles of the devil who beset the
Utah farmer. One of the veterans was designated as leader; probably he was also the ecclesiastical leader. Thus the
influence of the Church and Mormon control of land went
hand in hand through most of the habitable valleys of
Utah, and into parts of Nevada, Idaho, Wyoming, and Arizona. By the twentieth century Mormon settlements
reached from northern Mexico to Alberta.[26]

The Mormons ordinarily settled close together. The
houses and barns made compact units, centering about the
available water supply. Under this arrangement a mini-
mum of piping was needed and little time wasted in travelling back and forth for water. It also allowed a clear space
in the irrigated fields, a space free of houses and outbuild-
ings, and thereby, allowed for greater efficiency in placing
the irrigation ditches. Another factor, not to be forgotten
in these effete later days, is that the Mormon had to con-
sider defence against the Indian. There was little trouble
with the poor specimen of Red Man found in the Great
Basin; yet the Mormon believed in keeping his powder dry
against such a possibility. Thus the compact area of buildings could more easily be converted into a stockade than
could isolated ranches. Whatever the reasons, there was
one incontestable result: the people were near the Church
and under the immediate oversight of the local bishop.
Hence the economic and religious phases were brought
close together at the same time that the Church and its followers were closely united in community endeavor.

Another major problem in economics which Mormonism faced from the day of its origin was that concerning the distribution of wealth. Were the inhabitants of Zion to be divided into the "haves" versus the "have-nots"? The Mormon solution for this difficulty came to Joseph Smith in 1831. In that year a group of newly converted Saints, poor in the goods of this world, arrived in Kirtland from the western part of New York State. Bishop Edward Partridge was assigned to look after them and to care for their needs. These people were in dire need, and in answer to Bishop Partridge's question as to what should be done to supply their wants, Joseph Smith began a series of pronouncements. As a result of these pronouncements the Mormon leader advocated a new economic order among mankind, the United Order of Enoch, better known among the Mormons as the United Order.

According to Joseph Smith the individual Mormon was to surrender his property to the Church. This property was then divided by the Church authorities into two parts. The first of these was the inheritance or stewardship. This was the amount considered necessary for the individual to live upon and was returned to the individual who had given it. After its return this amount became a personal possession by clear title, so far as the Church was concerned. A second part, known as the surplus was "consecrated" to the Church and title passed. If possible, this surplus was placed in the bishop's storehouse, and used by that official for the poor and needy among the faithful.[27] The Church had a clear title to this as far as the individuals who had given it were concerned. Thus the United Order was an attempt to retain individualistic enterprise as the foundation of the economic order, and to build upon the surplus accumulated by individuals a store of goods held for the common benefit. The economic theory of Joseph Smith may be likened to a pyramid with individualism at the base supporting an apex of communism.

The revelation of Joseph Smith pertaining to the all-important question of earthly allotments was not specific. Bishop Partridge had the difficult task of dividing the "inheritances" among the people on the basis of equality according to families, according to wants and needs, and also according to circumstances.[28] This certainly was a piece of work that required no mean abilities. With a reassuring sense of calmness, the revelation in which the ideal of the United Order is set forth adds that in other respects Mormon economic relationships were to be carried on as usual.[29]

A revelation to Joseph Smith in July, 1831, gave the leadership in the United Order to a group of seven high priests, among whom were Bishop Edward Partridge and his two counsellors under the previous plan, Isaac Morley and John Corrill. [30] To make confusion worse confounded, a third body of control, the central council, was organized in April, 1832. Joseph Smith, Newell K. Whitney, Sidney Rigdon, and Martin Harris were members of this board which was "to manage the affairs of the poor and all things pertaining to the bishopric, both in the land of Zion [the Mormon Stake in Missouri] and in the land of Shinehah (Kirtland)."[31]

By 1836, according to the Mormon leaders, it became evident that mankind was not ready for the United Order. Therefore, on July 8 of that year, a new and lesser revelation, that of tithing, was announced. This revelation instructed the Saints to put their surplus property into the hands of the bishop for the construction of the Nauvoo Temple and for the payments of any debts owed to the presidency. It provided, in addition, that thereafter, "those who have been thus tithed, shall pay one-tenth of all their interest annually; and this shall be a standing law unto them forever."[32]

Since 1838 tithing has proved one of the main sources of revenue for the Church. By means of this system the temples at Nauvoo, Salt Lake City, Manti, Logan, and St. George, and the large office building at Salt Lake City were built. Payment in kind and in labor was accepted in the early days when money was scarce in Utah. According to the Salt Lake *Tribune* of June 25, 1879, the income of the Church from this source was placed at $1,000,000 a year, and during Brigham Young's administration the total receipts were estimated at $13,000,000.[33]

This fund and its use by a religious body have caused much criticism of the Mormon Church. Horace Greeley in his *Overland Journey* wrote of an interview with Brigham Young in which he asked the Mormon leader, "What is done with the proceeds of this tithing?" Young answered, "Part of it is devoted to building temples and other places of worship, part to helping the poor and needy converts on their way to this country, and the largest portion to the support of the poor among the Saints."[34]

Governor Eli H. Murray, of Utah, in his *Message of 1882*, referred to the custom of tithing and tried to have it abolished. He claimed that "the poor man who earns a dollar by the sweat of his brow is entitled to that dollar" and that "any exaction or undue influence to dispossess him of any part of it, in any other manner than in payment of a legal obligation is oppression."[35]

This may be compared with the statement of Brigham Young in the *Journal of Discourses:* "The people are not compelled to pay their tithing; they do as they please about it, it is urged upon them only as a matter of duty between them and their God."[36]

The views of the manner in which tithing is paid are irreconcilable. Such writers as Linn claim that even though paid without ulterior compulsion, there is a compulsion nevertheless. The non-payer of tithing could be left out of Church activities, a serious matter to the individual in the early days when the Mormon Church controlled almost all the functions of life in Utah. The delinquent could also be refused entrance to the Tabernacle, where ceremonies were performed which the Mormon believes absolutely necessary to his salvation. "To many of the Mormon people these consequences [incurred by non-payment of tithes] are more terrible than the consequences which may follow the neglect of other financial measures."[37]

T. B. H. Stenhouse, an Englishman who had joined the Mormon Church and who had left it in dissatisfaction, wrote of the Mormon tithing practices that Brigham Young as trustee-in-trust (that is, guardian of the tithing fund) "renders no account of the funds that come into his hands, but tells the faithful that they are at perfect liberty to examine the books at any moment."[38]

The number of sermons concerned with the delinquents in tithe-paying and the efforts made to hasten their payments show that with some Mormons this institution has as little popularity as tax-paying has among the Gentiles.[39] The Church authorities at the present day make public the amount of tithing paid to the Church, and also the manner in which it is expended.[40]

The Mormon ideal of economic organization had not been entirely forgotten by the Mormons when they left behind them the unpleasant memories of Missouri and had settled the Salt Lake Valley. Johnson, in his *History of Springville, Utah,* wrote that in the winter of 1853-54 the laws of consecration were taught to a considerable extent, and that the inhabitants of Springville were called upon to "consecrate their property to God which most of them did." He added that an invoice of the property to be thus "consecrated" was made. "None of the property," however, "ever left the hands of the donors, but it [the consecration] proved the people's willingness, at that time, to obey the command of the priesthood."[41]

With the approach of the rails of the Union Pacific Railroad nearer and nearer to Utah in 1869, the Mormon leaders once more saw before them the possibility of trouble with the Gentiles. In order to strengthen themselves the people were urged to make the United Order a fact as well as an ideal. The idea was energetically advocated in religious meetings. In addition, the Church papers, such as the *Millennial Star* and the *Deseret News*, during the years 1868 and 1869, published articles upon both the theory and the practice of the United Order. Heaven was not going to yield to mundane affairs without a struggle.

Although the Mormon communities in Utah during the late sixties failed to respond whole-heartedly to the economic plans of their leaders, some experiments in the proposed new order were made. Thus a coöperative branch was organized at Smithfield by a community organization which owned a tannery, shoe manufactory, harness shop, some lumber, shingle, and lathe mills, a brick yard, and a mercantile store.[42] In Price, Carbon County, people lived together as one large family. All material possessions except the clothes they wore were owned in common.[43] At Hyrum, Cache County, the people owned their own farms, cattle, and houses; but they subscribed for shares in a saw-mill, tannery, and a store and worked together to build necessary roads.[44]

In Springville, there was an undercurrent of opposition to the introduction of the United Order, although the community owned a meat market and store.[45] The people at Mount Carmel disbanded their common group by mutual agreement. About 180 of the people of Mount Carmel who wished to continue the experiment of the United Order went to Orderville, two miles away, and there renewed the experiment. This latter group chose an executive board of six directors. The whole community divided itself into working groups. The men were classified into three grades —boys, juniors, and men. All men were paid the same wages—$1.50 a day. The entire community ate at a common table, where eight people served the eighty families of the community. At the beginning of the experiment members had deeded their entire property, both real and personal, to the Order—all wealth was held in common.[46]

The leader of the Orderville experiment wrote of this attempt:

The members of the Orderville Ward entered into that communal association believing it to be a sacred duty to do so. We came together as strangers, each handicapped with individual weaknesses but all imbued with an earnest desire to overcome them. The very fact that "we had all things in common" tended to banish selfishness, and helped us to "love our neighbors as ourselves"; and it is a fact we became deeply attached to each other.[47]

This branch of the United Order broke up at the death of Brigham Young.

The most successful of these attempts to establish the United Order took place at Brigham City, about sixty miles north of Salt Lake City. Lorenzo Snow, later President of the Latter Day Saints, was credited with first putting this enterprise upon a successful basis. A mercantile establishment was started in 1864; successive expansions brought in about forty industries, including a model dairy with its herds and a cotton plantation in southern Utah for supplying the community cotton mill at Brigham City. A series of losses, twelve years after the plan had started, forced the

people to abandon it. The woolen mill burned down
twice.[48] A contract to supply timber to the Utah and
Northern Railroad could not be kept because thirty or forty
men were arrested upon the charge of unlawfully cutting
timber and, according to the Mormons, were unfairly convicted, by an anti-Mormon judge.[49] Another blow to the
Brigham City United Order came over the struggle with
the United States tax collector, O. J. Hollister, who
attempted to collect taxes to the amount of $10,200 on scrip
issued by the United Order. This scrip was issued by the
United Order to pay its employees, and, according to
Lorenzo Snow, passed as currency in the community.[50]
Grasshoppers destroyed one crop, causing a loss of $4,000.
A drought caused a loss of $3,000.

With the abandonment of the United Order in Brigham
City, these experiments lost their driving force. Once more
the plan of a better economic order was relegated to the
Book of Doctrine and Covenants, whence the faithful
Mormon believes it will again emerge and ultimately
achieve success. But though it had failed in practice, the
efforts illustrate the extent to which Mormon leaders and
their followers worked together at the problem of economic
coöperation.

Another pertinent problem for the Mormon leaders of
the fifties and sixties was caused by the dearth of manufactured articles in Utah before the coming of the railroad.
The Mormons were far off from industrial centres; as a
consequence the necessity of producing their own manufactures or else paying the heavy transportation charges
from the East fell upon the Mormons themselves. Quite
often the task was beyond the power and wealth of any
individual; therefore the Church assisted in solving this
problem also. The ecclesiastical authorities organized the
Great Salt Lake Valley Carrying Company for the trans-

portation of goods and passengers from the Missouri River to the Pacific Coast. With the cost of passengers $300 each, and with freight costing $250 a ton, the enterprise proved to be a profitable one.[51] Machinery for the production of sugar from sorghum cane was imported from Europe in 1852. The expensive undertaking of transporting this machinery across the plains was paid for by the Church. This enterprise required a train of forty-five wagons, each of which was drawn by four yokes of oxen.[52] At a later period the building in which this machinery was placed was remodelled by the Church and turned into a paper factory.[53] Fifty acres of mulberry trees were set out in Salt Lake and Utah counties, in an effort to introduce silk culture into the Territory.[54] Just before and during the Civil War, the Church experimented with raising cotton in southern Utah.[55] Improved breeds of cattle were brought in by the Church.[56] In the autumn of 1856 a number of young Mormons were called out on the plains to establish stations for a mail route; Brigham Young, governor of the Territory at the time, contracted to carry the mail on this route between Salt Lake City and Fort Leavenworth.[57] Ten years later the Deseret Telegraph Line, connecting northern and southern Utah with the transcontinental system, was projected, being completed by the autumn of 1867. Brigham Young sent a circular to the bishops, asking them to have the young people learn telegraphy. "The operators are to regard themselves as missionaries who spend their time without compensation."[58] Another example of the attitude of the Church in providing work may be seen by the taking of a contract by Brigham Young to build ninety miles of track for the Union Pacific Railroad. He sublet his contract to small contractors who employed thousands of men from the different settlements in need of work at the time.[59]

The arrival of the railroad made Utah an accessible
market for eastern manufacturers. Would the link between
the Mormon Church and its adherents be weakened by
this factor? Would the Gentile merchants reap the benefit
of Mormons' efforts? Would the old feuds of Missouri and
Illinois days be re-enacted? Would the Mormon Zion in
Utah become merely another Gentile territory? These were
questions asked in and out of Mormonism. The Mormon
authorities realized the situation and took steps to meet it.
A suggestion was made at the October Conference of 1868
that stores be formed and shares sold to as many Mormons
as would buy them.[60] Where the population of the community was almost exclusively Mormon, and if that part of
the community subscribed for shares in the store, the
prospect of other stores obtaining Mormon trade became
very dubious. Many outside the circle of the chosen
members would then be forced either to sell outright to the
new institution or else to give up the unequal struggle. The
formation of these so-called coöperative stores did, in fact,
bring to Utah a bitter period of readjustment for the
wholesale and retail merchants.[61]

This new economic adventure of the Church received
the name of Zion's Coöperative Mercantile Institute.
Branches were opened displacing the general merchandise
stores in Mormon towns. The one at Salt Lake City was the
parent institution of the Z. C. M. I. and was also the first
department store in the West. "So sacred were these cooperative organizations that those who were directly
identified with them entered into a 'covenant by re-baptism
to be subject to the priesthood in temporal as well as
spiritual things.' "[62] At first these coöperative stores mo-
nopolized business in some of the smaller communities.
After about ten years, however, individualistic competition
regained its strength. In time the name "coöperation"

attached to the village store was all that remained in many communities of this economic enterprise.[63]

It might be in point to quote some opinions of the Mormons themselves in regard to this aspect of participation of the Church in economic affairs of this earth and the corollary principle of individual coöperation with the Church leadership. In *Tullidge's Quarterly Magazine* for the year 1880 there is an editorial to the effect that "Coöperation is as much a cardinal and essential doctrine of the Mormon Church as is baptism for the remission of sins: and every Mormon elder who understands the philosophy of his own system could affirm that without coöperation society could not be saved."[64] Lorenzo Snow, the leading spirit in the Brigham City United Order, wrote in 1901:

That it will succeed in establishing Zion, in building the holy city, in gathering out the righteous from all lands and preparing them to meet the Lord when He comes in His Glory, no faithful Latter-Day Saint doubts. To this end it aims to institute what is known as the United Order, a communal system inaugurated by the Prophet Joseph Smith as early as February, 1831, but which owing to the Church's frequent migration and other causes has never been fully established. The purpose of the Order is to make the members of the Church equal and united in all things, spiritual and temporal, to banish pride, poverty, and iniquity, and to introduce a condition of things that will prepare the pure in heart for the advent of the world's Redeemer.[65]

CHAPTER III

CONFIRM THY SOUL IN SELF CONTROL

THE FUNCTION OF INTELLIGENCE

THE HEAVEN on earth ardently desired by Mormon leaders rested, of course, upon a firm foundation of economic well-being for the community. But a material base was not enough for, "man shall not live by bread alone." Architects of the Mormon social order wanted their followers to develop mentally as well as physically in order fully to realize their capabilities in this new exalted world. As an individual's intelligence developed, so would his full capabilities. It was possible, but not likely in the immediate future, for man so to develop his mental powers that .he would become a perfect human being. In other words, he would approach God. Thus, running along in parallel fashion with the Mormon economic teachings, ran a Mormon theology and philosophy which advocated the development of intelligence.

This Mormon theology, of course, arose out of the same background as did Joseph Smith and other early Mormon leaders.[1] The Mormon scholastics added a point here, subtracted one there, and came out with a philosophy that included many beliefs of other sects. Even to the believers in Jacksonian democracy, the Mormon leaders could point out that all Church officials were chosen by a display of hands in open meetings. To Catholics, of whom there were few converts, the Mormons offered a hierarchy and an authoritarian head who had the power of revelation. To

Methodists, they offered a system of bishops and some of the Methodists' own hymn tunes; and to Millennialists and Campbellites they offered a new dispensation. William Miller, with his flapping robes, offered a weak millennium as compared to that offered by Joseph Smith and Brigham Young. In addition to its concrete proofs that Mormonism had what other religions had, the Mormons had a Zion promised to its faithful supporters. True, the Zion had to change its earthly residence from Ohio to Missouri, from Missouri to Illinois, and from Illinois to Utah; but if earthly affairs were not yet prepared, a plan was. This plan is part of Mormon theology and philosophy. Since the plan has changed little since its early days, it is quite proper to discuss the pertinent beliefs of the present-day Mormon Church in this respect. No wonder, then, that out of this piling on of ritualistic and dogmatic practices, the resultant Mormon theology was eclectic.

The Mormons did add, at least, one very important belief to those in vogue on the frontier—their leader had the power, continuously renewed, of receiving new revelations. Few American sects have been promised as much—and achieved as much—as have the Mormons.

At the basis of Mormon philosophy itself lies their belief in the relationship between man and God. Their theology teaches that there had been an existence in the past and that this life is but a link in the chain leading to another existence. Orson Pratt's *Absurdities of Immaterialism* and the *Kingdom of God* are two philosophical explanations of this view, but perhaps the best literary expression of this concept may be seen in Eliza R. Snow's poem, "O, My Father,"

> O my Father, Thou that dwellest
> In the high and glorious place!
> When shall I regain Thy presence,

And again behold Thy face?
In Thy holy habitation,
Did my spirit once reside;
In my first primeval childhood,
Was I nurtured near Thy side.

For a wise and glorious purpose
Thou hast placed me here on earth,
And withheld the recollection
Of my former friends and birth;
Yet oft-times a secret something
Whispered, "You're a stranger here;"
And I felt that I had wandered
From a more exalted sphere.

I had learned to call Thee Father,
Thro' Thy Spirit from on high;
But until the Key of Knowledge
Was restored I knew not why.
In the heavens are parents single?
No; the tho't makes reason stare!
Truth is reason, truth eternal,
Tells me I've a mother there.

When I leave this frail existence,
When I lay this mortal by,
Father, Mother may I meet you
In your royal courts on high?
Then at length, when I've completed
All you sent me forth to do,
With your mutual approbation
Let me come and dwell with you.

According to Mormon philosophy, God Himself went through this chain of existence. And man can follow in His footsteps. As man now is, so God once was; as God now is, so can man become. God, in Mormon theology, is the greatest intelligence. By the best organization of his powers man can approach God, but never equal Him.[2] "The whole mortal existence of Man is neither more nor less than a preparatory state given to finite beings, a space wherein they may improve themselves for a higher state of being."[3] And a most essential feature of this improvement is the development of intelligence.[4] In the *Book of Doctrine and Covenants*, the guide book to Mormon theology, there is a statement that "The glory of God is intelligence,"[5] and that "It is impossible for a man to be saved in ignorance."[6]

Joseph Smith and his followers identify intelligence with knowledge.[7] Knowledge has two aspects, one of things divine and another of things in this world; if correctly understood the two are the same.[8] There are two avenues of approach to knowledge, one is by faith, the other by a study of ourselves and the world about us. The latter is gained by the combined use of reason and proper digestion of the "best books of wisdom."[9] It does not matter on which avenue one seeks knowledge, for one avenue eventually leads to the other. If there is any doubt, the Church authorities' rulings are the guides to follow.[10]

The knowledge gained in this life does not lose its value with the ending of this, our temporary existence. The first prophet of Mormonism asserted that "Whatever principles of intelligence we attain to in this life, it will arise with us in the resurrection,"[11] and "if a person gains more knowledge and intelligence in this life through his diligence and obedience than another, he will have so much more the advantage in the world to come."[12]

"Every good and useful gift," according to Brigham Young, "came from God." These gifts

. . . have been given with a view to prepare the way for the ultimate triumph of truth, and the redemption of the earth from the power of Sin and Satan. We should take advantage of all these great discoveries, the accumulated wisdom of ages, and give to our children the benefit of every branch of useful knowledge, to prepare them to step forward and efficiently do their part in the great work.[13]

This point—whatever was useful was from God, and whatever was from God was for the Saints—was continually emphasized by the Mormon leaders.[14]

In addition to their claims of being the founders of a new religious faith with better access to revealed knowledge than their predecessors, the Mormons planned to strike out on entirely new paths of learning and new modes of reaching truth.[15] W. W. Phelps well expressed this belief in 1850, when he wrote:

> The world of science was to be revolutionized, the theories of gravitation, repulsion, and attraction overthrown, the motion of atoms, whether single or in mass, being ascribed to the all-pervading presence of the holy spirit. The planetary systems were to be rearranged, their number and relations modified . . .[16]

This is an extreme statement, but it was made by a man whom the Mormons considered able enough to be regent of the University of Deseret and at one time was made a member of the High Council of Twelve.[17] Phelps seems, however, to have sipped too often but not drunk deeply enough of the waters of the Pierian spring of knowledge.

The attitude of Brigham Young and the Church leaders was to appropriate useful thought wherever they could find it. Immigrants were advised to bring books or articles which would be of value in giving information to the people of Utah. Those already in Utah were advised to spend their leisure profitably and absorb what they could of this world's knowledge.[18]

On the other hand, members of the Church were advised not to lose sight of God's laws as seen in the Bible, the Book of Mormon, and the various teachings of the Church as approved by the high presidency. Heber C. Kimball, when a member of the first presidency of the Church, pointed to the fact that both President Brigham Young and himself were men whose minds had not been halted in growth or cluttered with an accumulated hodge-podge of facts by a college education. He went on to say that "the education we have received from God has qualified me and my brethren to instruct kings, and rulers, and bring to nought the wisdom of their wise men."[19] If there was any doubt as to which could more easily be dispensed with, the knowledge gained through study of the ways of the world, or the word of God as revealed through the priesthood, there is no question but that the Mormon Church stood for the retention of the latter.[20]

Thus the individual searcher for truth was likely to run into conflict with the authorities. Here the Mormon Church found itself in the age-old conflict of authority versus individual will. Orson Pratt, one of the best self-educated men in the Mormon Church, openly acknowledged that intelligence should be subservient to God's will as interpreted by those who held the keys—that is, the Church authorities.[21]

Elder E. L. T. Harrison writing in the *Millennial Star* of October 8, 1859, insisted that those who were "without the pale" of the Mormon Church "do not understand the grand truths relating to life, death, and immortality; they do not realize the omnipotent truth that righteousness is the basis of celestial glory."[22] He pointed out, however, that educated persons, even if they had not accepted Mormon teachings, had a certain advantage over the uneducated:

These pleasures and perceptions of educated people come from reading works of intellectual and imaginative men, from viewing the exquisite productions of master minds in statuary, painting, poetry, and music, and from displays of wit and fancy, of which the educated mind alone can see the point and intensity.[23]

In the final analysis, however, Elder Harrison was forced

to the conclusion that the religious knowledge of the uneducated man was of more weight than the earthly knowledge of the educated man. But the article taken as a whole gave an unusually high place to those who were educated, even though not members of the Mormon Church.[24]

The Book of Mormon and Joseph Smith's revelations did not ordinarily attract educated persons. But there was no such unanimity of dissent among the educated men of Mormonism as that ascribed to them by John Hyde, Junior, who had, at one time, been a member of the Church. Hyde claimed that all educated men apostatized from the Mormon Church.[25] Some of the educated men found the road rather difficult—Orson Pratt, for example, who at one time in his career had found himself cut-off from the Church.[26] Pratt had acquired by self-study a methodology in philosophy and a knowledge of mathematics equal to that of any other man in the Church during its formative years in Utah. He evidently had a love of learning for its own sake, not for any utilitarian purpose. He was an unusual person among a group which believed that learning should be of practical worth and of immediate value, both here and hereafter. Parley P. Pratt, a brother of Orson, was another self-educated man. Suffice to say that the latter always remained in good standing and was a leader in Church activities until the time of his death in 1857.

Some of the early Mormons had gone beyond elementary training. Albert Carrington, for example, at the end of his life was a prominent member of the Church, although at one time in his career he too had been cut-off from membership.[27] Carrington had graduated from Dartmouth College in 1833 and eight years later had joined the Mormon Church at Wiota, Wisconsin.[28] In 1844, he went to Nauvoo and became prominently identified with the

Church as a missionary. He became well known in Utah as the private secretary to Brigham Young, a position which he held for twenty years, and in which he gained, according to Bancroft, the sobriquet of "The Mormon Wolsey."[29] Carrington held various other positions of prominence in both Church and Territory, such as first clerk of the High Council in Salt Lake City of Zion. During the years 1868-70, 1871-73, and 1880-82, he acted as president of the European Mission. This jack-of-all-trades in Church affairs also edited the *Deseret News* at one time and for a long period was one of the Twelve Apostles.

Lorenzo Snow was another prominent Mormon who went beyond the elementary grades in his schooling. It is stated that he attended school at Oberlin, Ohio. Since the register of Oberlin College does not contain his name it may be that he attended an academy at Oberlin which prepared students for Oberlin College. He joined the Mormon Church soon after completing his work at Oberlin.[30] Snow remained a member of the Church until his death. His work in the missionary field, in the coöperative enterprises at Brigham City, and finally as President of the Church gives evidence that he was a vigorous Mormon leader. Doctor John M. Bernhisel, a graduate of the medical department of the University of Pennsylvania in 1827, served as delegate to Congress from the Territory of Utah during the years 1851 to 1859 and also remained a member of the Church until his death.[31] George M. Teasdale, one of the early teachers in Salt Lake City and later one of the Twelve Apostles, was educated at the University of London.[32] No Mormon was more eager to spread the Church doctrines than Orson Spencer, a graduate of Union College in 1824 and of Hamilton Literary and Theological Institute, New York, in 1829. He had taught and studied law in Georgia and acted as a Baptist minister for twelve years before joining the Mormon Church in 1841. His lameness did not hinder his missionary endeavors, in the midst of which he died, at St. Louis, on October 15, 1855.[33] Although the university founded at Salt Lake City had not prospered under Spencer, it did advance under another college-trained man, Doctor John R. Park. The latter had attended Ohio Wesleyan University and New York University, and in 1869 was appointed president of the University of Deseret.

Thus some Mormons had received university or college degrees and therefore had at least a modicum of education in the estimation of the faculties and boards of trustees who had the power of granting degrees. Franklin D. Richards, as well as Orson Pratt and Parley P. Pratt, was a man who could be considered educated because of his interests and accomplishments, even if he lacked degrees. By whatever standard one measures education—either by that shadowy claim, possession of a university diploma, or else by actual interests in intellectual affairs—the generalization that all educated men apostatized from the Church is far too sweeping.

On the other hand, one can note the few in this group as compared with the thousands who were in the Mormon Church. There must also be taken into account the evident lack of educated men who were with the Church in the days of Joseph Smith. Some of the regents of the University of Nauvoo had the degree of "doctor" attached to their names, either because of proved proficiency or because the title appeared formidable to the unknowing. Not much evidence beyond their names and the titles remains concerning these men. Almost all of these individuals left the Church before their deaths.[34]

In the year 1867 a group of men who were influential in forming opinion in Utah broke with the Church. This group supported those who questioned Brigham Young's attempt to build up coöperative enterprises under the aegis of the Mormon Church. Among these protestors were E. L. T. Harrison, editor of the *Utah Magazine;* T. B. H. Stenhouse, editor of the Salt Lake City *Daily Telegraph;* E. W. Tullidge, and H. W. Lawrence. Eli B. Kelsey at a Church meeting voted against the excommunication of the men who had differed with the ideas of Brigham Young, and thereby found himself cut off from the Church because of his temerity.

In contrast to this group which believed that individual reason led to conflict with those who held the leadership of the Church, there was the great mass of the Mormon people, numbering, according to the census of 1870, over eighty-five thousand in Utah.[35]

The great majority of the Mormons had not gone beyond the three "R's" of the common schools. [36] Joseph Smith, during his youth, had little of the education that is gained in schools. Brigham Young, the second president of the Church, as well as his two counsellors, Heber C. Kimball and Daniel H. Wells, were forced to give up school at early ages to earn money.[37] The biographer of John Taylor, third president of the Church, wrote: "John Taylor attended school at Beetham [England] . . . It was in those days that he got 'mixed up' as he puts it 'with ploughing, reaping, hay-making, and other farm work' "—all before he was fourteen.[38] Wilford Woodruff, the fourth president of the Church, attended school in New England until he was fourteen.[39] Parley P. Pratt at the age of sixteen had his last schooling for many years.[40]

The leaders of the Church were not ashamed of the fact that many of them were not educated in the learning of the world. In a prayer given at the opening exercises of the University of Deseret in December, 1862, Brigham Young

displayed a vein of thought that is not ordinarily associated
with his forceful personality. "Bless all," he said, "who
take an interest in the improvement of the minds of Thy
people, and wilt thou instruct them by the revelations of
Thy Spirit; for we realize that we are ignorant, and our
opportunities to be taught in the learning of men on earth
have been few.[41]

Thus in the Mormon Church, knowledge and intelligence were advocated as part of the preparation for the
hereafter. And as this life may be but a step in preparation
for the next, the Mormon adherents were advised to obtain
all the knowledge they could in the present. It is also
possible that by fully developing themselves in this life the
conditions of heaven can be realized on this earth. This was
the philosophy of the Church. What was its practice?

CHAPTER IV

GOD MEND THY EVERY FLAW

EDUCATION

MORMON THEORIES and practices in regard to education followed paths similar to those of older states. This is true particularly in the question of financial support of a free public school system. The struggle and wrangling over this question show that the Mormon attitude was but little different from that of the rest of the United States.[1] The unbounded optimism of the followers of Joseph Smith about the possibilities of educational endeavor among Mormons could doubtless be duplicated elsewhere as a frontier phenomenon; Mormonism was normal in this boastfulness and hope. But few frontier communities had as direct a control from headquarters as did the Mormons in Utah. Therefore, the problem differed to some extent from that of other frontier communities.

The problem of educating both Mormon young and old was one that had to be faced sooner or later by those who guided Mormon opinion. The constitution of the State of Deseret, adopted in Salt Lake City, March 15, 1849, and unsuccessfully proposed to Congress as the basis of admission to statehood, does not mention education or schools.[2] One, however, of the first ordinances passed, February 28, 1850, by the legislative assembly of the Territory empowered a chancellor and a board of regents to incorporate the University of Deseret.[3] The first general act relating to common schools in Utah was passed on December 30,

1854.[4] The main provisions in this act gave control of
schools in the Territory to a chancellor and a board of
regents. The chancellor was to "hold his office during the
pleasure of said board," and his duty was to report school
conditions in the Territory to the board of regents and to
fulfill such other duties as the board required of him.
County courts were authorized to divide the Territory into
school districts; the inhabitants of these districts were
empowered to elect school trustees for a period of one year.
These courts were also authorized to appoint a board of
examiners in each county. The popularly elected trustees
had the power of assessing and collecting a tax upon all
taxable property in their respective districts, at a per-
centage ratio to be decided upon by the vote of the district
meeting. Out of such funds the trustees were to erect
buildings, keep them in repair, and see that fuel was supplied. The board of examiners received the reports of the
trustees concerning income and expenditures and the condition of buildings. The board also examined prospective
teachers and had the power of appointments.

An act was passed in 1865 amending and consolidating
the school laws of 1854.[5] The act of 1865 in turn was re-
pealed by another act, January 19, 1866,[6] which added
some officials to the list authorized by the act of December
30, 1854. The new act provided for the election of a Territorial superintendent of common schools by the legislature instead of appointment by the board of regents, as
had been done since 1854. A county superintendent, to be
elected every two years by the people of the county, was
also added to the list of school officials. The act of 1866
was more specific than earlier acts in defining the duties of
the trustees. It also allowed a sustenance tax of one *per
cent* to the trustees by consent of the voters of each district. Without specifying what funds or their amount, the

act mentions that certain sums due from corporations were to be added to the school fund.

An act of February 21, 1868, defined common schools as those which the trustees of each district should organize and control. It forbade the alienation of any portion of the school fund to private or other schools which were not under the direction and control of these trustees.[7] This prohibition was evidently a barrier against the obtaining of any of the school fund of the Territory by the newly arrived mission schools which were being erected in Utah by Presbyterians, Catholics, and other Gentile religious groups, hitherto negligible factors in Utah.

In 1873, the Territorial Teachers' Association "realizing the inefficiency of the condition of our educational affairs" presented a petition to the legislature to improve the school system of the Territory.[8] The petition went on to recommend that a board of education chosen by the legislature be placed at the head of the entire system of the Territory. This board was to have control of all educational matters not otherwise provided for. The main proposal was to have more officers, both appointed and elected, in order to obtain greater efficiency. The legislature was asked to add to the school fund one-half of the liquor tax, all fines for drunkenness and disorderly conduct, profits from sale of estrays, revenue obtained from the sale of valuable franchises to corporations, escheats, and one mill on all taxable property in the Territory. But even from this Territorial Teachers' Association there was as yet no recommendation concerning free schools in the Territory. One would have expected this class, above all others, to have favored this type of school within Utah. There were no free schools at the time of the petition, nor did the teachers' petition recommend that any of them be established.

The first legislative assembly to meet after the publication of the Territorial Teachers' Association petition required the county superintendents to make a yearly report of the number of children from four to sixteen years of age in each district. The Territorial superintendent was also required to show the yearly distribution of the school funds in proportion to the school population of each district. In order to receive any share of the school fund, amounting for the entire Territory to $15,000, schools were to remain open at least three months in the year.[9]

An act amending—but in reality, because of its scope, replacing—all preceding school acts, was passed on February 18, 1876.[10] The passing of this act marked another step in the evolution of popular control over schools. The Territorial superintendent and the county superintendents were to be elected by the people. The county courts retained their power of appointing the county boards of examiners. The sum of $25,000, instead of $15,000, was henceforth to be the school fund. Twenty thousand dollars of this sum went to the district schools and $5,000 to the university, on the condition that the latter would instruct forty pupils in a normal-school department. These forty pupils, in return for free tuition, were required to serve the Territory for one year as teachers in the district schools.

The achievements of the Territorial legislative assembly show, however, but one aspect of the struggle which Utah, in common with many other sections of the country, went through, in order to obtain free schools. In this contest one finds that the governors, who were appointed from Washington, repeatedly pointed out to the Utah legislature the desirability of a free school system. The first Gentile Governor of Utah, Alfred Cumming, in his message of December 11, 1860, praised the inhabitants of the Territory for their increasing interest in building schools and commended President Young for building "a college for the

instruction of youths in the higher branches of education."
But "as yet, you have no free or common schools; and I
would again impress upon you the vital importance of appropriating a portion of the Territorial revenue to the
establishment and maintenance of such schools."[11] Governor S. S. Harding repeated this plea for free schools in even
stronger terms in 1862, emphasizing the fact that the legislature was appropriating money to objects of far less
importance, such as the Nauvoo Legion.[12] Governor Charles
Durkee in 1886 proposed a memorial to Congress, asking
for financial aid in the cause of education, for he doubted
the financial ability of the Territory to provide free education for all of its childern. Acting-Governor E. P. Higgins
in 1869 and Governor G. L. Woods in 1872 spoke about
the lack of interest in providing free schools.[13]

Governor George P. Emery, in his first message to the
Legislative Assembly in 1876, admitted that he could not
bring the matter of free education to the attention of that
body more forcibly than his predecessors had done; yet
he asked for legislation upon the subject.[14] In his message of 1878 his recommendations were more specific. He
spoke of Salt Lake City alone as annually spending on
private tuition more than thirty thousand dollars, which
was enough to educate the entire school population of the
city, whereas only one-fifth of that population were being
benefited. He wanted teachers appointed "for their moral
worth and qualification as[15] teachers, regardless of their religious bias."

But the acts of the legislative assembly and the messages of governors of Utah Territory tell only part of the
story of the beginnings of the school system in early Utah.
These official utterances provide merely a skeleton outline
of what was going on. For the flesh and blood story one
must penetrate beyond the statutes and the speeches de-

livered from the governmental tribune. The leader of the
Mormon people, Brigham Young, was a force which had
to be considered before any move of importance could
be made, as some of the governors of Utah Territory found
to their chagrin after their arrival in Utah. Hence Mormon
practice and Brigham Young's attitude on the subject of
schools outweigh in importance the acts of the legislative
assembly or the speeches of the non-Mormon governors of
the Territory.

Those in charge of the early Mormon educational enterprises had somewhat exaggerated ideas about what their
followers could achieve. This overstressing of their power
to achieve results may be seen in some of their early attempts in Nauvoo. Simultaneously with the granting of a
charter to the City of Nauvoo, a charter was granted to
a university contemplated for that city.[16] John C. Bennett,
a Mormon for the time being, was appointed chancellor
of the university. On the board of regents were a number
of prominent Mormons—William Law, Joseph Smith, Hyrum Smith, William Marks, Sidney Rigdon, Daniel H.
Wells, N. K. Whitney, John Taylor, and Heber C. Kimball.[17] With Orson Pratt teaching mathematics and English literature; Sidney Rigdon, church history; and Orson
Spencer appointed to fill the chair of modern languages,
the *Times and Seasons* of December 15, 1841, modestly
noted that these positions were "occupied by some of the
most able men the nation affords in their respective de-
partments."[18]

According to one writer "a site for a building was selected and plans of the structure were drawn."[19] If this
were done, it is one of the few accomplishments of those
who inaugurated the University of Nauvoo. Another
achievement of these men consisted in the granting of two
honorary LL.D. degrees—one of these to the fiery James

Gordon Bennett, whose New York *Herald* had gained the approbation of the Mormon leaders.[20] The Mormon population both inside and out of Nauvoo was neither ready nor able to support this institution of higher learning; its name soon disappeared from the pages of the two Mormon publications of the period, the *Times and Seasons* and the *Millennial Star*.

Not at all daunted by the lack of response at Nauvoo, the Church leaders decided in 1850 to establish the University of Deseret, at Salt Lake City. In fact, the chancellor and regents of the new university stood optimistically as upon a "peak in Darien"—but not silently—when they perceived the future possibilities of Mormonism and of their university, for the two were to advance hand in hand. In a circular addressed to the "Patrons of Learning" dated Salt Lake City, April 17, 1850, they wrote:

Multitudes of all ages come from under the heavy hand of oppression, and desire instruction in order to be free, useful, and happy. This boon must be given to them, without respect to age or means. The emigrants and outcasts of all nations will here find an asylum of safety, and a nursery of arts and sciences available upon the cheapest terms. Here, instructions by means of lectures or otherwise, will be brought to the level of the laboring class of every grade—of every religious faith—of every political or social creed, and of every living language. It is neither arrogant or extravagant to say that this institution is forthwith prepared to teach more living languages practically, than any other university on the face of the earth; and as to the matter of dead languages, we leave them mostly to the dead. The known industry of this people in rearing up cities and temples, with almost magic celerity, is not least visible in their system of diffusing a knowledge of the sciences throughout the popular mass. It is interwoven in the very fabric of this peoples' organization and progress to educate the mass, and elevate all the people to the fullest extent of their capacity.[21]

This Mormon circular compares interestingly with the purpose behind the founding of Harvard College in 1636.

The intent of the Harvard fathers recorded on one of the gates to Harvard Yard reads:

After God had carried us safe to *New-England,* and wee had builded our houses, provided necessaries for our liveli-hood, rear'd convenient places for Gods worship and setled the Civill Government: One of the next things we longed for, and looked after was to advance *Learning* and perpetuate it to Posterity; dreading to leave an illiterate Ministry to the Churches, when our present ministers shall lie in the Dust.

The University of Deseret had an appropriation of $5,000 voted to it by the Territorial Assembly; but this amount, which would have been a substantial contribution at the time, proved to be chimerical, for the Assembly found itself unable to pay the appropriation.[22] About a year later the vote on this appropriation was rescinded without the university's having received any aid.[23] At the time the University of Deseret was chartered, a committee was appointed to draft a memorial to Congress concerning education in the Territory, but the plea fell on uninterested ears.[24]

The university opened its classes in November, 1850, under the name of "Parent School."[25] A Doctor Cyrus Collins, en route to California, stopped in Utah long enough to be chosen principal. By the beginning of the second term Doctor Collins had resigned. Chancellor Orson Spencer and W. W. Phelps, a member of the board of regents of the university, took immediate charge of the teaching. Forty pupils were registered; and the tuition, which had been eight dollars a quarter, was reduced to five. The third term, which began on October 27, 1851, found Orson Pratt added to the teaching staff. Four terms proved to be the life span of this new school. In 1852, at the close of the fourth term, classes were discontinued.

If education were to be a widespread benefit to the Territory, a normal school would be a necessity. Therefore, during the last days of the Parent School, methods of resuscitation were unsuccessfully tried by turning the school into a training school for teachers. But this aspect of the common school system—teachers' training—received little consideration until the advent of Doctor John R. Park at the revived University of Deseret in 1869. During the sixties Robert L. Campbell, Territorial superintendent for the common schools had consistently called the attention of the legislature to the need for trained teachers. His advocacy of a normal school was supported by the Gentile governors of the Territory and at times by groups of citizens in the Territory.[26] There was little active leadership by the heads of the Church in filling this need.

In April, 1860, an article in the *Deseret News* described the schools of Salt Lake City. Henry I. Doremus, a graduate of the College of New Jersey in the class of 1832 and a member of the Mormon Church, had a school of "about fifty scholars, mostly under fifteen."[27] He cautiously told the writer of the article that if a sufficient number of older pupils presented themselves, he would surrender the younger pupils and teach those who were more advanced. The article stated that there was another school of about fifty pupils taught by a Mrs. Hulda Kimball, and also the Union Academy. After mentioning these three schools the writer of the article concludes, "What other schools there are in the city we are not prepared to state."[28] The same issue contained an advertisement that the City Academy in the Sixteenth Ward would open its doors for the summer session on April 16, 1860. Reading, writing, and "numbers" would be taught at the rate of four dollars per quarter, "the higher branches" at six dollars for the same period; board and tuition for the term of twelve weeks could be obtained for sixty dollars.[29]

The Union Academy was one of the schools which received definite attention from the President of the Church. His support of this school was assured by an article in the *Deseret News* of February 22, 1860. This article emphasized the teaching of algebra, surveying, and other higher branches of mathematics, astromomy, chemistry, mineralogy, geology, and modern languages. The president had hopes that the students would soon learn to use and develop their practical energies.[30] As evidence of his practical support, President Young gave the school $2,500.[31] Later developments showed that there was little necessity of limiting the enrollment, for when the school opened on April 9 and 10 only twenty-six pupils were ready to take advantage of the offer.[32] But though the response showed that there was no great demand for such an institution, this Academy managed to survive.[33]

To note what was practicable and then to urge its adoption with all the power at his command was one of the strong points in Brigham Young's leadership. Advocacy of the university in the early fifties would have been a waste of effort. Therefore, Brigham Young paid no attention to that question. By the sixties the question was reasserting itself in another form. Education in practical subjects was needed, or so Brigham Young felt; therefore he sent out a trial balloon. Under his patronage the Union Academy opened. Once the academy was ushered into the cold practical world, it had to find its own light, heat, and enthusiasm within itself. The leadership and the care exercised by the Church authorities were not so strongly evidenced in the sphere of education as in their economic paternalism.

In a frontier country settled by a group composed, as were the Mormons, of many people who lacked elementary education, the problem of the common school was a more important one for the community to solve than that of the university. There seems to have been little done about common schools before the Mormons reached Utah. In June, 1831, when the Church was barely one year old, Joseph Smith had a revelation and then told William W. Phelps:

> You shall be ordained to assist my servant Oliver Cowdery to do the work of printing, and of selecting books for schools, in this Church, that little children also may receive instruction before me as is pleasing unto me.[34]

The temple at Kirtland had a school room—whether for children or for adults is not mentioned.[35] At Nauvoo, the chancellor and regents of the University had charge of the common schools, and appointed the school wardens and adopted text books for each district in the city.[36] Here also some of the men who became prominent as teachers in Salt Lake City gained experience—among these men were Jesse Fox, who opened the first school at Manti, Utah; Eli B. Kelsey; and Julian Moses.[37]

As soon as the settlers in Salt Lake Valley had built themselves shelters, schoolhouses began to appear. Often these buildings served also as meeting-houses, dance halls, lecture halls, concert halls, and theatres; but these uses were secondary, except where there was no meeting-house available; in that case the religious claim superseded all the others.[38] Captain Howard Stansbury, of the United States Army, who spent the winter of 1849-50 in Salt Lake City, noted that "School-houses have been built in most of the districts, both in the city and country, which are attended by old as well as young, and every effort is made to advance the mental improvement of the people."[39] Other visitors who followed Stansbury confirmed his observation about schoolhouses. In 1855, Remy recorded thirty schools in the city.[40]

As the settlers pushed north and south from the chief city of the Territory, school buildings appeared in regions where a short time before sage brush and sand had held solitary sway. In the smaller settlements the manifold functions of the school buildings were especially notice-able.[41] Springville was settled by several families under the leadership of A. Johnson in 1850.[42] Two years later the town boasted a schoolhouse "forty-three feet by twenty-seven, two stories high."[43] Nephi's first settler, Timothy B. Foote, arrived with his wife and six children in the fall of 1851.[44] Before the year was finished several additional families and a schoolhouse were added to the settlement.[45]

Elder Amasa Lyman wrote, June 22, 1852, from the Mormon colony founded at San Bernadino, California, the previous year: "The bowery is occupied during the week by our Day school of one hundred and twenty-five scholars under the direction of two well-qualified teachers."[46] Logan City was a houseless plain on September 1, 1859; by March 6, 1860 "there are nearly one hundred houses, a tabernacle and three schools."[47] One enthusiastic letter-writer wrote to Albert Carrington, editor of the *Millennial Star*, in 1870; "I have never been in a settlement of fifteen or twenty families that did not contain a meeting-house and a schoolhouse."[48]

But, as Remy noted in his trip through the Salt Lake Valley, the number of schoolhouses erected does not indicate an interest in knowledge any more than does the well-stocked library of a rich man imply an interest in learning.[49] That schoolhouses were erected is an indisputable fact; what amount of studying was done and what interest evoked for learning cannot be determined quite so easily. John Hyde, Jr., who tried teaching school in Utah, severely criticised the Mormon people and their leaders on this score. Remy drew many of his facts and conclusions from the work of Hyde;[50] and much of what Remy recorded about the common schools came from the observations of Hyde. But several other travellers who mention this feature of Utah life agree with Hyde that the Mormon people were not particularly interested in education.

Chandless, that capital observer of the human element in Mormon life, spent his time in the Territory mingling with the Mormon families, selecting the children as the especial object of his attention. This was done by Chandless not as an inquisitor, but as a friend and impartial observer. He summarized his observations of Mormon education by noting that "All the children old enough were sent to the school of the ward; but the education there is entirely secular; nor did I ever find Mormons very anxious for the early instruction of their children."[51]

Richard F. Burton, who wrote one of the best works on Mormonism during the period before 1869, said of their education:

The object of the young colony is to rear a swarm of healthy working bees. The social hive has as yet no room for drones, bookworms, and gentlemen. The work is proportioned to their powers and inclinations. At fifteen a boy can use a whip, an axe, or a hoe —he does not like the plow—to perfection. He sits a bare-backed horse like a Centaur, handles his bowie-knife skillfully, never misses a mark with his revolver, and can probably dispose of half a bottle of whisky. It is not an education which I would commend to the generous youth of Paris and London, but it is admirably fitted to the exigencies of the situation. With regard to book-work, there is no difficulty to obtain in Salt Lake City that 'mediocrity of knowledge between ignorance and learning' . . . Every one learns to read and write . . . The Mormons have discovered, or, rather have been taught, by their necessities as a working population in a state barely twelve years old, that the time of school drudgery may profitably be abridged. A boy, they say, will learn all his memory can carry during three hours of book-work, and the rest had far better be spent in air, exercise, and handicraft.[52]

Phil Robinson, who visited Utah a few years after the death of Brigham Young, saw some children in Monroe, Utah, wandering to school in a haphazard and lackadaisical manner. This observation led him to write:

I thus had an opportunity of observing the curious happy-go-lucky style in which "schooling" is carried on, and I was sorry to see it, for Mormonism stands urgently in need of more education, and it is pure folly to spend half the revenue of the Territory annually in a school establishment, if the children and their parents are permitted to suppose that education is voluntary and a matter of individual whim. Some of the leading members of the Church are conspicuous defaulters in this matter, and do their families a gross wrong by setting "the chores" and education before them as being of equal importance. Even in the highest class of the community children go to school or stay away almost as they like, and provided a little boy or girl has the shrewdness to see that he or she can relieve the mother or father from trouble by being at home to run errands and do little jobs about the house, they can, I regret to think, regulate the amount of their own schooling as they please.[53]

The Mormon teachings may have advocated more education among the faithful, but it was a case of even though "the spirit was willing the flesh was weak." One may explain this weakness in accomplishment, and so to a slight extent excuse the short-comings of the leaders in this respect.

One factor involved was the inferior economic status of the teacher. Evidently some most noble souls thought that teachers should receive a living wage in this heaven on earth envisioned by the Mormon leaders. Remy, travelling south from Salt Lake City to California, saw a poster nailed on the door of a schoolhouse in southern Utah which read:

NOTICE

I, schoolmaster to all the brethren, greeting, Monday, the 19th of November, the anniversary of the massacre of one hundred and

eighty-five thousand Assyrians by the angel of the Lord, has been
fixed upon for the reopening of my course on the divine sciences
and reading, and on writing, with the art of orthography; and
wheras we are in a state of famine, in consequence of the seventh
year after our establishment in the country, the charges will be
fixed for each scholar, boy or girl, in the following way:—for one
month, a bushel of wheat or maize, or two bushels of potatoes.
And whereas it is winter, each must bring a cedar log every
fortnight. And whereas those who cannot pay in grain or Irish
potatoes, may be able to do it in some other way, bears' flesh,
squirrels, and dried pumpkins will be received, as well as salt
pork and cheese. And whereas, I have nothing whatever to eat, I
must be paid a month in advance, inasmuch as I am in want.[54]

Hyde also gives instances of this neglect of the teacher.[55]
An incident is told of an early teacher at Ogden who received a buckskin in payment of tuition fees.[56] Accounts
of this type are magnified by Hyde, who wrote as if they
were part of a premeditated plan of the Church leaders to
keep their followers in ignorance. Mrs. Hannah Cornaby,
a Mormon writer, shows a different attitude towards this
state of affairs from that taken by Hyde, whom it embittered. Although Mrs. Cornaby's husband had been appointed assistant United States deputy marshal and remained as a teacher in Salt Lake City, the members of his
family were often in want, in spite of efforts to economize
on the two salaries. At times the family had to rely on the
charity of Judge Elias Smith to tide them over difficult periods. But Mrs. Cornaby and her husband realized that life
in a frontier community was no easy task nor was teaching
school a sinecure in a society where laborers, craftsmen,
and farmers were in great demand.[57] For a number of years
the educational theories of the Mormons had to confront a
stubborn economic fact. Food, clothing, and shelter had
to be provided before education. For this reason Mormon
leadership was diverted from fulfilling its theories regard-
ing education until late in the sixties, when the physical

life of the frontier was not constantly and relentlessly con-
suming the major part of the community's energies and
resources.

Indirect evidence showing a lack of regard among the
inhabitants of Utah for school matters may be found in the
remarks made by the superintendent of common schools
for the Territory in 1862.[58] One of the duties of this official was to collect statistics on attendance, number of
schoolhouses, and other educational affairs which seemed
of importance to the territorial legislature. It was the duty
of the trustees in each district to furnish the superintendent
with these statistics; yet the latter official continually complained of the trustees' lack of interest in supplying grist
for his statistical mill. In 1868-69, the superintendent stated
that the statistics were especially incomplete because many
of the trustees, busily at work building the transcontinental
railroad, had no time to make school reports.[59]

Another problem in early Utah was that of obtaining
text books. A letter published in the *Millennial Star* of
April 1, 1851, stated that "Brother" Woodruff had arrived
in Salt Lake City with two tons of school books. After the
long haul a third of the way across the continent, probably
the weight of the school books was of more significance to
the letter-writer than their contents.[60] Imigrants to Utah
were urged to "bring books, charts, and other useful
things."[61] One means of solving this lack of school books, a
solution which had an added merit in the opinion of the
Church leaders, was to bring into use as text books the
Bible, the Book of Mormon, and the *Book of Doctrine and
Covenants;* for a greater supply of these than of any other
books had been brought into the Territory. Although a
printing press was imported into the Territory in the early
days, there was still the question of obtaining paper. By the
time the paper supply was adequate, books could be pur-

chased in the East and transported to Utah at lower rates than they could be published in the frontier community.

In keeping with the attitude of the Mormon leaders towards the learning of the world, which they once had attempted to revise by means of the University of Nauvoo, was their attitude towards the written language with which they had to contend. The *Eleventh General Epistle* of 1854 read:

> The Regency have formed a new alphabet, which it is expected will prove highly beneficial, in acquiring the English language, to foreigners as well as to the favourable consideration of the people, and desire that all of our teachers and instructors will introduce it in their schools and to their classes. The orthography of the English language needs reforming—*a word to the wise is sufficient.*[62]

Orson Pratt and W. W. Phelps devised this new alphabet, the Deseret alphabet. Each character in the Deseret alphabet represented a syllable of the English language, necessitating thirty-eight characters.[63] At one fell swoop the difficulties of spelling and reading were to be eliminated. Included in the Territorial Assembly appropriations for 1855 is listed one of $2,500 to purchase a font for the new alphabet.[64] Some primers, the Book of Mormon, and a few articles in the *Deseret News* were printed in its type, but the artificial method did not gain popular support.

A motive not mentioned in the official announcement of the Church's support of the Deseret alphabet became evident when the Church reopened the question about the year 1867 and, for a few years, continued proposing the use of the new alphabet. This was the period in which the transcontinental railroad was approaching Utah. And in that fact may lie the explanation for introducing the Deseret alphabet into the common schools of Utah.[65] It was part of a drive that took place on many fronts with the purpose of giving Mormonism a strong group consciousness before the wave of the first Gentile invasion, which was sure to reach Utah, should arrive. But in 1869 the characters of the new alphabet were no more able to gain popular support than in 1855. Bancroft assigns as the causes of the alphabet's failures the difficulty of obtaining uniform pronunciation and orthography, and also the monotony of its tailless characters, which made words difficult to distinguish.[66] Even if these obstacles had been removed, there would still have been the difficulty of introducing a new alphabet, *ex-cathedra*, among a people accustomed to another system and who, whether they wished them or not, had numerous relations with the outside world and an old established alphabet.

In a pioneer community that wished to adopt the beehive as its symbol, signifying the industry of its members, few adults were able to spend any part of the day in remedying past defects in their education. But, for those who wished to carry on their education, evening schools were opened. Newspaper items frequently mention evening classes for adults; quite often, but not always, these items refer to lectures in which the lecturer did all of the work except sitting and listening to his own voice.[67] During the winter months evening schools had to be squeezed into a weekly schedule of evening prayer-meetings, lyceum lectures, and dancing.[68]

Salt Lake City had two free evening schools for adults in 1860, one in the Fourteenth Ward under R. L. Campbell and another in the Sixth Ward under a Mr. Findlay.[69] In 1859, Provo had organized an evening school.[70] Another town had night classes for instructing the Danish Saints in the use of the English language.[71] A letter from Fillmore City, February 22, 1863, stated that:

The long winter evenings have passed off very agreeably and profitably to the young people of this place, by the establishing of an evening school, which was commenced last fall under the supervision of Benjamin Robison, and has been taught successfully by him, assisted by other qualified teachers who have given their time and talent gratuitously to this valuable institution.[72]

The evening schools were evidently of a sporadic nature. They were introduced as each community felt the need. As other interests intervened, attendance stopped. The popularity of dances and lectures helped detract from the interest in the evening schools.[73] But the desire to create literary and debating societies—to many a much more sociable way of spending spare time than attending school—showed that these schools, none of which seemed to have continuity, did not entirely satisfy the social and intellectual desires of the people in Utah.[74]

The Mormon Sunday Schools may also be considered as part of the educational system of Utah during the years 1847 to 1877. Almost all the children of the period came into contact with the religious principles taught there. Previous to the year 1877 these schools had been conducted by individuals in the different wards, acting independently of each other.[75] The publication of the *Juvenile Instructor*, the first number of which appeared on January 1, 1866, with Apostle George Q. Cannon as editor, helped to bring the scattered Mormon Sunday Schools closer to each other. Cannon was also a leader in the formation of the Sunday School Union, an organization which centralized all the Latter Day Saints' Sunday Schools into one group, the union taking place on November, 1867.[76]

One of the outstanding features of the school union was the interest in music which it was able to create in the students.[77] The teaching of music had occupied a prominent place in these schools. At the organization meeting Apostle

Cannon stated that Elder David O. Calder volunteered to
teach the tonic-sol-fa system of musical notation to the Sunday School teachers, if a sufficient number of them desired
it. Soon after, a group was learning the new method.[78]

At various times distinct groups under Church leadership entered the field of education. These groups, composed
of the Mormon élite, were formed under Church guidance
and were known as the School of the Prophets, the classes
of elders, and the Deseret Theological Institute—the last
being an institution founded by Brigham Young in 1855.
The purpose of these groups was, theoretically, the study
and development of theology. But Mormon theological doctrine was not only concerned with the theological principles of the Medieval Church as enunciated by St. Jerome,
St. Augustine, Abelard, or William of Champeux. Mormon
discussions also included such worldly topics as cattle feed,
human well-being, and irrigation, as well as questions
about the Holy Trinity and the Logos. For a large and important part of the population of Utah, these Church institutions provided contact with the thought of such Church
leaders as Joseph Smith, Parley Pratt, and Brigham Young.

As with many other Mormon practices, the original idea
for these training schools in the higher realms of theology
came from Joseph Smith, who founded the School of the
Prophets in Kirtland.[79] The school's primary purpose was
to prepare the officers of the recently organized Church for
their duties in the ecclesiastical hierarchy. It limited its
membership to Church officers, which in practice meant a
large portion of the adult male members of the Mormon
Church. In his *Journal* under the date of December 1, 1834,
Joseph Smith wrote that the school was well attended

. . . and with the lectures on theology, which were regularly
delivered, absorbed for the time being everything else of a temporal nature. The classes being mostly elders, gave the most

studious attention to the all-important object of qualifying themselves as messengers of Jesus Christ, to be ready to do his will
in carrying glad tidings to all that would open their eyes, ears,
and hearts.[80]

Discussion concerning Church doctrine occupied much
of the time, but history, geography, literature, and philosophy were touched upon in their meetings. In the winter of
1835 Joseph Smith presided and, at times, lectured on
grammar.[81] On November 20, 1835, Oliver Cowdery, the
amanuensis of the Book of Mormon, arrived in Kirtland
with a supply of Hebrew books. Work on these books and
the study of Greek occupied the Church elders in their
spare time.[82]

During the first week in January, 1836, classes in
Hebrew were organized under the direction of Joseph
Smith; a short time afterwards a Mr. Joshua Seizas of the
Hudson Seminary, at Hudson, Ohio, arrived to take charge
of this study for a fee of three hundred and twenty dollars
a term.[83] It was to members of this school that Sidney Rigdon gave a series of lectures on faith. Three of the school's
leading spirits—Sidney Rigdon, Frederick G. Williams, and
W. E. McLellin—were among those who apostatized from
the Church before it reached Utah.[84]

Parley P. Pratt described in his *Journal* his relation with
this school during the summer and autumn of 1833. He
wrote that:

A school of elders was . . . organized, over which I was called
to preside. This class to the number of about sixty, met for instruction once a week. The place of meeting was in the open air,
under some tall trees, in a retired place in the wilderness where
we prayed, preached, and prophesied and exercised ourselves in
the gifts of the Holy Spirit. Here great blessings were poured out
and many great and marvelous things were manifested and
taught. The Lord gave me great wisdom, and enabled me to teach

and edify the elders, and comfort and encourage them in their preparations for the great work which lay before us.[85]

The members of the school were hurriedly preparing themselves for their great proselyting campaign. During the enthusiasm of the early days, the school continued. After the departure from Kirtland in 1837 there is little mention of the efforts of this Mormon seminary.

In 1855, several societies were spontaneously formed by various people in Utah for intellectually and socially improving their members. The Deseret Theological Institute was formed by the Church in an effort to centralize the efforts of all these societies under the aegis of the ecclesiastical leaders. The effort of centralizing was perhaps too successful, in that all but one of the societies gave up the ghost. The Deseret Agricultural and Mechanical Society was the only group that remained in existence a few years later. The Deseret Theological Institute showed that the idea, at least, of the School of the Prophets was still in existence in 1855, although at that date there was not enough interest to keep the school alive.

The late sixties proved to be a critical period in the field of Mormon educational development as well as in that of economic development. The School of the Prophets could perform in one field services similar to that performed by the Zion Coöperative Merchantile Institute in the order. In fact, the initial impetus behind the coöperative movement of the period came from the School of the Prophets. This gathering of the Mormon leaders may be compared to the English cabinet. Policies concerning the whole Church were discussed in this group. Many an English prime minister would, however, give much to be able to hold a whip-hand over Parliament similar to that held by Brigham Young over the School of the Prophets.

The School of the Prophets was revived during the year 1867. A letter to Franklin D. Richards, head of the British Mission, from Wilford Woodruff on January 6, 1868, told that the School of the Prophets had been reëstablished.[86] A letter to Richards from his brother on February 2, 1868, also told of the revived School of the Prophets and that "the theological class numbers between 200 and 300 of our principal elders."[87]

Since Mormonism was a religion that was concerned with affairs in this world, as well as the next, the subjects of discussion included quite practical affairs. For instance, on February 2, 1868, S. W. Richards reported that the subject of astrology never would be an aid or a help to the priesthood; so probably that pronouncement terminated the study of astrology in the school.[88] Usually, however, the topics were not quite so far distant from this world as astrology. In May, 1869, the question under consideration centred about the best measures to be adopted in order to put the work of grading the transcontinental railroad before the people. "Its advantages to us just now as a people were presented in a very favorable and satisfactory light."[89] An earlier letter from George Goddard told that Brigham Young was the head teacher and added:

The subject of oneness or union is sustaining ourselves commercially &c., also the World of Wisdom, a revival of our fast day observance, attending meetings, and offerings for the poor are being taken hold of by the Saints.[90]

In April, 1868, Brigham Young wrote:

The members of the School of the Prophets have become so numerous that yesterday we adjourned to meet in the old Tabernacle; the scholars are very punctual in their attendance, spirited in their remarks, and anxious to improve in correct understanding and conduct.[91]

During the same period branches of the School of the Prophets were reported in Ogden and in Provo. L. E. Harrington wrote from American Fork, a short distance from Provo, on May 20, 1870:

> On Monday, President Young, Elder A. O. Smoot, and Elder McDonald attended our Theological School which was well attended by the brethren of Lehi, Alpine, Pleasant Grove, American Fork, and Cedar Valley at which much valuable instruction was given by all the aforesaid brethren and a great impulse was given to the Provo factory which when completed will be of great use to the citizens of Utah and surrounding counties.[92]

Here one may see the difference in emphasis between Joseph Smith's period of leadership and that of Brigham Young. In the early period, Greek, Hebrew, and the Scriptures received the major emphasis. In the latter period attention was directed to questions of a material nature. The educational and religious elements were present, but the emphasis was now upon the practical side of Mormonism.

But not only was the School of the Prophets being revived at this time. All Mormonism was on the alert. Education for the inhabitants of the Territory as a whole now had to be considered in a new light. The lack of resources had hitherto been a problem. By 1867 this problem was becoming less acute, for Utah's wealth and population were increasing at a rapid rate.

In 1851, the assessed wealth of the Territory had been $1,160,883.80;[93] by 1860 it had become $4,673,900.00.[94] For 1868-69 the assessed value was reported at $10,533,872.-00.[95] This, in turn, had doubled by 1874,[96] and in 1875 had become $23,289,180.00.[97] The population also was increasing: in 1850 it was reported at 11,380;[98] in 1860, at 40,273;[99] in 1870, 86,786;[100] and in the census report of 1880, 143,-963.[101] The *per capita* wealth in 1850 was over $86.00;[102] in

1860, it was $139.00;[103] and in 1880 $172.09.[104] In 1850, the legislative assembly received an auditor's report calling for payment—on account of the University—to the regents of $157.16.[105] This is the sole item which can be credited to education, unless the $56.00 donated for music books used by the Nauvoo Legion may be included under education.[106] The auditor's report for 1860 contained a bill of the Utah library for $600.00; and under sundry expenses, there was a charge of $30.00 by Elias Smith for printing blanks to be used for school purposes.[107] But in the report of 1869 one notes a change; $5,101.74 was spent in procuring books for the common schools, and $800.00 was spent for incidentals and stationery and as salaries for the various superintendents.[108] By 1874, there was a common school fund of $24,152.50 to be used for education.[109] Thus, the increase of wealth meant that education received more attention.

In addition to this increase in available funds, a new factor entered the Utah field of education. The effort of Brigham Young to consolidate the Mormon community as a commercial entity has already been noted in the campaign that gave birth to Zion's Coöperative Mercantile Institute. The Mormon leader realized the part which education would have in the future of Mormonism, especially with Gentile influences penetrating into Utah. Thus, a renewed energy was applied to the schools of Utah—a subject which the attitude of the community and its leaders had hitherto allowed to drift whither it would.

The Mormon control of education in Utah was first encroached upon in 1867 by an Episcopal grammar school, which gained an enrollment of sixteen pupils.[110] The Methodists followed with a school of twenty-eight pupils, founded on September 20, 1870.[111] In 1875, both the Roman Catholics and the Presbyterians founded schools.[112] Three years later the Congregational Church opened a school in Salt

Lake City.[113] The majority of these schools were established with the purpose of counteracting Mormon teachings by offering their own brands of sectarian education. They did draw some students away from the Mormon-controlled public schools; they had also the effect of forcing Mormon leadership to view anew the inconsistency between its educational theory and its practice.[114]

On April 8, 1867, President Young sounded the rally call with a rousing sermon delivered in the Salt Lake bowery to the Saints gathered there at conference time, urging them to study the arts and the sciences.[115] The Utah *Kulturkampf* then began in earnest. The Mormon leader recommended to his audience a previous speech made by "brother" Wells advocating the introduction of the Bible, the Book of Mormon, and the *Book of Doctrine and Covenants* into the schools "that our children may become acquainted with . . . [their] principles, and that our young men, when they go out to preach, may not be so ignorant as they have been hitherto."[116] Brigham Young advised the Mormons to study useful things, such as arithmetic and surgery, instead of French and German. In closing his speech, President Young said:

In these [useful studies] and all other branches of science and education we should know as much as any people in the world. We have them within our reach, for we have as good teachers as can be found on the face of the earth, if our bishops would only employ and pay them, but they will not. Let a miserable little, smooth-faced beardless, good-for-nothing Gentile come along without regard for either truth or honesty, and they will pay him when they will not a Latter Day Saint. Think of these things. Introduce every kind of useful studies into our schools . . . Do this instead of riding over the prairies, hunting and wasting your time, which is property that belongs to the Lord, our God, and if we do not make good use of it we shall be held accountable.[117]

In the speech preceding President Young's, Daniel H.

Wells had said: "Let us provide schools, competent teachers, and good books for our children, and let us pay our teachers."[118] The charge that Utah teachers received pittance wages made by John Hyde, Jr., in the late fifties, received support in 1867 from Brigham Young's second counsellor, D. H. Wells.[119] This Mormon leader in his argument for better pay for Utah teachers quoted the teachers of the Territory as complaining in the past: "We cannot afford to teach school, for the wages is too low, and low as it is we cannot get it when it is earned."[120] In Wells's opinion the time had now arrived to change the status of Utah's teachers.

At the next conference, October, 1867, George A. Smith, who at this same conference became first counsellor to President Young, advised the foreign Saints to learn English, and "preached to all classes—all the boys and girls under ninety—to go to school and educate themselves." He then asked the bishops to "stir up" everybody on the subject of education and to encourage it in all possible ways.[121] These three speeches came after a period in which there had been a lack of concentrated effort by the Mormon leaders in educational affairs. It was during these same years of 1867-69, while "the hosts of Israel were girding up their loins to protect Zion," that the reëstablishment of the University of Deseret took place. Instead of the subjects which were to revolutionize the learning of the world, as had been announced in the circular of 1850, commercial subjects were to hold the main place in the curriculum of the reorganized University of Deseret, which opened on December 2, 1867.[122]

Among those present at the opening exercises of the university were Presidents Brigham Young, H. C. Kimball, and D. H. Wells; Elders Orson Pratt, Wilford Woodruff, George Q. Cannon, and Joseph Smith of the Twelve Apostles; and several members of the board of regents, "with a large number of bishops and leading men of the city."[123] Chancellor Carrington, according to the *Millennial Star*, rejoiced "that the Presidency had seen fit to make a move in the direction of re-opening the University."[124] David O. Calder, who had been President Young's chief clerk and was considered a leading figure in Salt Lake musical circles, was present as principal of the institution.[125] He announced that he would teach commercial subjects by having the students perform the actual duties of keeping books, act as tellers, and perform similar clerical duties that were required of clerks in the business houses of 1867.[126]

From this restricted start, which promised all the greater success because of its being confined to what the community actually needed, the university slowly expanded into other fields under the leadership of Doctor John R. Park, who became principal in March, 1869, following D. O. Calder's resignation.[127] Dr. Park, educated at Ohio Wesleyan and New York universities, had gained a reputation as teacher in the Drapersville section of Salt Lake City.[128] By June, 1870, a classical and a normal course had been added to the commercial course at the University of Deseret.[129] In 1871, Dr. Park was appointed, in company with the instructor of French at the university, C. L. Bellerive, to a mission in order to study the school systems of the eastern United States and Europe. C. L. Bellerive's letters describing the results of this mission are published in the *Millennnal Star*.[130] As soon as the work of education was decided upon, the Mormon leaders displayed energy in studying methods and enlarging the educational possibilities of Utah.

A branch of the University was organized at Provo in April, 1870,[131] and continued for about three years. At one time it enrolled approximately two hundred pupils.[132] Brigham Young, owner of the university building and grounds at Provo, deeded the property to seven trustees, all of whom were members of the Church, to found an academy at Provo. Part of the deed of trust read:

> The beneficiaries of this academy shall be members in good standing in the Church of Jesus Christ of Latter-Day Saints, or shall be the children of such members, and each of the boys who shall take a full course, if his physical ability will permit, shall be taught some branch of mechanism that shall be suitable to his taste and capacity; and all pupils shall be instructed in reading, penmanship, orthography, grammar, geography, and mathematics, together with such other branches as are usually taught in an academy of learning, and the old and New Testaments, the Book of Mormon, and the *Book of Doctrine and Covenants* shall be read and their doctrines inculcated in the academy.[133]

Karl G. Maeser was appointed principal to carry out the ideas of Brigham Young—"that the heart and the hand should be educated together."[134]

The question of who was going to pay for the education of Utah children still remained to be settled. The Gentile governors had spoken in favor of a free common school system supported by territorial taxation. Undoubtedly there was some hesitation among the inhabitants of the Territory in taxing themselves for this purpose before Utah became a state. Once the Territory achieved the desirable status of statehood, it would become entitled to receive 500,000 acres of the public land.[135] Until then, ways and means had to be devised by the Territorial legislature.

Robert L. Campbell, superintendent of common schools from 1862 until his death in 1874, advanced some actual facts which would have to be taken into consideration before Utah could successfully have a system of free schools by its own efforts. An assessment that would be willingly borne by some of the counties would not be accepted by the legislators of poorer counties, but in this sense the taxation for this purpose would not differ from any other assessment passed. At another time Campbell pointed to the need for preparation. If free schools were to be adopted, an adequately trained corps of teachers and a sufficient number of buildings would be necessary to meet the new demands.[136] In his recommendations Superintendent Campbell did not, however, deny the desirability of free schools.

But one person at least in Utah was opposed to free schools, and the attitude of the head of the Mormon Church must be taken into consideration in any movement of importance that took place while he was alive. Brigham Young gave vent to his feelings on this subject while speaking at St. George Temple, on April 6, 1877, five months before his death. He said:

> Many of you have heard what certain journalists have to say about Brigham Young being opposed to free schools. I am not opposed to free education as much as I am opposed to taking away property from one man and giving it to another who knows not how to take care of it. But when you come to the fact, I will venture to say that I school ten children to every one that those do who complain so much to me. I now pay the school fees of a number of children who are either orphans or sons and daughters of poor people. But in aiding and blessing the poor I do not believe in allowing my charities to go through the hands of a set of robbers who pocket nine-tenths themselves, and give one-tenth to the poor. Therein is the difference between us, I am for the real act of doing and not saying. Would I encourage free schools by taxation? That is not in keeping with the nature of our work; we should be as one family, our hearts and hands united in the bonds of the everlasting covenants; our interests alike, our children receiving equal opportunities in the school-room and the college.[137]

This strikes one as the very human complaint of the wealthiest man in Utah fighting against a tax he dislikes. In considering the attitude of Brigham Young, whose fight against public taxation for the support of schools was successful during the period under discussion,[138] one must take into account the fact that states far wealthier than the Territory of Utah had but recently abolished the rate bills, by which parents had paid a *per capita* charge for their children in school. Connecticut and Rhode Island had abolished the rate bill in 1868, Michigan in 1869, and New Jersey in 1871.[139] The question whether the community as a whole or parents should pay the cost of education had virtually been settled when New York State decided in 1867 that the community should pay the bill.[140] Thirteen years after Brigham Young's speech, in 1890, the Territory of Utah decided that the community as a whole should not leave education to the parents' ability to pay or to charity, but that the charge should be a definite part of the Territorial expenses. After that year the Mormons maintained some colleges and academies of their own, but the history of the common schools followed that of the country as a whole.

What did the Church do in this field before 1877? The evidence given by men such as Burton, Robinson, Hyde, and Remy showed that there was a laxness in this development of the life of the people. The reports of the Territorial superintendent of schools confirmed the observations of these travellers and sojourners in Utah, as did the incomplete statistics and the messages of the governors. The universities of Nauvoo and of Deseret showed that the Mormons placed a value upon education, especially if that education had a different tinge from the education of the "outer world." Thus, one can balance the sheet in Mormon educational work—the ideal was there, and it savored of a Mormon learning different from other learning. Actually, the Mormon leaders were lax in carrying out the details; the laxness, was caused to some extent by lack of wealth, but also by a lack of interest by both the Mormon believers and by their leaders. After 1867 the growth of mission schools and the increase of wealth in Utah lessened the gap between the ideal and the practical.

CHAPTER V

AND EVERY GAIN DIVINE

VARIOUS GROUP INFLUENCES

IN A SOCIETY—such as that of Mormonism in early Utah —with a well-organized directorate at the controls, formal schooling would be but one means of transmitting the beliefs of the leaders to their followers. The lecturer, the actor, the painter, the musical director, the editor—all of these could be used in furthering what were considered group interests. These various influences were especially necessary in a group which had many individuals trained in patterns of thought other than those of Mormonism. These influences, of course, were all at work during the same period with varying degrees of strength. But they are best treated by analyzing them one by one—a method which isolates influences that were united in practice. The Mormon newspapers were one means of influencing the Latter Day Saints.

1. Newspapers

The list of Mormon newspapers is not lengthy, but it tells a story of persecution, smashed printing presses, vitriolic articles, sulphuric editorials, and personalities attacked with bitterness. The tumultous career of Mormon journalism started peacefully at a Church conference in September, 1831. As a result of these deliberations, W. W. Phelps, who was travelling from Kirtland to Independence, Missouri, was directed to purchase a press and type in Cincinnati for a newspaper. With this equipment at their disposal the Mormons brought out the *Evening and Morning Star* at Independence in June, 1832. In the summer of 1833 the Mormons thought it the better part of wisdom to remove their newspaper headquarters to Kirtland, for the Missourians were at that time seemingly anxious to eradicate everything from their midst that savored of Mormonism. In October, 1834, *The Latter-day Saints' Messenger and Advocate* appeared in Kirtland as the successor of *The Evening and Morning Star*. This paper in turn gave way to the *Elders' Journal of the Church of Latter-day Saints,* a monthly publication, as the others had been. The last-named paper followed the Saints in their travels from Kirtland to Far West, Missouri. During the troublous days of 1838 in Missouri, its publication was discontinued.

The following year the Mormon press, with other things Mormon, found a refuge in Nauvoo. The newspaper published in that industrious beehive of Mormon farmers reflected the feeling of security which the Mormons enjoyed from 1839 to 1844. The first number of the *Times and Seasons,* published at Nauvoo in July, 1839, while that town was still known as Commerce, stated that the paper proposed to give news of the progress of the Church to Saints who were scattered abroad. It planned also to give to the world a history of their "unparalleled persecution in Missouri." Interesting experiences and items were solicited from the elders who lived or were travelling outside in the Gentile world which seemed at times to those in Nauvoo to be a world apart from that of the Saints. From July to December, 1839, there is a gap in the issues of the publication.[1] In December, 1839, the regular monthly issue began. Previous to its final issue in February, 1846, the *Times and Seasons* was being published semi-monthly.

In keeping with its purpose, the greater part of the paper was filled with theological articles and the story of Joseph Smith's life. Much of the heavy artillery of the editorial pen was directed against those who attacked the Saints and their beliefs. Minutes of Church conferences, exhortations, and tales of evil disasters befalling the world outside of Nauvoo occupied much of this paper's columns. In some of their lighter moments the editors, however, gave up worrying about the all-pervasiveness of Satan and his hoofed and horned assistants in their successful sway over the Gentile world and found space for matters less fraught with religious tension.

Poetry, strongly tinged with sad thoughts of foreboding, was in the prevailing mode of the period. Thus one volume of the *Times and Seasons* contained poems by Mormon writers on "My Epitaph," "An Apostrophe to Death," "The Hero's Reward," "Saturday Evening's Thoughts," and "The Three Witnesses"—the last dealing with the witnesses of the gold plates from which the Book of Mormon was transcribed.[2] After observing a wind storm in southern Illinois, S. A. Prior expressed himself in the following manner:

> A house or two by it destroyed
> The men with terror filled
> And many animals annoyed,
> And two or three were killed.[3]

All attempts were, however, not so awkward as this, for on the same page was an "Ode to Spring" by Miss Eliza R. Snow, which began

> Welcome Spring, estranged from sadness
> Paragon of Nature's gladness.[4]

This poem went on in a mood more joyful and imaginative than the ordinary run of poems in the *Times and Seasons.*

In May of 1840 another publication of the Church, the *Millennial Star,* appeared in Manchester, England, with Parley P. Pratt as editor. The purpose of this magazine was, in the words of the editor, to explain "the fullness of the gospel—the restoration of the ancient principles of Christianity."[5] The first and succeeding volumes retained this ambition as the fundamental purpose of the publication. The early numbers digressed at times into articles such as "Awful State of Things in America," "Duties of Women," and "The Flood in France."[6] One article advised elders to investigate both sides of questions, for

almost everything has two sides. The world has two sides—else how could the Lord turn it upside down? Man, beast, bird, fish, insect, and vegetables have two sides each, . . . not so with truth . . . which has but one side. Since the Saints wish to know the Truth, they ought to investigate a proposition in order to distinguish its false principles from those that are true. Adopt the true principles and let either one of the Twelve or the editor of the *Millennial Star* know the true principles.[7]

As the *Millennial Star* increased in size, poetry received a proportionately greater amount of space. None using poetry as a means of expression surpassed or even approached the power of imagination or facility in the use of words possessed by Miss Eliza R. Snow. Among some of the other regular contributors who attempted writing in poetic form were W. W. Phelps, John Lyons, John Jacques, and W. G. Mills. The last-mentioned writer had a weakness for themes telling about "the sweet flower of early spring" or about a young lady, aged fourteen years whom, "death . . . with ruthless hand had seized."[8]

Although religious ideas dominated the magazine—as was appropriate, because this journal's main purpose was

to be the European mouthpiece for the Church—aspiring
writers both in prose and verse of non-religious topics were
given a means of expression by the editors. Much of the
prose was of a didactic nature, such as "On the Proper Improvement of our Time,"[9] the "Degeneracy of Public Mor-
als,"[10] or the "Cultivation of the Mind."[11]

After the fall of Nauvoo, Latter Day Saint news in the
United States was at first printed in the *Frontier Guardian,*
a newspaper which prospered under the editorship of
Orson Hyde, at Kanesville, Iowa, from February, 1849, to
March, 1852. The *Deseret News,* which was started at Salt
Lake City on June 15, 1850, eventually became the favorite
paper of the Saints in Utah. At various periods during its
career publication was discontinued because of the scarcity
of paper,[12] but in time weekly editions appeared quite regularly, and the editorial desk was accepted equally with the
pulpit as a vehicle of Church thought.

William Richards, second counsellor to President Brigham Young, from 1847 to 1854, was the first editor of the
Deseret News. Upon his death Albert Carrington, who had
been business manager of the *Times and Seasons* in Nauvoo, and had occupied the same position on the *Deseret
News,* took charge of the newspaper. Judge Elias Smith and
George Q. Cannon were the other editors of the paper until
1873. The first, a cousin of Joseph Smith, had been manager of the *Times and Seasons* at Nauvoo. George Q. Cannon
was private secretary to Brigham Young from 1864 to 1867.
While Cannon was editing the *Deseret News* in 1868:

Joseph Bull [was sent] to the Eastern States to obtain advertisements from the merchants who held the Utah trade, or desired
so to do. Bull carried with him an autographed letter from President Young, and the Eastern merchants saw the commercial wisdom of sustaining the Salt Lake *Deseret News.* The mission of
Bull to the states was a marked financial result, and thus by a

business *coup de main*, Cannon made a business success of the *Deseret News*.[13]

D. O. Calder and Charles W. Penrose continued the tradition of the office, being prominent members of the Church while they edited the paper.

The news columns contained articles which would interest readers in an agricultural settlement far from other sources of information and whose religious outlook upon life smacked of the Old Testament. The religious beliefs of the Mormons as well as their defensive attitude towards the outside world found expression in their paper. The columns of the *Deseret News* were also open to those who desired to write verse or short stories.

A typical number was that of March 12, 1856, which contained extracts from the *History of Joseph Smith* (written by himself), the sermons given in the Tabernacle, a short story ending in the approved manner—"Virtue, innocence, and kindness will ever triumph, and be the victor; while pride, hatred, and ill-will, will always be overcome." In a second tale in the same number, "The Drunkard's Good Angels," the drunkard's children turn out to be the angels. Space was given to political news from the East, to notices of marriages and deaths, and to the recent forgiveness of Brother John Pack by a council of Seventies from the charge that he was selling flour contrary to the counsel of the Church. The advertisements contained notices of school books for sale at "states'" prices, notices of strayed cattle, and sales of machinery, clothing, and lumber.

The first magazine published in Utah, as distinguished from the weekly newspapers such as the *Deseret News*, the ephemeral *Mountaineer*, or the Gentile *Valley Tan*, was the *Peep o' Day*—a magazine devoted to "science, literature and art." Theatrical reviews, articles on music, short stories, and poetry appeared in the six weekly numbers which were the life span of this magazine. A shortage of paper brought about its end. An incident connected with its publication caused comment at the time, and is interesting in the light of later developments. E. L. T. Harrison and E. W. Tullidge, the editors, were compelled to have their printing done at the United States army post, Fort Douglas, situated about three miles east of the city. Why did these men leave the Mormon metropolis to have their printing done? Why did they go to a United States army post? Was it possible that all was not well with newspaper editors in Zion. Rumor had it that these men had failed to ask counsel of the Church leaders before they started publication of the magazine in October, 1864.[14] Five years later these editors of the *Peep o' Day* were prominent in the group which criticised Brigham Young's leadership of the Church.

On January 11, 1868, a rejuvenation of the *Peep o' Day* appeared in a weekly publication, the *Utah Magazine*. E. L. T. Harrison was editor. Many of the literary articles were written by the assistant editor, E. W. Tullidge. This magazine also was devoted to "Literature, Science, Art, and Education." Years before coming to Utah, E. L. T. Harrison had written an article in the *Millennial Star* pointing out to the Saints that though they had the revealed word of God, they should not neglect that knowledge which men had gained by study and had stored in the great books and works of art during the ages of recorded history.[15]

This attitude eventually lead to conflict. In 1869, a group which believed that each individual's reason would lead him to the Truth came into conflict with the Church authorities, who believed that in the final analysis an individual must submit his reason to the leadership of the Church. The leaders of the group which refused to accept Brigham Young's authority over each and every act of their lives included men who had been prominent in the intellectual and economic development of Utah. Among these were W. S. Godbe, E. L. T. Harrison, E. W. Tullidge, John Tullidge, H. W. Lawrence, Eli B. Kelsey, and T. B. H. Stenhouse. The *Utah Magazine* was their vehicle of protest.

The movement was primarily a protest against Brigham Young's direction of economic affairs in the Utah of 1869.[16] This was the year in which Young advocated the founding of Zion's Coöperative Mercantile Institute. The "revolters" refused to accept the choices which the Mormon leader had placed before them. Brigham Young offered them the alternative of either entering the Mormon scheme of coöperation or of staying out and being boycotted as well as ostracized. Brigham Young had another bone to pick with these independents. They had refused to follow Brigham Young on the question of developing the mining resources of the Territory. The Mormon leader warned his followers that mining wealth and its attendant evils was not for the community of the Saints. Some of the Mormon merchants saw with apprehension that the mineral wealth of Utah would be entirely in the hands of Gentiles if Mormons did not enter the field very soon. To those who disagreed with Brigham Young the time seemed favorable for a protest because there was the possibility of gaining the support of the laborers and mechanics of Salt Lake City.[17] A resolution had recently been passed in the School of the Prophets favoring a standardized scale of wages for the workingmen of the city—laborers were to receive one dollar a day, and mechanics one dollar and a half—wages lower than they were then receiving under the accepted laissez-faire status. The Insurgents, or Godbeites, made a bid for the support of the workers of the city.

W. S. Godbe doubted Brigham's business ability, and in his protest to the School of the Prophets he pointed to the failures he had suffered in the past because he had followed Brigham Young's leadership in investments.[18] Godbe's scepticism caused H. W. Lawrence, who had already invested thirty thousand dollars in Brigham's coöperative enterprise, to announce his doubts concerning the business acumen of the head of the Church. Lawrence then made haste to withdraw his financial support from Zion's Coöperative Mercantile Institute and immediately came to the open support of his friend, Godbe.[19]

The protesting group claimed that its principles were more in accord with the progressive spirit of Mormonism than were those of Brigham Young. They did not deny that under his leadership a society had been founded in Utah. They contended, however, that since the settlement in Utah was now an accomplished fact, other methods than absolutism were necessary for the best physical development of the Territory.[20]

The spark of dissatisfaction sputtered at first. Two sons of Prophet Joseph Smith arrived in Salt Lake City in the summer of 1869 and denied that Brigham Young was the true inheritor of their father's power. In spite of the known opposition of Brigham Young to these men, and in spite of his undoubted influence in the city their talks drew large audiences in Salt Lake City. Many, of course, came out of curiosity to see David Hyrum Smith. The rumor spread that his father had once predicted the leadership in Zion would fall to the lot of this son.[21]

The *Utah Magazine* tried at first to act as umpire between the disputants. To go even thus far savored of heresy in the minds of the faithful. But the editors went further and touched a vulnerable spot in Brigham Young's feelings. There was a rumor in Utah that Young was training one of his own sons to succeed him as the leader of the Church. On September 4, 1869, an editorial in the magazine of the

Godbeites was obviously aimed at any aspiration which
Young may have had in this respect. The editorial read in
part:

> If we know the true feeling of our brethren, it is that they never
> intend Joseph Smith's nor any other man's son to preside over
> them, simply because of their sonship. The principle of sonship
> has cursed the world for ages, and with our brethren we expect
> to fight it till, with every other relic of tyranny, it is trodden
> under foot.[22]

Other articles by some of the ablest writers in the Territory were devoted to an analysis of the absolutism of Young
in all phases of Utah life. Eli B. Kelsey wrote to show the
Mormon people "How the World Has Grown."[23] E. W.
Tullidge wrote on "Great Characters"—demonstrating
with obvious intent, but without mentioning the leader of
Mormonism, that there were others in the world who were
entitled to fame besides Brigham Young.[24] E. L. T. Harrison wrote an article explaining the philosophical basis of
faith.[25] The battle was not far off when Godbe wrote of "the
possibility of honest error."[26] The editor of the *Utah Magazine* stated the point of the dispute in his article on "Steady-
ing the Ark" by the statement that he doubted if "God
Almighty intended the priesthood to do our thinking."[27]
Brigham and the High Council thought otherwise; therefore the entire group was cut-off from the Church.

What about this paper and its supporters who possessed
the nerve to twist the lion's tail? No paper or magazine
published in Utah before 1877 had writers who were su-
perior in breadth of interest or in point of view to those
writing in the *Utah Magazine*. The insurrection against
Brigham Young, was, of course, the paper's *raison d'être*.
But the editors sought also to make their publication a re-
pository for the musical and literary compositions of Utah

inhabitants. This source of literary production failed to materialize; therefore excerpts from the *Pickwick Papers* and from Bulwer-Lytton's, *Harold, The Last of the Saxon Kings* were used. The third volume, which appeared during the period when the actual break with the Church occurred, showed more vigor and native strength than any production favored by the Church. E. W. Tullidge wrote a serial entitled "Terese, The Hebrew Maiden or Not all Dross," a story which had as its background members of the far-off English nobility mournfully wending their way through treachery, storms, and "Black Death." But even the nobles in this story realized the value of celestial marriage in orthodox Mormon fashion.[28] Articles on music abounded, reviews of books published in the East appeared, articles on the theatre, and poetry—both by home authors and excerpts from other magazines and from the writings of well-known poets. This ambitious periodical, once the reform movement was under way, gave place to the weekly *Mormon Tribune*. An article in *Tullidge's Quarterly Magazine* published in 1880 by E. W. Tullidge, one of the journalists prominent in Godbe's support, stated that the literary enterprises of W. S. Godbe cost that man over fifty thousand dollars.[29] Measured in terms of finance, the *Utah Magazine* was Godbe's greatest literary enterprise.

Just as this first flight into the field of literary publications was not sponsored by Church leadership, neither was the second attempt—*Tullidge's Quarterly Magazine*, the first number of which appeared in October, 1880. This was, of course, three years after the death of Brigham Young. John Lyons, William G. Morris, and George A. Mears were among the prominent Mormons who assisted in this attempt with their stories, poems, and essays. This journal had articles on sociology, natural science, history, religion, music, and the drama. Both Mormons and Gen-

of Virgil. For the worldly-minded there were volumes of
Macaulay's *History of England* and a number of novels,
which were on sale at a dollar each or for rent at ten cents
a volume.[33] Five years later Burton speaks of a few book-
stalls in the city.[34]

A writer in the *Utah Genealogical Journal* tells of the experience of A. H. Lund, who came to Utah in 1862 and
went to one of the smaller settlements. The writer states
that to A. H. Lund "as to many others who have come to
Utah, the first impressions of the new country were rather
discouraging. He missed his books more than anything
else."[35] This deprivation, however, had an advantage, for
good use of the one book available was made—a handbook
on astronomy. The newcomer had time thoroughly to
master, by supplementing the text with home-made maps,
the contents of his one book. But if there was a scarcity
of books in Utah, there were some books with which the
Mormons were familiar. They were well acquainted with
the Bible much to the discomfort of many of their theological adversaries. There were few people in Utah who did
not have access to a copy of the Book of Mormon, with its
turgid sentences, its monotony, and its Biblical plagariz-
ing. Their *Book of Doctrine and Covenants* was another
doctrinal work with which the Mormon public was familiar.

The shortage of school books combined with the absence
of book advertisements in Utah newspapers shows, at least,
that the use of books was not especially widespread in the
Utah of the fifties.[36] In addition to these factors there are
very few references to the contemporaneous literary life of
the period by the journalists of the Territory. This is particularly true of the period from 1847 to 1869.

Authors, who might have provided a substantial foundation for a unique Mormon development in literature,

were given no special marks of favor by the Church, except as the Church magazines and papers provided the
medium for publication. The major share of Mormon
writings are concerned with theological questions. In this
sphere, after the days of Joseph Smith, the two outstanding
writers were the brothers Orson and Parley Pratt. In addition to his theological works on Mormonism, Orson Pratt
published a work on the cubic and biquadratic equations,
as well as writing a manuscript article on the differential
calculus. But few of the Mormon leaders ventured so
far away from theological matters.

The list of those who received space in the papers has
already been mentioned. Some of the women, like Mrs.
Hannah Cornaby and Eliza R. Snow, ventured to publish
their poems in book form. Scenes and incidents connected
with the history of the Church gave Mormonism a vital
interest which Eliza R. Snow used with feeling and effect
in her works. This woman, already mentioned as a contributor to the *Times and Seasons* in Nauvoo and to the
Millennial Star, became known as "The Mormon Poetess."
She had been the wife of Joseph Smith; in Utah she became
the wife of Brigham Young. One source of her power was
her willingness to write of the scenes through which she
passed—the assassination of Joseph Smith, the expulsion
from Nauvoo, and other incidents in the life of the
Church.[37] A compilation of her work was published in two
volumes by the Church press in 1877.

Closely connected with the question of book supply in
Utah was the question of libraries. The Church, through
the organized seventies, here played a prominent part.
Even before Utah was known to the Mormons, the seventies had become interested in collecting books for the use
of their members. In an article published in the *Times and
Seasons* of January 1, 1845, a reporter announced that:

Among the improvements going forward in this city [Nauvoo], none merit higher praise, than the *Seventies* Library. The concern has been commenced on a footing an[d] scale, broad enough to embrace the arts and sciences, everywhere: so that the Seventies while travelling over the face of the globe, as the Lord's "Regular Soldiers", can gather all the knowledge, inventions, and wonderful specimens of genius that have been gracing the world for almost six thousand years.

Ten years ago but one *Seventy* and now *fourteen Seventies* and the foundation for the best library in the world. It looks like old times when they had "Kirjath Sapher", the city of books.[38]

In the precarious days during the expulsion from Nauvoo, this library must have disappeared, for there is no trace of it in early Utah. The first actual library came into existence when the United States Congress appropriated five thousand dollars for the foundation of a library in Utah.[39] Doctor John M. Bernhisel, the delegate from Utah, selected the books which arrived in the Territory in the fall of 1851.[40] Early in 1852 the Territorial assembly appointed William C. Staines librarian and voted to pay him four hundred dollars a year for his services.[41] In 1864, the library had a total of 5458 books and over four hundred additional tracts, loose sheets, and files of newspapers.[42] A public reading room was connected with this Territorial library; Chandless, in commenting upon reading facilities during his visit to the chief city of Utah, in November, 1855, does not mention this reading room.[43] Perhaps it was not open during his visit, but there were periods when its material was available to the inhabitants of the city, for Remy and Burton both mention this reading room during their respective visits to the city in 1855 and in 1862.[44]

Bancroft wrote of a reading room that was opened in the council house in Salt Lake City during the year 1853.[45] Here the Mormon with spare time, evidently a *rara avis* in a community watched over by Brigham Young, could while away the hours by reading "newspapers and magazines from all parts of the world." This source of entertainment, or learning, had evidently gone out of existence as far as general use was concerned by 1862, for in that year an article in the *Deseret News* spoke of the revival of the seventies' library and hoped that a reading room which would be connected with it might be used as an adjunct to the lectures planned for the winter of 1862-63.[46] On April 29, 1863, the *Deseret News* announced that the reading room at the seventies' council hall would be open to the public on three days a week, from 9 to 12 A.M. and from 1 to 6 P.M. Saturday of each week was reserved for ladies and for country visitors.[47] Here again the seventies made an organized effort to advance the cultural interests of Utah.[48]

To some extent the provincial areas followed the lead of Salt Lake City. The *Deseret News* of July 30, 1853, announced the establishment of the Mount Nebo Literary Association at Nephi City. Gifts of books, pamphlets, and mathematical instruments were solicited for the new organization.[49] The following year the Lehi City Council appropriated seventy dollars for founding a public library in that city, but either the amount or the enthusiasm aroused was not sufficient, for the library did not materialize.[50] By 1864 the Ogden Library Association had been formed with Chauncey W. West, Bishop of Weber Stake, as president. This association hoped to have reading matter by the following winter.[51] In 1874, the Ogden *Junction* was still seeking a public library, a lecture hall, and a reading room for that city.[52] The Sunday Schools and young peoples' societies of the Mormon Church carried this work of the seventies on to completion.[53] Salt Lake City, as the most populous and leading town in the Territory, was the most likely to lead the way in this respect, and it was not until 1864 that the seventies' library was a success there.[54]

3. Lectures

The seventies took the lead in another aspect of Mormon development—that is, in utilizing the lecture platform.[55] It would have been strange, indeed, if the Mormons had failed to utilize this method, for the lecturer was at the height of his popularity during the period in which Mormonism was founded.[56] Joseph Young, elder brother of Brigham, was the senior president of the seventies in early Utah. His grandson, Levi Edgar Young, writes of him: "His life dream . . . was to have the Seventy the scholars of the Church. He travelled up and down Utah awakening the Seventies to this end of the Mormon people."[57] Here was a method by which the Church, through its organization, tried to widen the intellectual horizon of its adherents.

In actual practice the bishops and ward leaders who were entrusted with guiding the temporal interests of their community made use of the lecture both as a means of education and of recreation. In some districts it was also used as a means of modifying the isolation of pioneer life as well as of bridging the chasms in many a Mormon's schooling. Isaac Higbee, one of the Church officers in Provo, shows how the lyceum fitted into a somewhat busy life in Provo during the winter of 1852. In February of that year he wrote to the editor of the *Deseret News*:

We have no time nor place for dancing at present. On the Sabbath, preaching; Sabbath evening, prayer meeting; Monday evening, singing school; Tuesday evening, lyceum; Wednesday evening, seventies' meeting; Thursday evening, prayer meeting; Friday evening, spelling school; and Saturday evening, the meeting of the lesser priesthood; and day school which takes up time.[58]

James S. Brown, writing of the first years in the Great Salt Lake Valley, shows the essentially useful character of these lectures at that period. He wrote that:

Some of the most practical and best informed men in the community were called upon to deliver free lectures on farming, stock-raising, etc., for many of the people had come from manufacturing centers and had no experience in agricultural life, consequently these people needed instruction and it was given in every industrial pursuit that was practicable at the time. . . .[59]

In 1852, a course of twelve lectures was given in Salt Lake City. Orson Pratt gave four lectures on the subject of astronomy; and G. D. Watt, a clerk in the Church offices, gave lectures on "phonography," that is, stenography.[60] In 1862, the *Deseret News* announced a series of evening lectures to be given each week during that winter season—the first lecture to be delivered by Joseph Young, Sr., on the History of the Rise, Progress, and Persecution of the Church of Jesus Christ of Latter Day Saints." The article announced that among the numerous subjects already selected for the lectures that coming winter were astronomy—the favorite choice of Orson Pratt, who gave his time unsparingly to this work—geology, architecture, mechanics, elocution, witchcraft, hydrophobia, Mahommedanism, evidences of divinity in Mormonism, and general history.[61]

At the lecture of November 18, 1862, by John Romney on "The Study and Advantages of History," Brigham Young, probably having in mind the thousands of youths back East who were at that time living warlike history before Richmond and Vicksburg, spoke to the audience

. . . complimenting the youthful lecturer, and expressed a desire to see other young men brought up in the same way. He defined history to be a fair account of events we have not seen. Continuing the subject of the evening, he painted in glowing colors the evils attendant upon youth reading warlike history.[62]

The winter of 1863-64 found the seventies' hall crowded every Thursday evening.[63] E. L. T. Harrison, Orson Pratt, T. B. H. Stenhouse, Karl Masser, J. V. Long, E. W. Tullidge, and James McKnight, all prominent in Church affairs, lectured. Joseph Young, Sr., exercised general supervision. Stenhouse, who had worked on a New York newspaper, gave some of his experiences in journalism to the Salt Lake audience. E. W. Tullidge spoke about ancient and modern literature. G. M. Ottinger, who had done the interior decoration work on the theatre, lectured on "Harmony of Colors." George A. Smith, historian of the Church, lectured on the ever-thorny question of the "History of Ireland."

In 1867, the lectures were transferred from the small seventies' hall to the more commodious Thirteenth Ward assembly rooms.[64] A subscriber to the *Utah Magazine* suggested during February, 1868, that diagrams, charts, chemicals, and geological specimens ought to be introduced to make the lectures more truly popular; and, he said in closing, "the settlements would soon follow suit."[65]

Not only were some of the settlements interested, but the wards of Salt Lake City followed the lead of Joseph Young's example. A letter to John Jaques, published in the *Millennial Star*, describes conditions in the Salt Lake City in February, 1871. "This winter, instead of dancing every other night and intermediate nights too, there has been a large number of lectures delivered in the various Wards."[66]

The settlements also had their lecturers. James S. Brown was sent in the winter of 1855 with a number of fellow Mormons on a mission to the Green River Indians.

They built a blockhouse and "in our religious and social arrangements, we held regular meetings, had lectures on different subjects, organized a debating society, and had readings."[67] In the winter of 1859 a lyceum was started at Provo.[68] By 1862-63 the Provo Literary Association was sponsoring lectures every Thursday evening on "scientific and practical subjects."[69] During the same winter a letter from Ogden City described the condition of the drama in that town and stated that under the auspices of the Ogden Literary and Scientific Institute lectures had been delivered once, and sometimes twice a week, to large audiences. The course of lectures was similar to that of the Salt Lake course in 1862—mineralogy, astronomy, navigation, the Ionian Islands, and education are some of the subjects treated. The writer said that the president of the society spoke at the opening lecture at some length upon the benefits to be derived from such institutions. He also encouraged the members of the association "to be diligent in the pursuit of that knowledge which will refine their feelings, dignity and enable their minds and exalt them in the scale of intellectual being."[70]

Fillmore organized a course of lectures early in 1864. The correspondent in the *Deseret News* who announced this fact wrote at the close of his letter:

We would like to hear of other places as well as Fillmore moving in matters of education and instruction. We are satisfied that there are hundreds of men in the settlements able and willing to devote a portion of their leisure during the winter evenings to the instruction of the youth of the Territory and in imparting general information to the people were they only encouraged to such labors. Brains will yet count for something.[71]

The question of whether the audience received any intellectual stimulus from lectures was discussed at the time.

Remy tells of the difficulties encountered by some of the able men of the period.

[They] have several times undertaken to give in the Social Hall, public lectures on astronomy, Hebrew, comparative physiology, and religious history. But under the penalty of otherwise speaking to empty benches, they were obliged on these occasions to confine themselves to lectures in which they treated the subject in the most general way, without being ever able to succeed in establishing a systematic and continuous course of instruction.[72]

This feature of the lecture course was noted by those in charge of the lectures, and an article in the *Deseret News* of December 2, 1863, reported that those most deeply interested in the advancement of the people had questioned the value of the lectures in Salt Lake City. Joseph Young called a meeting of the elders to discuss the question, and their proposals were submitted to President Brigham Young. The outcome of these discussions resulted in a continuation of the lectures. The committee in charge decided, however, to limit each lecturer to forty minutes; then a period of questioning was permitted for twenty minutes. The decision was reached that topics of a practical nature would be the most likely to become popular. Illustrations were favored, as was the introduction of a choir, to add variety to the program.[73]

The leading lecturers in early Utah were frequently men who had seen much of the world outside of Utah. If travel educates an individual, then the Mormon men could have some claims to being educated. Almost all of them had acted as missionaries; this task made them *ipso facto* travellers. Orson Pratt crossed the Atlantic Ocean sixteen times in his missionary work. T. B. H. Stenhouse, born in Scotland, had spent various periods at work for Mormonism in England, Italy, and Switzerland.[74] Joseph Young, the president of the seventies, had journeyed to England

on a Church mission.[75] These men, to mention but a few,
were the leaders in the seventies and in the lecture work
of early Utah.

But the rank and file of the Mormon men were as widely
acquainted as their leaders with modes of life outside of
Utah. Often men in the obscure and remote settlements
of the Territory had travelled widely. Thus, Erastus Snow,
who had taken a prominent part as organizer of the
Church settlements in southern Utah, had also organized
a branch of the Church in Denmark. Many communities
had individuals who could duplicate the travel experiences
of the bishop of Snowflake Stake, Arizona, and his assistant. Jesse H. Smith, bishop of this remote region, had done
missionary work in the Scandinavian countries from 1861
until 1865 and from 1868 until 1870. His first counsellor,
Lorenzo H. Hatch, had performed missionary work in England and among the Navajo Indians. Missionaries on their
way to and from the Pacific coast passed through this
bishop's diocese and told of life in far-off places. Any typical list of Mormon men shows a high proportion of names
of individuals who had seen more than the western fron-
tiers of the United States. Some of these had travelled as
missionaries, others had come to Utah as immigrants from
foreign lands.

Many of these individuals, especially the missionaries,
were eligible candidates for the lecture platform. Through
these speakers the whole audience could have a vicarious
trip to places where the beliefs and customs were different
from those holding sway in Utah. Intelligent minds made
comparisons. Joseph Young's interest in the education of
the Mormons by means of the lecture system was aroused
after a trip to England. It was after an European missionary trip that George Q. Cannon became interested in a
stronger Sunday school union among the Latter Day Saints

and became instrumental in bringing about that union.[76]

Hard to measure, but nevertheless present as an educational factor, was the effect of these talks about far-off places and of ships sailing the seven seas when heard by boys in arid and remote Utah farming settlements. From the rude hewn benches in the adobe meeting-house a boy's curiosity and nimble imagination could be aroused. The lecturer took the place of the present-day travel films. One could travel in imagination through the green fields and along the winding lanes of England or even go to far stranger lands on the shores of the Pacific with companions like Marco Polo and Long John Silver. If necessary, one might even think of himself as another Robinson Crusoe marooned on an oceanic island. The possibility of religious persecution or of Gentile ridicule merely made the honor of Mormon achievement seem the more heroic. In spite of the leaders' dreams of a paradise in Utah, Mormon youths kept their interest in the affairs of the profane Gentile world.

These lecture courses were but an addition to another series of lectures—that given at the various religious meetings of the Saints. At meetings for prayers, for funeral services, or for Sunday meetings, topics of all varieties could be introduced without any sense of impropriety. Religion entered every phase of their lives; therefore, every phase of their lives seemed appropriate in their religious services. The Mormons boasted that their religion was not of the one-day-a-week variety; nor was their God, they said, one that remained inside the portals of the church building in order to avoid contact with the dross and hardships of men's lives. Heaven was here on earth, and some aspects of earth would be found in heaven. All observers of Mormon belief note this intermingling of the now and the hereafter, of the temporal and the spiritual. To the

Mormons there is no inconsistency. The perfect temporal existence would be a perfect spiritual existence—a perfect earth would be a heaven on earth.

As an example of this aspect of Mormonism one may take the subjects discussed during the April conference of 1852. Brigham Young spoke upon such completely different topics as "The weakness and impotence of the strength of man as compared with that of God," "The Millennium," "Education of Children by Their Mothers," "Self-Government," "Tithing," and "Adam as our Father and our God." During this same conference the Mormon leader also told his hearers in a lengthy address that recreation and amusement in themselves were not sinful.[77] At the conference which followed in October, 1852, among the topics discussed by Heber C. Kimball were "Building the Temple," "Blessings of Faithfulness," "Education of Children," and "Materials for the Temple."[78] Part of Brigham Young's address at this same conference included advice on "Paying Debts," and "Keeping Store."[79] The majority of the topics given at the religious meetings centred about Church doctrine and purely theological subjects such as "Celestial Marriage,"[80] "Keeping the Commandments,"[81] or the "Divine Authenticity of the Book of Mormon."[82] But a large minority were on topics concerned with the work, debts, material prosperity, and farm crops of the Mormons. Another series of talks at the religious meetings advised the hearers how to improve their health and how to use their recreation. Stories of travel were very popular. Some of these travel talks were the main topics at Sunday services—as for instance, the talk given by Elder Amasa Lyman in the Salt Lake City bowery on June 7, 1857.[83] Another talk of this type was given by Elder G. A. Smith in a report of his trip to southern Utah which was the *pièce de résistance* in the Salt Lake bowery meeting on Sunday afternoon, September 13, 1857.[84]

Thus the pulpit served as a lecture platform as much as did the speaker's stand at the seventies' council hall. Missionaries told of their experiences or travels. If the bishop of a ward had any ideas concerning either celestial or terrestial coöperation, the Sunday pulpit was deemed an appropriate place from which to give his views. There were risks, of course, in using the pulpit for these purposes. Individual speakers could give vent to their hobbies or to their favorite subjects. When the presiding officer at a meeting called upon some member present to give the sermon for that meeting, the individual called upon would quite naturally revert to his own worries—perhaps about his crops, his business, or his horses. But Mormon audiences are not alone in taking chances.

4. Clubs and Societies

Some groups not having the official connections with the Church at the start as did the seventies were organized in the chief city of Utah during the winter of 1854-55 to further the cultural interests of the Saints.[85] The printers of the city banded together in the Deseret Typographical Association.[86] A group of young men organized the Deseret Literary and Musical Association.[87] The Polysophical Society was organized under the leadership of Erastus Snow, one of the Twelve Apostles of the Church. Another of the Twelve Apostles, Lorenzo Snow, was appointed president of the Polysophical Society upon its actual organization.[88] During this same period there was organized a Horticultural Society, which later expanded into the Deseret Agricultural and Mechanical Association, the one hale and hearty survivor of these various societies.[89] Prominent in the organization of the Horticultural Society was Wilford

Woodruff, who was elected its first president. At the same
time he was at the head of the newly formed Universal
Scientific Society, organized February 19, 1855.[90]

A copy of the constitution of the Universal Scientific
Society published in the *Deseret News* of March 14, 1855,
states its object to be "the improvement and elevation of
the intellectual powers and pursuits of its members."[91]
This cultural improvement was to be achieved by means of
lectures on every branch of useful arts and sciences. A
library and a museum were also proposed to further these
objects; but in common with all these groups except the
Horticultural Society, the formation of the Universal Scientific Society seems at the first glance to have been pushed
forth prematurely into a society that could not yet support
such ventures. But is this the complete explanation?

John Hyde, Jr., gives another reason for the decline of
these various organizations. This man, embittered by the
experiences he had endured as a member of the Church,
left the fold as soon as he could quit Salt Lake City; therefore his remarks must be accepted with caution. He blames
the officials of the Church for autocratically interfering
with these non-ecclesiastical ventures. There is much cir-
cumstantial evidence in favor of Hyde's explanation of the
death of these societies—that it was the purpose of Brigham Young to control all institutions within Utah that
were likely to become so powerful as to influence public
opinion, which in the Utah of the fifties and early sixties
meant Mormon opinion.[92]

Whatever his motive, Brigham Young organized the
Deseret Theological Institute at the April Conference in
1855. The purpose of this Institute, as explained in the preamble to its constitution, made the other organizations superfluous at that period of Utah's growth. The preamble
read:

Having in view the promotion of knowledge, and the extension of those principles of light and truth which we have received through the instrumentality of the Holy Priesthood; and believing that the science of Theology embraces a knowledge of all intelligence, whether in heaven or on the earth, moral, scientific, literary, or religious, and being desirous of receiving and imparting such light, wisdom, and principles as have or may come to our understanding, for the benefit of society, and the building up of the kingdom of our Lord upon the earth . . . we form . . . the Deseret Theological Institute.

The officers of the newly organized Deseret Theological Institute were also the outstanding functionaries in the other societies formed during this period. Brigham Young was president of the new Institute; Heber C. Kimball, Jedidiah M. Grant, then Mayor of Salt Lake City, and George A. Smith were vice-presidents.[93] Among the directors were Wilford Woodruff and Lorenzo Snow, who had been prominent in the organizing of the Universal Scientific Society, the Horticultural Society, and the Polysophical Society. Heber C. Kimball, who at the time was First Counsellor to President Brigham Young, wrote to his son, then in England on a mission, that the Deseret Theological Institute met for lectures in the Social Hall once a week.[94] The Deseret Theological Institute was not the first attempt to organize this type of society in the Church. It harked back to the days of the Prophet in Kirtland and his School of the Prophets. But soon the Theological Institute vanished into a limbo of lost and forgotten things.

The story of these societies is one that was repeated in other fields of Utah group development; the first impulse was received from individuals acting independently of the Church, but once the movement had prospects of becoming successful or strong, it found itself embraced by the Church and made subsidiary to the plans of the ecclesiastical organization. Evidently there was a demand for some intellectual activity in the Utah of 1855. In guiding a ship through the social straits of Utah the societies had to avoid on one side the Scylla of being too interested in religious discussions while on the other side was the Charybdis of not discussing theological matters in a community where God was present at all times. The Church settled the difficulty by taking control of the ship when it first appeared in sight, and no audible protests were expressed by the former pilots.

During the year 1855, Mormonism went through a process of "reforming." The reins of ecclesiastical control were tightened; religious revivals took place both in Salt Lake City and in isolated hamlets throughout the Territory. It was a period of emotional strain and stress. These societies formed for intellectual jousting at such a critical time might go beyond the limits of the tournament and develop into real battles. Hyde claims this was the reason the Church took these societies under its wings.[95] Whatever the reason, the Deseret Theological Institute became the coördinating power in this plan of centralization. Soon afterwards the whole group of societies atrophied.

Interest in the organizing of social and intellectual groups seemed alive in the Utah of 1855. Then definite signs of a healthy organism, about to bring forth cultural societies, manifested themselves within the Mormon body. But within a short time these symptoms of a new life gradually died away. Why did these indications of health so soon give way to signs of decadence? For it was not long before organized cultural groups departed from this earth in what seemed to be a swift and painless death. A diagnosis of symptions before death made it appear that the embryo had vitality. What does the autopsy show? In the first place it is evident that Brigham Young evinced little desire to coördinate the efforts of individuals haphazardly struggling to organize congenial groups. In addition, the Mormon president was the only man in Utah who, after these organizations were once formed and under ecclesiastical control could have kept these groups alive. Did Brigham Young show his practical opportunism once more by diverting these interests into channels that would be ecclesiastically safe? The answer seems to be that he did. The overpartiality of the societies to theology proved to be too indigestible for the gusto, éclat, and enthusiasm with which these groups started. A cold shower of rigid ecclesiastical control put out the feverish fires which might lead individuals to question how heaven and earth were to be made synonomous. The ultimate result of these societies, if they remained untrammelled, would lead to a chaotic millennium. To the orderly and dominating Brigham Young such a chaos would be an absurdity. As head of the Church, Young held the keys to heaven. He was willing to use his power to see that all Utah was headed safely and securely on the narrow path chosen by himself as the Mormon leader.

The Horticultural Society, the sole survivor of the groups formed in 1855, went on to further honors and glory. It auspiciously entered the land of the elect when it was incorporated by the legislature of the Territory, early in 1856. At the time of incorporation its name was changed to "The Deseret Agricultural and Manufacturing Society." The purpose of this incorporated organization was to promote "the arts and domestic industry, and to encourage the production of articles from the native elements in this territory."[96] At the annual fair of this society the artists of Utah received public recognition. At the fair held in the fall of 1856 oil and water color paintings, specimens of photography, of penmanship, and of engraving were offered in competition for prizes.[97] The society conducted exhibits until 1881, offering an opportunity of public exhibition for those home artists who cared to show their work.[98] An obvious reason for the continued life of this society, while all the others disappeared, was the fact that its direct interest in horticulture, industry, home economics, and stock-raising came very close to a corresponding interest in the minds of the early settlers. And for many years the Territory remained primarily a community whose economic life depended almost exclusively on agriculture.

The interest in literary and debating societies which had been evident in Utah during 1855 appeared again in the late sixties and had received definite recognition by the end of the following decade. The *Utah Magazine* appeared in 1868;[99] the University of Deseret was reopened during this period;[100] and a number of literary societies were founded in the various wards of Salt Lake City. An unusually strong society was formed in Ogden under the guidance of Franklin D. Richards for the purpose of the moral and intellectual improvement of the young people of that city.[101] By 1876 similar organizations had been organized in the Fifth, Sixth, Tenth, Thirteenth, Sixteenth, Seventeenth, and Twentieth Wards of Salt Lake City.[102] The *History of Springville* records an organization of a similar type in that town during the year 1867.[103] Here was a situation in which the intellectual and social interests may be compared to those which had taken place during the winter of 1854-55.

In June, 1876, Junius F. Wells was appointed by Brigham Young to organize all these groups into a unified Young Men's Mutual Improvement Association "so that we shall know who and where they are, so that we can get our hands upon them at any time for any service that may be required."[104] In a short time all of the ecclesiastical divisions of Utah and Idaho had branches of this organi-

zation with headquarters at Salt Lake City. Its purpose
was the same as that of the organization formed by Franklin D. Richards at Ogden, "to further the moral and intellectual progress of all classes, especially the young."[105]
Free-for-all debates were frowned upon, as leading to in-
fidelity. The formation of libraries and the collecting of
interesting specimens and oddities were encouraged.[106]
At the meetings of these young men written essays and
questions were handed in and discussed by the group.
Members gave both prepared and extemporaneous talks.
Brigham Young favored the giving of testimonies in these
meetings, a proposal which was adopted, as well as the plan
of singing hymns, and the custom of having a prayer at
the opening and closing of each meeting.[107] A parallel organization for girls had been recently formed. So by the
time of Brigham Young's death the young people's group
interests were under the Church control.

Junius F. Wells, writing of his interview with President
Young in which the young people's association was suggested, asserted that the inspiration for this movement
came, not from any of the societies then in existence, but
from God.[108] But there were many worldly facts influencing that inspiration. The Wasatch Literary Society and the
Zeta Gamma, a debating society at the University of Deseret, contained younger members from many families that
had thus far played a leading part in the affairs of the
Mormon Church; some of Brigham Young's children were
in the group.[109] The non-religious tone of these societies
and its effect upon those who took part in its meetings were
before Brigham Young's eyes. At the same time there was
a demand for societies of this sort, as was evidenced by the
growth of similar organizations throughout Utah. Therefore, the Church took the step of combining all these societies and organizing new ones under its protecting wings.

Of the various efforts at intellectual improvement made
during Brigham Young's life this one was the most notable
and most permanent.[110] The organized activities of the
young people were combined into a branch organization
of the Church. Training in public speaking and in management of assemblies was given to numerous young people.
And as many adolescents attended the young people's society early in life for recreation and "mutual improvement," in a similar manner many adults continued to attend parents' classes which were closely akin to the lectures; and both the giving of recreation and the imparting
of information were organized by the Church. The organizations formed in 1876 were primarily based on the
non-religious interests of the members. The religious interests were not absent; however. The leaders and patrons
still considered that the interests of God were of para-
mount importance, both here and hereafter. But in 1876,
as compared with 1854-55, the theological and dogmatic
weights were not so heavy as to stifle future growth.
Furthermore, the control in 1876 from headquarters was
decentralized as contrasted with that exercised by the
Deseret Theological Institute twenty-one years earlier.

5. Artists

The artists of Utah received little encouragement from
the Church beyond commissions for the painting of scenery
in the theatre and for some interior decorating of a simple
sort in the large buildings of Salt Lake City. Utah itself
contained many possibilities for the landscape artist or for
those who enjoyed contrasting colors and distant perspec-
tives. The clear air and the blue skies gave sharply defined
silhouettes to the copper-colored peaks of the Wasatch and
Ocquirrh ranges, which were in sight of Salt Lake City.

The regions which surrounded the southern settlements of Kanab or St. George added the coloring of the desert to the scenic possibilities of the Territory. Later generations of artists and of visitors were to marvel at the color effects of Cedar Breaks, Zion National Park, and Bryce Canyon—all within the Territorial boundaries of Utah.

But if Nature was profuse in her offerings of color and scenery, the eyes of the early Utah settlers could not afford the diversion of admiring such a colorful siren. To be courted she demanded time and money, and the Utah settler had more immediate demands on his hours and wealth. There were few individuals who possessed more than the essential means of living. For the first thirty years of her existence, Utah lacked persons with the wealth necessary to patronize artists. Nor did the Church as yet deem it necessary to encourage all branches of art. Education and the drama had practical benefits, as did music, in holding the community together. Painting and sculpture required a more individualistic training for the understanding of their worth and an appreciation of their values.

William Majors, whose works were principally small profile portraits in water colors, was probably the first professional portrait painter in the Territory. Whether or not he found the place uncongenial or unprofitable, he left Utah for England, where he died in 1853.[111] William Ward, a sculptor, remained in Utah long enough to model the lion which lies couchant on the portico of the "Lion's House," Brigham Young's residence in Salt Lake City. After doing this work Ward left Utah in the early fifties and returned to the East.[112]

A group of men, arrivals in the emigrant trains during the year 1861, gave to Utah several individuals who were interested in painting. Dan Anthony Weggeland, one of the newcomers, had been a native of Norway and had studied at the Royal Academy of Fine Arts in Copenhagen. While painting portraits in the north of England, he decided to emigrate to "Zion." A writer in *Tullidge's Quarterly Magazine,* in telling of Weggeland's work, writes, "It is probable that an adherence to one branch of art—either that of historical painting or *genre*—would have more fully developed his abilities; but the demands of a new country for pictures have not been sufficiently active to admit of such concentration. . . ."[113] William Ottinger, a Pennsylvanian of German extraction; William V. Morris, a Welshman; and Alfred Lambourne, who later gained local fame as a writer, arrived in Utah at the same time and found employment in decorating the theatre which was being erected in 1861-62. E. L. T. Harrison, trained as an architect in England, also arrived in the autumn of 1861, and was called upon to assist his fellow-countryman, H. B. Folsom, in designing the Salt Lake Theatre. John Tullidge, who had learned the trade of house and decorative painting in his native England, came to Utah in 1863. He was more fortunate than some of the others with artistic abilities, for he received the patronage of the Walker brothers, the leading Gentile merchants of Salt Lake City.

In the summer of 1863, the men living in Salt Lake City who were interested in fine arts proposed to found the Deseret Academy of Fine Arts. In their prospectus offered to the public they gave as their reasons:

Our circumstances as a people have hitherto constrained our attention mainly to matters of utility and necessity; but everything now indicates that Providence, which established a people in these mountains, and led out the minds of our leaders in plain, practical direction, is now shaping our career as a nation towards a day of refinement and polish.

Living as members of a religion which views art, skill, and beauty as emanations and inspirations of divinity, associated with a creed that allies art with immortality, and assigns it an endless field of progress beyond the grave, every ordained Priest of the Most High must of necessity be an ordained patron of science and art: to all such, therefore, we look for patronage and support.

The founders of this academy proposed to give their time and labor without any compensation; pupils were expected to furnish their own materials and pay a tuition fee of five dollars a quarter. Any person who produced a work of art acceptable to the canons of the society under whose auspices the academy was founded thereby became a member of the original society, and received free instruction for himself, although expected to assist in the work of instructing others. The curriculum included drawing, oil and water color painting, architecture, engineering, topographical drafting, sculpture, modelling, and photography. The efforts to found this surely proved to be premature, for within a few months the Deseret Academy passed out of existence.[114]

6. Museums

If landscape and portrait painters seemed superfluous in early Utah, museums were not quite so badly off. It was not until 1869, however, that the followers of a religion which was presumably based upon the excavation of some gold plates in western New York could boast of an archaeological museum in their chief city. Immediately upon the reopening of Mormon immigration after the settlement of Utah, the newcomers to that Territory were advised to bring "their treasures of precious metals and those of general utility, the curiosities of art and nature."[115] Remy, in 1856, noticed the wish of the Mormons to found a museum. He wrote that:

They have already got together a considerable quantity of objects, and their numerous missionaries to all parts of the world materially contribute to their opportunities of forming a very valuable collection. Brigham Young, who thinks this a useful and practical institution, takes a particular interest in its development; but it is much to be regretted that for want of a person sufficiently qualified to direct the collectors and classify the objects, the institution is to this day nothing more than a lumber-room of disorder and confusion.[116]

This was probably the same collection that was exhibited at the annual affair conducted by the Deseret Agricultural and Manufacturing Association. Among the items shown at the fair in the autumn of 1858 were "works of art from Hindoostan" owned by A. M. Musser and "relics from Africa, India, and Europe exhibited by Brigham Young."[117]

Early in 1869 the *Utah Magazine* had advocated a "polytechnic, or museum" in Salt Lake City because "of the great strides recently made in our midst."[118] John W. Young, later counsellor to Brigham Young, was the owner of an institution which contained a cross-section of Mormon life from the days of Kirtland down to 1869— home manufactures, paintings, and daguerreotypes were some of the articles in this collection. For the scientifically minded there were collections of the minerals of the Territory and specimens of the zoölogical life of the area, the crania of Red men, and articles connected with Indian life. One of the prize exhibits in 1874 was "Kit Carson's boat from the Lake."[119]

An article published in the *Millennial Star* in 1871 told of

. . . a curious relic of the past [that] had been ploughed up near the mounds in the vicinity of Spanish Fork. It is a piece of metal, seemingly copper about 1¾ inches by 1⅜ inches, on one side of which is engraved the figure of a man in priestly robes with a censer in his hand; an altar on which the fire is kindled; a tree, probably emblematical of the tree of life, and above the tree a representation of the sun.[120]

If this did not find its way to the museum, others similar to it did.

Phil Robinson, an English journalist who visited Utah in the early eighties, was especially impressed with the attempts to found a museum at Orderville, one of the towns which was settled by a group attempting to live under the rules of the United Order. He described the rudimentary museum as a place

... where the commencement of a collection of the natural curiosities of the neighborhood is displayed. What this may some day grow into, when science has had the chance of exploring the surrounding hills and canyons, it is difficult to say; for nature has favoured Orderville profusely with fossil strata and mineral eccentricities, a rich variety of bird and insect life, and a prodigious botanical luxuriance. Almost for the first time in my travels, too, I found here a very intelligent interest taken in the natural history of the locality; but the absence of books and of necessary apparatus, as yet of course prevents the brethren from carrying on their studies and experiments to any standard of scientific value.[121]

These are the two isolated incidents available concerning museums in Utah. At the time of the *First Epistle* in 1849 it appeared that the Church planned to further this work, but years later the most extensive collection of relics and oddities in Utah was still in private hands.

7. Woman's Work In The New Order

If the Mormon leaders were lax in collecting museum material, Mormon women made up for this disinterest in the past by developing to its limits another field—that of genealogies. According to Mormon belief, baptism can be performed vicariously for those who lived and died before the New Dispensation of Mormonism had been announced to mankind. Thus Mormons, particularly the women, delved into the past of family trees and went through the rites of baptism for their deceased relatives. These searches into the past created a stream of Mormon group consciousness linking the past with the present, and the living with the dead—a continous functioning between heaven and earth, the now and the hereafter.[122]

Even the Mormon pioneer women who were too busy with their every-day tasks to delve deeply into the genealogical past were doing their share in community enterprises. In March, 1842, a "Female Relief Society" was organized in Nauvoo at the request of Joseph Smith.[123] The group, as the name implies, functioned as a charitable organization. After 1844, the organization is not mentioned as a group until the Utah settlements were made. Small unorganized groups worked sporadically in Salt Lake City and its vicinity during the fifties and sixties. The present organization dates from 1866. Then Brigham Young called Eliza R. Snow to head a mission for organizing female relief societies in all wards of the Church. From that time the women's organization has coöperated with the male leaders of the Church as a subsidiary and semi-independent group. Handling of relief cases, managing bazaars and quilting-bees, calling upon the sick, acting as mid-wives, caring for the dead in settlements where there were no undertakers, running coöperative stores—all these tasks were handled by the Relief Society.

In addition to their charitable work the Relief Society proved itself useful to the ecclesiastical leaders in some specific enterprises. The development of the silk industry was left to the women by Brigham Young. But in spite of his urging and their efforts, silk culture did not succeed.[124] Another enterprise in which the men had failed, but in which the women were comparatively successful, was the gathering and saving of the surplus wheat in the community. By the end of 1877, after one year's effort, the Relief Society had saved more than 10,000 bushels of wheat, more than 7,000 pounds of flour, $329.00 in cash and "quilts, carpets, and other products of the sisters' handwork which they intended to dispose of to buy wheat."[125] Another enterprise of the women may be seen in their publication, *The Woman's Exponent,* which gives an interesting insight into the part played by women in building up heaven on earth. In this Mormon paradise women were necessary, but everywhere in practice the men determined policies.

In group enterprises, at least, the women were subordinate to the men. How affairs were managed in the Mormon homes is another question. Fortunately, it is not the task of this writer to ferret out who ruled the Mormon home. There is evidence that even Brigham Young knew when he was bested by the females. One of his obsessions —or was it merely practical sense when he had twenty-seven[126] wives and thirty-one daughters[127] to support?— came to the surface when women's clothes were discussed. Young thought that the money wasted by women on clothes could be used to better advantage in purchasing grain for storage. His discourses are replete with his ideas on what is proper for the well-dressed Mormon woman to wear.[128] He organized the female members of his own household into a society for dressing more sensibly and cheaply.[129] Out of this society came the Young Women's Mutual Improvement Association, which paralleled the work of the Young Men's Mutual Improvement, already mentioned as being formed under the leadership of Junius F. Wells. But although the women's societies have functioned down to the present day as an integral part of Mormon life, on the lesser issue of reforming women's fashions Brigham Young went down to defeat, as have so many other mere males both before 1877 and since.

CHAPTER VI

THINE ALABASTER CITIES GLEAM

THEATRE

As LATE AS 1860, the Puritan taboo on the theatre still exerted its influence among religious sects on the frontier.[1] But the attitude of the followers of Joseph Smith towards the theatre was but one more point of differentiation between the religion of the Mormons and that of their neighbors. To many good people of the early nineteenth century the Mormon sanction of the theatre offered additional proof —unnecessary perhaps—that Mormonism could not be a religion, guided from above.[2] Joseph Smith, however, was not restrained by the anxieties haunting stand-patters of the early nineteenth century. At Nauvoo the leaders of the Mormon Church not only allowed, but even took an active part in theatricals.

The Church's sanction of the theatricals is in keeping with several other aspects of Mormon development. What had been a vague and indefinite idea in Joseph Smith's period became a concrete and definite reality under Brigham Young. Attempts to develop a theatre began in Nauvoo. The leading man in the plays there was Thomas A. Lyne, a well-known actor in the East, who had been converted to Mormonism by his brother-in-law and fellow actor, George J. Adams. While in Nauvoo, Lyne played in *Pizarro, William Tell, Virginius, The Iron Chest,* and *Damon and Pythias.* The first stage experience of Hiram B. Clawson, later a leading actor and theatrical manager in

Salt Lake City, was gained in Nauvoo. In this same town on the banks of the Mississippi, Brigham Young received favorable comment for his role of high priest in *Pizarro*. But the drama of Nauvoo was soon transferred from the make-believe world to the realm of actuality which began with the march from Nauvoo. For several years the proscenium gave way to the covered wagon, and the declaiming of the actor gave way to other interests as thousands of apprehensive refugees fled westward. The drama of the stage was unnecessary under these conditions.

Late in 1850, interest in dramatics appeared in Salt Lake City. The Nauvoo Brass Band, an organization formed by Joseph Smith in Nauvoo, provided the nucleus for a new organization, The Deseret Musical and Dramatic Association.[3] Even before this group gave any performances there is evidence which leads one to believe that individuals had been trying out their dramatic talents in the Seventeenth Ward of Salt Lake City.[4] The roster of the Deseret Musical and Dramatic Association included names which later became prominent in the theatricals of early Utah. Among these were John Kay, H. B. Clawson, Philip Margetts, James Ferguson, and H. E. Whitney.[5] The first play of this organization, *Robert Macaire*, was given late in the autumn of 1850.[6] Performances were held in the bowery, a building in the southeast corner of the temple grounds.[7]

In the fall of 1852, the Deseret Musical and Dramatic Association reorganized and became the Deseret Dramatic Association. About this same time Brigham Young began to take an active interest in the actors and in their work. There probably is significance in the changing of the Association's name and in the omission of the word "Musical." This supposition is strengthened by the fact that Brigham Young appointed Bishop Alonzo H. Raleigh to preside over the new group.[8] Bishop Raleigh had been baptized into the

Mormon Church by George J. Adams, the same actor who
had converted Thomas A. Lyne and who seems to have
had more than an ordinary interest in theatricals.[9] For
three years Bishop Raleigh devoted his evenings to the
interests of the organization under his care.[10]

In 1853 the Church erected a building in Salt Lake City
in order to provide an amusement centre for the people.
This new building was so arranged that it could be used
either as a banquet hall or as a theatre. When used as a
theatre about three hundred could be seated. This early
type of community centre, which had appliances for cooking and serving food in the basement, was dedicated on
New Year's Day of 1855. The editor of the *Deseret News*
felt that the theatrical efforts which would be shown in
this Latter Day Saint theatre would resurrect the genuine
drama, not the counterfeit plays of the devil.[11] For ten
years this building served as the centre of the social, musical, and dramatic life of Salt Lake City. The list of plays
given at the social hall is nowhere available, but George A.
Pyper has a list of some of the plays given during the
season of 1855 and 1856. Among these were *Ingomar, She
Stoops to Conquer, Othello, Luke the Laborer, New Way
to Pay Old Debts*, and *Richard the Third.*[12] One of the favorite plays was Bulwer's *Lady of Lyons.*[13]

Theatricals, as well as all other phases of Utah life, were
thrown into confusion when messengers brought the news
to the Mormons, assembled for a picnic at Big Cottonwood
Canyon on July 24, 1857, that an army was on its way from
"the States" to invade Utah in order to reassert Federal
authority.[14] In addition to this disturbing element to Salt
Lake life, some of the leading personalities of the Salt Lake
Dramatic Association had been called to the European mission field. Among these were Philip Margetts, John T.

Caine, James M. Barlow, William C. Dunbar, and James Ferguson.[15]

After a compromise had been arranged between the United States commissioners and the Mormon officials, the United States troops marched through a deserted Salt Lake City and went into permanent quarters at Camp Floyd, thirty-six miles to the southwest of Salt Lake City on the shores of Lake Utah, where Sergeant R. C. White, a man of some dramatic ability, organized a theatrical group among the soldiers. As the soldiers lacked players for the female parts, a Mrs. Tuckett, one of the leading Social Hall players, was secured to play at Camp Floyd.[16] Her departure from Salt Lake City was a distinct loss to the Deseret Dramatic Association, and may have been one of the reasons which led Brigham Young to give the Salt Lake actors better facilities.[17]

Probably one of the best illustrations of the hold which the drama gained in Utah during the fifties may be seen in the popularity of the theatre in the settlements outside of Salt Lake City. Thus, during the early winter of 1854, a group of local players in Provo gave its first performance, using a log schoolhouse as a theatre.[18] The next event of significance in Provo theatricals occurred on April 27, 1861, when the local players organized an amateur dramatic association.[19] Material assistance came to this group from Camp Floyd, for when that post was evacuated, the new dramatic association managed to obtain much-needed stage accessories at bargain rates.[20]

Lehi, a town situated between Provo and Salt Lake City, evidently had its amateur actors organized before Provo. On February 16, 1865, William Burgess secured a license from the Lehi City Council giving the Lehi Dramatic Association the privilege of performing in that city without paying the required tax.[21] "Tallow candles were used for footlights, and wagon covers painted with charcoal and red paint—the latter from the hills above Lehi—formed the scenery and the drop curtain."[22]

A letter from a correspondent in Parowan appearing in the *Deseret News* of March 9, 1859, stated that the "The Parowan Dramatic Association is about closing its season, having performed a variety of plays in a manner that has given general satisfaction, considering the many disadvantages under which its members have been laboring." Here again ingenuity often must have been called upon to satisfy the players, if not the audience, in this small hamlet, in a region surrounded by deserts and mountains two hundred and fifty miles south of Salt Lake City. Frequently, stage properties and make-up were not available. The pioneer's imagination had to work overtime in designing costumes for the parts. Frequently the resourcefulness of the costume man was taxed in making the available costumes fit the players. In addition to these difficulties many of the cast were amateurs.

Nine years before the United Order had been organized at Brigham City, Lorenzo Snow tried to make the theatre a community affair in that town. During the winter of 1855-56, he converted part of his unfinished house into a theatrical hall. He then organized a dramatic company, inviting the actors to perform and the audiences to witness the performances—the latter without charge. In order that all citizens might be entertained, the audience was invited according to a definite schedule.

Lorenzo Snow, in connection with the voluntary actors furnished the entertainments—he held the strings, not allowing anything of a demoralizing character to be presented—carefully examining the plays before they were exhibited on the stage, and only accepting such as would create innocent merriment or inspire elevating and refining sentiment.

The effect was very satisfactory not only in producing pleasurable recreation at the time, but was one of the aids in arousing the partially dormant energies of the people.[23]

The following season the Dramatic Association of Brigham City was organized, larger quarters were obtained, and an actor with considerable experience on the Salt Lake stage was hired. A wind storm in the spring of 1857 blew down the building in which the theatre was situated, ruining the stage and the theatrical scenery. For a time this loss put a damper on the town's theatrical ambitions.[24] In spite of discouraging circumstances, however, the Dramatic Association of Brigham City reorganized; and, according to Mrs. E. R. S. Smith, the biographer and sister of Lorenzo Snow, it was "justly acknowledged as the best dramatic company in the Territory outside of Salt Lake City."[25]

From 1857 to 1859 theatricals in Salt Lake City itself had not prospered. In the autumn of 1859, the Mechanics' Dramatic Association, a recently organized group, enlisted many of the members of the then almost-defunct Deseret Dramatic Association and began giving plays. The unfinished house of one of the members of this new group served as a theatre, and the heads of the Church were invited to the performances. Brigham Young accepted an invitation to one of its plays and after the last act made a significant speech.

He complimented the company. He encouraged them to go ahead, and told them that before long he intended to build a good big theatre, where they could have ample room to develop their dramatic art, observing in his characteristic way that the people must have amusement.[26]

Upon Brigham Young's espousal of the idea of building a new theatre, Mormon participation in theatricals received new life. The difficulties involved in a pioneer country, such as carrying heavy timbers down from the mountains miles away, obtaining laborers, or the still more difficult task of obtaining the skilled workers, were all taken care of by Brigham Young. Even the murmurings of those who wished to see the Temple built previous to any theatre quieted before the practical leadership of Brigham Young.[27] Camp Floyd, which was being evacuated at this time by Federal troops who were moving east for the Civil War, supplied necessary material to the Salt Lake Theatre, as it did to the Provo players. Hiram B. Clawson was sent with $4,000 to the army camp, where he purchased such articles as glass and nails at prices far lower than similar articles could be bought in the East. Nails, for instance, which ordinarily sold at $40 a box, were auctioned off at Camp Floyd for $6 a box.[28]

Many incidents were told in later Salt Lake history illustrating the efforts of the builders in getting material wherever they could in order to finish the large theatre— large, that is, for an isolated frontier community. For instance during the march of the United States troops to Utah in 1857, Mormon scouts had burned a number of army supply wagons. What was left of these wagons remained on the plains until Mormon teamsters returning with immigrant trains gathered the cast-off iron and brought it to Salt Lake to be made into nails for the new theatre.[29]

In addition to the building material there was the problem of obtaining the necessary labor. Here again the Church stepped into the breach. Through its centralized power, the Church was able to gather the craftsmen necessary to build the theatre. Carpenters, masons, and builders could be found among the newcomers from Europe as well as from the pioneers who had training, or who were willing to undertake any type of work.[30] One person writing reminiscences concerning the building of the Salt Lake

Theatre fifty years after the event remembers that Brigham Young called out all the sailors—men used to working on high levels—to work on the new building.[31] The incoming immigrant trains brought an Englishman, E. L. T. Harrison, an architect, and George M. Ottinger, an American scenic painter, in time to assist in the decorative features of the theatre.

Besides gathering in the laborers, the Church had to help finance the construction costs of the theatre. In a speech before the curtain on Christmas night, 1862, the stage manager, John T. Caine, said that the cost of the theatre had been $100,000. Only group endeavor and the sponsoring of the idea by the Church head could have carried this project to completion in the Utah of 1862.[32]

After the completion of the building in 1862, the theatre was a show place for visitors and an object of a civic pride to the inhabitants of Salt Lake City.[33] The external appearance of the building, with its Doric columns, added in the decade after 1862, adobe bricks, and plain surface, had a pleasant simplicity about it that was in keeping with its surroundings. Architecturally the simplicity of the Salt Lake Theatre was a great contrast to the ornateness of the Salt Lake Temple, which took over forty years to build.

The great desideratum in the case of the theatre was to have it constructed and ready for use; the opening exercises were held before the seats had been completed or before any heating arrangements had been installed. The theatre had to fill an immediate need in the community. That might explain the simplicity of the exterior architecture of the Salt Lake Theatre. The external decorations were few and simple—as befitted this temple in the midst of a hard-working, farming community of Saints. But the interior of the building was a different matter. Were the interior decorations a compensation for the hard work and simple life of those who attended the plays?

One tourist considered the interior of the building commonplace, with its dreary audience of a dozen or two people under the dim lights of medieval-looking oil lamps.[34] The majority of travellers, however, who have left us their impressions of the interior disagree with Justin McCarthy's opinion. John Sheepshanks, Bishop of Norwich, England, who visited the Salt Lake Theatre in the sixties, described the interior as spacious and handsome.[35] Samuel Bowles, editor of the Springfield *Republican,* wrote in 1865:

> The building [Theatre] is itself a rare triumph of art and enterprise. No eastern city of one hundred thousand inhabitants—remember Salt Lake City has less than twenty thousand—possesses so fine a theatrical structure. It ranks alike in capacity and elegance of structure and finish, along with the opera houses and academies of Boston, New York, Philadelphia, Chicago, and Cincinnati.[36]

F. H. Ludlow, whose book *The Heart of the Continent,* is an attempt to probe beneath the surface of events in Utah, gives an interesting picture of one reason why the Salt Lake Theatre was unique.

> I was greatly astonished to find in the desert heart of the continent a place of public amusement, which regarding comfort, capacity, and beauty has but two or three superiors in the United States . . . My greatest surprise was excited by the remarkable artistic beauty of the gilt and painted decorations on the great arch over the stage, the cornices, and the moulding about the proscenium boxes. President Young, with a proper pride, assured me that every particle of the ornamental work was done by indigenous and Saintly hands.
> "But you don't know yet," he added, "how independent we are of you at the East. Where do you think we got that central chandelier, and how much d'ye suppose we paid for it?"
> It was a piece of work which would have been creditable to any New York firm, apparently a richly carven circle, twined

with gilt vines, leaves and tendrils, blossoming all over with flaming wax-lights, and suspended by a massive chain of golden lustre. So I replied that he probably paid a thousand dollars for it in New York. "Capital!" exclaimed Brigham; "I made it myself! That circle is a cart-wheel, the wheel of one of our common Utah oxcarts. I had it waxed, and gilded it with my own hands. It hangs by a pair of ox-chains which I also gilded; and the gilt ornaments of the candlesticks were all cut after my patterns out of sheet tin."[37]

The Salt Lake Theatre was one of the most impressive buildings in the city. Few, indeed, were the visitors who failed to notice it. All did not see eye to eye concerning its merits. Some compared the building with similar structures in older and wealthier centres. Some of these men failed to appreciate the difficulties of constructing such a building before the railroad came to Utah. In fact, those visitors who arrived in Pullmans and with dining-car waiters at their beck and call frequently failed to appreciate the effort put forth to construct a community theatre in Salt Lake City in the sixties. To these individuals Salt Lake City did not mean the promised land, as it did to those who came by stage coach.[38] To these latter, after hundreds of miles of barren canyons, sagebrush, and cactus, any sort of large edifice or large town was a welcome sight.[39] Thus the theatre, even with its modicum of appointments, was likely to be viewed favorably by those who had travelled the weary stage-coach route to Salt Lake City.

Soon after the opening ceremonies took place in the Salt Lake Theatre, the managers heard that Thomas A. Lyne, the veteran actor of Nauvoo days, was playing in Denver. They sent for him and engaged him to coach the Salt Lake Stock Company. Lyne did the coaching for a time, but soon was once more acting the leading parts of his favorite plays before the Salt Lake audience.[40] The precedent of bringing in stars, whenever they were available in the mountain region, was followed from the time of Lyne's engagement. Mr. and Mrs. Selden Irwin, who had also been playing in Denver, appeared on November 4, 1863, remaining throughout that season until April 9, 1864. From Salt Lake City this couple went on to Virginia City and from there to California, stopping at the chief ports of call for actors between Salt Lake City and the western coast. One of the outstanding events of the Irwin engagement in Salt Lake City was *Othello,* a production in which a Salt Lake actor, Bernard Snow, created a favorable impression by playing the title role, while Mr. Irwin played Iago and Mrs. Irwin, Desdemona.[41]

T. A. Lyne reappeared for a second series of plays on June 25, 1864, with some of his former successes *Damon and Pythias, Pizarro, The Octoroon,* and *William Tell.*[42] Then, again by way of Denver, came an English actor who electrified both the audience and the stock company by his realistic acting and strong characterizations—George D. Paunceforte. He produced *Hamlet* on Christmas Eve, 1864, and *Macbeth* on January 4, 1865; in the latter play he had the assistance of one hundred voices from the Tabernacle choir for the witches' chorus.[43]

On July 26, 1865, a dramatic company entered Salt Lake City from the west after having completed a tour of California, Oregon, Montana, and Idaho. After a week's run in Salt Lake City, the managers of the Salt Lake Theatre engaged two of its players, Mrs. Julia Dean Haynes and George B. Waldron, to continue playing with the Salt Lake Stock Company.[44] The loss of these two stars broke up the travelling company, whose manager, John S. Potter, with the assistance of Thomas A. Lyne, attempted to open a rival theatre in Salt Lake City. The new theatre had no prospect of success in trying to rival the popularity of Mrs. Haynes. Her acting kept the lead for the old theatre during

her stay in Salt Lake City from August 11, 1865 to June 30,
1866.[45] This proved to be longer than her competitors could
remain. Among the plays given by Mrs. Haynes were
*Romeo and Juliet, East Lynne, Macbeth, The Merchant of
Venice, Pizarro, The Octoroon,* and three plays by Salt
Lake authors, E. W. Tullidge's *Eleanor De Vere,* and Edward L. Sloan's *Osceola* and *Stage and Steam.*[46]

The railroad connecting Salt Lake City with Ogden and
points east and west was completed early in 1870, thereby
making Salt Lake City easily accessible to actors travelling
between the Pacific Coast and the cities of the East and the
Middlewest. The Salt Lake Stock Company assisted the
stars who visited the theatre until the year 1874. During
the interims when no stars were visiting, the performances
were given by the stock company. Among the well-known
actors who played with the local stock company during this
period were C. W. Couldock, Madame Scheller, Anette
Ince, John McCullough, James A. Herne, Lucille Wester,
Fanny Morgan Phelps, Charles Wheatleigh, George D.
Chaplin, Kate Dennin, and Charlotte Thompson. By 1874,
the individual star who travelled about the country and
gave plays supported by local stock companies was becoming a creature of the past. The railroad brought to Salt Lake
City a new type of theatrical production which had already
influenced Eastern cities. After 1860, entire casts went
from city to city, needing no local assistance in their productions. The Salt Lake Stock Company, like the local
stock companies of Philadelphia, Boston, and other American cities, eventually succumbed to these more highly
organized and standardized groups.[47]

After 1862—the year in which the Salt Lake Theatre was
built—items concerning dramatics in the smaller towns
of Utah appeared with greater frequency in the columns
of the *Deseret News.* Perhaps the editors and people of

Salt Lake City were becoming more interested in that phase of life in the settlements, or else the people in the settlements themselves were becoming more interested because of the attention aroused by the building of the large theatre at the metropolis of Utah. Whatever the cause, more is said about the theatre after 1862 than had been said previously.

A possible link between the building of the Salt Lake Theatre and the increase of theatricals in Utah outside of Salt Lake City may be seen in the presentation of special performances during conference time. Groups of Mormons from the settlements came to Salt Lake City to attend these conferences. A holiday as well as a holy day atmosphere ruled in the Mormon metropolis. Camping in the public squares and on the outskirts of the city, the pilgrims with their camp fires and their covered wagons were a picturesque sight. And an essential part of the pilgrimage to their Mecca involved a trip to the theatre. Here was the cue for the settlements to follow; and follow they did, for items of plays in the settlements soon appeared in the *Deseret News.*

On July 24, 1862, the *Gamester,* and a farce, *The Widow's Victim,* were given at Logan.[48] The same day the Tooele Dramatic Association gave its first performance in Tooele City. A correspondent wrote that "as yet the association is in its infancy, but from it may be expected Stars to arise whose light may possibly be reflected in larger bodies."[49] A year later the same correspondent reported the Salt Lake Thespians acting for six successive nights at Tooele City. In a postscript he showed the unique relation of the stage and pulpit in early Utah. "Most of the membert of the [Thespian] association," he wrote, "have this day spoken in the bowery upon the principles of the gospel, showing that in the midst of play they do not forget their religion."[50]

The *Deseret News* of March 11, 1863, contained a summary of theatrical work in Utah County during the winter of 1862-63. Among the items was one that the managers of the Springville Theatre closed their season on February 23 with the play of *Virginius,* which attracted large audiences for three consecutive nights. On the same evening the Payson Amateur Association played *She Stoops to Conquer,* before a "crowded audience [which] bore evidence that the labors of the Association were appreciated." The Provo Association played at Spanish Fork on February 25 and on February 26 and 27 at Payson. This latter engagement was in return for a similar compliment which had been paid them by the Payson Association which previously had played at Provo. On March 2, Bernard Snow and the Springville Association visited Provo and played *Retribution, or Justice in Cuba.* The following evening they presented *William Tell.*[51]

By February, 1863, Santaquin had organized a "corps of dramatic amateurs."[52] In the same issue announcing the Santaquin organization, a correspondent in the *Deseret News* wrote from Ogden City that his town was occasionally favored by the plays of the Ogden City Dramatic Association.[53] Thus one reads the reports from the Mormon settlements scattered about Utah. Some of the items told of benefits being given for the Temple fund, others that the money gained was to be used for musical instruments.[54] The sponsors of these plays were generally leading members of the Church in the locality. Thus the Cluff family, prominent in the Church annals of Provo, provided the nucleus for the Provo Dramatic Association. The position of Lorenzo Snow in Brigham City has already been mentioned. Bernard and Erastus Snow were as prominent in the theatricals of their respective localities as they were in their church work.

Under the leadership of Brigham Young the actors and the theatre of Salt Lake City were an example to other sections of Utah. What was Brigham Young's motive in adopting the theatre as subsidiary to the religious organization, while at the same period to many people of other sects in the United States the theatre was still looked upon as an abomination? Brigham Young himself gives his reasons in two places—first, in a letter to the *Deseret News* which was published in the issue of that newspaper of January 11, 1865, and, secondly, in a somewhat rambling discourse, "The Capacity of the Human Body and Mind for Improvement and Development," delivered at the dedicatory exercises held at the Salt Lake Theatre on March 6, 1862.[55]

If Brigham Young desired merely to provide amusements for his people when he first publicly proposed building the theatre in 1859, his purpose had expanded into something more significant by March 6, 1862. In his dedicatory speech Young said that it was the privilege of man, and also his duty, to scan all the works done by mankind from the days of Adam until the present, "and thereby learn what man was made for, what he is capable of performing and how far his wisdom can reach into the heavens, to know the evil and the good."[56] Brigham Young added that the stage could be made to aid the pulpit in showing to the people the difference between virtue and vice, "which we cannot do unless we also understand the evil and the good."[57]

The Mormon leader wrote a letter to the *Deseret News* of January 11, 1865, which so fully described the place of the theatre in the life of a people that it is given in its entirety in the appendix as an evidence of what the Mormon leader believed in this respect. In this letter Brigham Young emphasized three points; first, the theatre is of value to the community as a means of recreation; secondly, it is a means of improving the community's taste; and, thirdly, it is a means of differentiating the Mormon use of the theatre from that of the outside world. The theatre among the Mormons was not only to provide recreation for "those whose bodies and brains were weary with toil and close application to business,"[58] but also was a place where "good thoughts would be inspired,"[59] and where the proper acting would have "an elevating and pleasurable effect upon the audience."[60] In all this it is the duty of the priesthood to take the lead.[61] The actors, also, Young hoped, would develop "in native refinement and grace."[62] Here again the Mormons contrasted their attitude with that of "the outer world"; Young evidently desired a more rigid control of actions and words than the "level of the wicked world" allowed.[63] Here, too, the Mormon leader refered to the attitude of which he spoke in his speech of March 6, 1862, as that of "the tight-laced religious professors who have horror at the sound of the fiddle" and to the father who says, "My Son, you should not attend the theatre for there the wicked assemble . . . You should not be found playing a ball, for the sinner does that."[64]

Thus, amusements, as well as knowledge, were for the Saints. Brigham Young, in treating of amusements in general, once wrote, "We are here to learn how to enjoy the things of life—how to pass our mortal existence here. There is no enjoyment, no comfort, no pleasure, nothing that the human heart can imagine, with all the spirit of revelation we can get, that tends to beautify, happify, make comfortable and peaceful, and exalt the feelings of mortals, but what the Lord has in store for his people."[65] As the Mormons viewed the teachings of the religious sects about them, it seemed that those sects had an attitude towards pleasure—at least, in regard to the present—which the White Queen in *Through the Looking Glass* had towards jam when she told Alice ". . . jam to-morrow and jam yesterday—but never jam today." The "Hairy Gown and Mossy Cell" of Milton's *Il Penseroso* were not for the Mormons, but rather the "Hence, loathèd Melancholy" of *L'Allegro*. Their attitude was that man should have heaven as well as hell on this earth.

A pertinent question to ask concerning the Mormon use of the theatre is whether or not the people found recreation in their theatre? The almost unanimous opinion of the travellers who have left their impressions of Salt Lake audiences would lead one to believe that they did enjoy the plays; and they were the same plays that were popular in the East at the time: *The Octoroon, The Charcoal Burner, Damon and Pythias, The Lady of Lyons,* and *The Pride of the Market,* to mention but a few of the favorites.[66]

One writer noted the frankness and lack of sophistication shown by the audiences in Salt Lake City.[67] The Reverend Mr. Jones who was so displeased with everything Mormon wrote about the audiences: "Nobody dresses for the performance and there is a good deal of talking between whiles. The piece was 'A New Way To Pay Old Debts.' . . . It was badly acted, but the audience laughed on small provocation, and seemed to enjoy itself."[68] Chewing apples and sandwiches, visiting, and other forms of sociability were much in evidence during the intermissions. Frequently the fraternizing of the group proved to be as much a means of recreation as the play itself.

The Tabernacle and the theatre were two places where visitors could view Mormons gathered together in a group. The resulting effect upon the visitors who have left us their impressions is a varied one. Mrs. Ferris described a performance at the Social Hall on January 17, 1853:

> The play was the "Lady of Lyons", and the performance so much better than we anticipated that I should have enjoyed it well enough had it not been for some side acting in the crowd, which must preclude us from going again to the same place. How thoroughly and horribly poisoned is everything in this society![69]

Over two years later, in November, 1855, Chandless witnessed a play in the same Social Hall and set down in writing its effect on him:

> The audience which had listened attentively but with as little enjoyment as myself to *Othello*, entered thoroughly into this piece [a lighter piece which followed *Othello*] and laughed and applauded from end to end . . . and so we separated in good humor; and many a merry word slipped out, and laughter glanced on pretty faces with a radiant phosphorescence, as with downward-turned but not dejected faces we picked out for ourselves and the ladies a safe route over the many running streamlets that hasten down towards the plain along either side of the moonlit streets of the Mormon capital.

If, in Chandless' estimation, the selection from the act of *Othello* was poorly played, the following selection was well performed, especially in the part that required a country girl, "for there was the absence of the traditional tone of the rustic and she was pretty and unpainted."[70]

At times the editors of the *Deseret News* were conscious of rowdyism, as evidenced by an article in their paper of April 3, 1861:

> The audiences have been respectable, decorous yet unrestrained, and seemingly have enjoyed highly the fleeting moments. The introduction of a few easternisms, and rather boisterous, clamorous encores could well be dispensed with. A few noisy whistling youths might profit by a hint, and one or two young ladies would lose nothing by remembering what they have been; if they had changed society modesty need not be altogether dispensed with.[71]

John Sheepshanks, Bishop of Norwich, England, might
not have been an experienced critic of the theatre when
he visited Salt Lake in the early sixties; for when he told
Brigham Young, upon the latter's invitation to witness a
play, that it was not his habit to attend the theatre,
Young replied, "No, I dare say not, and with good reason.
But if you come to our theatre you need not leave your
religion at the door."

The wary bishop overcame his qualms and attended the
theatre. He tells of one effective method for stopping
rowdyism in the Salt Lake Theatre. "The President, it was
well known, did not like much noise and if the applause
became vociferous, his well-known face would be seen
protruding from the curtain of his box and looking round,
and lo! at once all was hushed." The Bishop, however, said
of the audience:

They applauded the noble and democratic sentiments in a boy-
ish way with clapping of hands and hurrahing greatly preferable
to the shrill whistling and vile noises of country theatres in England . . . there was perfect decorum of behavior throughout. The
young women of whom there were many in the house, behaved
with exemplary propriety and modesty and conversed during
the intervals of the play chiefly among themselves . . . at the conclusion of the entertainment there was no loitering about, no
congregating at the entrance, but on emerging from the doors all
walked quickly away as if the next thing to be done now was to
go quietly to bed. The parents went off with their children, and
young girls who had perhaps come alone, walked away separately
and quietly as if not in the least fearing rudeness or molestation.
Altogether I came away pleased with what I saw, glad that I had
taken advantage of the President's suggestion, and mentally
wishing that we could have recreation of the same sort in England.[72]

In addition to the method mentioned by Bishop Sheepshanks which Brigham Young employed to keep order,
other means had to be employed. No liquor was sold in

the building. An editorial of the *Deseret News* of October
14, 1863, said: "In the announcement of this evening's
play we are glad to see that special notice, which objects
to the admission of persons carrying firearms or other wea-
pons." The arms were piled on a table at the entrance and
tagged, the owners reclaiming them on leaving the playhouse. The problem of disposing of young children was not
settled so easily. At first younger children were forbidden
entrance. But this was as effective as Canute's command
to the waves to cease. The managers of the theatre then
hit upon a more effective scheme. Posters were hung saying "Prices of admission, same as usual. Babes in arms
$10 extra." The success of this scheme is unrecorded.

One can find little concerning the views of those who
sat on the rough wooden benches. A scene painter in the
Salt Lake Theatre tried to express the thought of these
people when he wrote:

> Many a man who watched the play at night had done the
> roughest of pioneer work during the day. Perhaps he had "grub-
> bed" sage for an order for a theatre ticket; perhaps he had toiled
> in the fields; irrigated an orchard, or dug a water ditch. Perhaps
> he had helped at building a saw mill, or at blazing a trail up to
> the mountain pines. It may be that he had brought down a load
> of logs and stood, thereafter, for many hours in the rain or shine,
> in the woodyard opposite to the Play-house, until he had sold
> that load of fire wood and the pay that he received for it might
> have been partly used for his theatre admission fee.[73]

A problem which Utah theatricals had to meet was that
of finding actors. Hepworth Dixon told how this was
solved:

> [Brigham] Young understands that the true work of reform in
> a play-house must begin behind the scenes; that you must elevate
> the actor before you can purify the stage. To this end, he not
> only builds dressing-rooms and a private box for the ladies who
> have to act, but he places his daughters on the stage as an ex-

ample and encouragement to others. Three of these young sultanas, Alice, Emity, and Zina are on the stage . . . from Alice's lips I have learned a good deal as to her father's ideas about stage reform. "I am not myself very fond of playing," she said to me one day as we sat at dinner—not in these words, perhaps, but to this effect—"but my father desires that my sisters and myself should act sometimes, as he does not think it right to ask any poor man's child to do anything which his own children would object to do." Her dislike to playing as she afterwards told me, arose from a feeling that Nature had given her no abilities for acting well . . . Brigham Young has to create, as well as to reform, the stage of Salt Lake City; and the chief trouble of a manager who is seven hundred miles from the next theatre, must always be with his artists. Talent for the work does not grow in every field; like a sunflower and a peach tree; it must be sought for in nooks and corners; now in a shoe shop, anon in a dairy, then in a counting house; but wherever the talent may be found, Young cannot think of asking any young girl to do a thing which it is supposed that a daughter of his own would scorn.[74]

Actors and actresses received calls to perform on the stage similar to the calls which sent some Mormons to preach the word of Mormonism in Australia or in Norway. The actor was as truly called to perform a mission as was the travelling preacher. Miss Nellie Colebrook, at one time the leading lady in the Salt Lake Stock Company, had been called to the stage when sixteen years of age.[75] Mrs. Ann Eliza Webb, in her *Mormon Bondage,* tells of receiving and accepting a similar call.[76] This control of whatever ability there was in Salt Lake City helped make the theatre a community affair.

These actors, gathered from the farms, shops, and stores of the city, brought forth no first-class performers who adopted the stage as a career, but several of the stock company were evidently above the average in ability, among whom were David MacKenzie, Bernard Snow, and James M. Hardie. One of the most capable performers, John S. Lindsay, did become a professional actor after the stock company began to disintegrate.[77] During the early days of the Salt Lake Theatre members of the stock company served without pay; as the demands on their time became more and more frequent, their dissatisfaction with this state of affairs increased. If the management could afford to pay outside stars, could it not afford to pay the home talent, too? Lindsay records a protest meeting which met one day in the green room of the theatre and expressed dissatisfaction with the economic, or non-economic, status of the Mormon actor in the Salt Lake Theatre. A delegation was sent to Brigham Young. The ultimatum succeeded before a strike was necessary, and the players were allowed to give benefit performances for themselves.[78]

In other respects also Brigham Young had to make concessions. In his speech at the dedication of the theatre, he said, "Tragedy is favored by the outside world; I am not in favor of it."[79] He had expressed himself similarly at the time he decided to build the Salt Lake Theatre, giving as his reason the fact that "this people have had enough of tragedy."[80] One must, however, take into consideration what Young meant by tragedy—it was really the frightful melodramatic play that he feared—"murder and all its horrors and the villainy leading to it portrayed before our women and children; I want no child to carry home with it the fear of the fagot, the sword, the pistol, or the dagger, and suffer in the night from fearful dreams."[81] Nevertheless, Salt Lake patrons were soon enjoying the great tragedies of the stage, *Hamlet, Macbeth,* and *Othello,* as well as the lesser attractions of *Nick of the Woods, Under the Gaslight,* and *Ten Nights in a Barroom.* Plays given in New York soon found their way to Salt Lake City; in this respect the Mormons were following the trend in the United States at large.[82]

When one takes into consideration the active proselyting

character of the Mormon Church, it seems odd that, with their belief in the possibilities of the stage, so little was done to utilize drama as a means of expressing their beliefs. There is record of a play given in Provo with the experiences of Mormon missionaries in the Sandwich Islands as a theme. William W. Cluff portrayed the part of a Mormon missionary so well in this play, *The Mormon Converts,* that he soon afterwards went to the Sandwich Islands to enact the actual rôle.[83]

There were few original dramas by Utah writers of the period. Edward Tullidge wrote two plays, both with European settings. The first, *Eleanor de Vere,* was played by Julia Dean Haynes during her stay in Salt Lake City.[84] This piece so pleased Miss Haynes that Tullidge wrote another for her entitled *Queen Elizabeth,* which she intended to play in New York. This intention, however, was never fulfilled; for the very successful production of the Italian Giacometti's play of the same name with Ristori in the title rôle forestalled any competition in this respect.[85] *Osceola* and *Stage and Steam,* by Edward L. Sloan, editor of the Salt Lake *Herald,* and *Under One Flag,* by John S. Lindsay, the first two relying mostly on action and stage effects to hold the attention of the audience, seem to complete the list of Mormon productions. The play by Lindsay was given at one of his own benefit performances. About all that is known of this production is that it was played at least once and had the Civil War as its background.

During the gold rush days of California, Salt Lake City found that its location had certain advantages. Actors and actresses considered the Mormon metropolis a convenient stopping place on their journey to the West Coast. After days of being tossed about in a stage coach, the actors had to limber their stiff joints and relax their muscles. While doing this, the Salt Lake Theatre offered them a chance to exercise their dramatic ability and an opportunity to make extra money at the same time. For the stars the pay was not niggardly. Julia Dean Hayne, for example, received $300 a night for playing in 1865.[86]

Plays were regularly given in Salt Lake City from the time of the Social Hall days. The *Deseret News* of February 5, 1853, reported that the "Dramatic Association were in full bloom nearly every evening, during the week before last, and several evenings last week, and the [Social] Hall generally filled with attentive and interesting assemblies."[87] The ordinary schedule of plays during the first few seasons in the Salt Lake Theatre usually listed two performances a week. During conference time extra performances were given in order to provide entertainment for the visitors to the city and also to help balance the theatre's budget.[88] The engagement of Mr. and Mrs. Selden Irwin in November, 1863, inaugurated the practice of having a Saturday matinée and three night performances weekly.[89] In 1869, the theatre was open 285 nights.[90] Productions continued to be given throughout the hot summer evenings, as the audience waited for cooling breezes to come down from the canyons, and during the regular winter season, when icy winds from the selfsame canyons had to be braved in order to reach the theatre.[91]

What became of the receipts received from the faithful? The answer to this question is a matter of uncertainty. Brigham Young, of course, was the master of proceedings. He also was master of the finances. Was Brigham Young managing and directing the theatre as his own personal property, or was he directing and managing this institution as guardian for the Church?

Bowles had no doubt concerning Brigham's relation to the box-office of the theatre when he wrote:

President Young built and owns the theatre, and conducts it on
his own private account, or on that of the Church, as he does that
of many of the other profitable institutions of the Territory . . .
and as he is at no expense for actors or actresses and gets good
prices for admission, he undoubtedly makes a good thing out of
the theatre.[92]

This statement seems verified by the fact that on April
23, 1860, Young gained possession of the corner upon
which the theatre later stood.[93] One of Young's most vulnerable spots was this overlapping of cash accounts—his
own and that of the Church. Mormon critics have shot
many a barbed arrow into this Achilles' heel of Young.
The Salt Lake Theatre receipts probably went into the
Church fund, for which Young was accountable to no one.
The property became involved in litigation after the death
of Young, whose will transferred the theatre and its
grounds to John Taylor, Trustee in Trust for the Church,
for the sum of $125,000.[94]

The management of the theatre also had its difficulties. Clawson and Caine managed the theatre from its
opening until February 23, 1867.[95] For about eight years
thereafter several managers tried their hands at making
the theatre pay, but none was successful. The entire business was deeded to Brigham Young in May, 1876, and for
a period affairs were run successfully from the office of
the President of the Church.[96]

The Mormon leaders acquiesced in Young's actual, as
well as theoretic, control of this property and its management. With his extensive powers he seemed to have been
more successful than any of the other managers. One need
not imply anything dishonest in Young's management by
saying that the question is still confused. As in the economic sphere, this close and yet vague connection between

Young and the financial affairs of the Church has caused adverse criticism.

On the other hand, it is evident that the Mormon leader realized the social value of the theatre. The continued existence and adoption of theatrical entertainments throughout Utah show that the drama filled a need of the people. If it had no other reason for being, this social aspect would justify its existence. Dramatic literature received scanty additions from Utah, in spite of the dramatic and unusual elements in the life of the Mormon people. Actors from the East were accepted as readily as plays from the East. The East, in turn, had frequently received its plays from Europe. If there had been any chance of building a distinct type of actor and play in Utah, the actors on the way to California proved too much for the managers of the Salt Lake Theatre to resist. Hiring trained actors was easier than going through the laborious work of instructing local stock companies. Once this method of hiring travelling players was adopted, the Salt Lake Theatre and its actors lost their importance in the history of the Territory. And when the railroad came to Utah, the theatrical history of that locality merged with that common to the remainder of the United States.

CHAPTER VII

O BEAUTIFUL FOR PILGRIMS' FEET

MUSIC

IF DANCING and dramatics were considered outside the pale by many religious people in the early decades of the nineteenth century, certain forms of music were more favored. Even the Puritans and the Pilgrims—with many grave doubts, it is true—had allowed psalm-singing.[1] Evangelical sects on the frontier after 1800 vigorously shouted hymns in their camp meetings. This was particularly true of the Methodists, from which sect Mormonism gained many of its followers as well as many of its tunes and hymns.[2] The Mormons were also able to find Biblical justification for the use of music in their services. Had not the sons of Asaph, Jeduthum, and Heman been chosen musicians in connection with the sacred ordinances of the Temple? The Psalms of David and the display of music at the opening of the Lord's Temple by Solomon gave additional proof that music was in vogue among the inhabitants of ancient Israel—the former-day Saints.[3]

With this precedent as a support, music had, in addition, an immediate practical value. It could be used to express the religious ardor of the community, and the Mormons frequently expressed their aspirations in their hymns. Parley P. Pratt, for example, published a hymn in the first number of the *Millennial Star*:

The morning breaks, the shadows flee

Lo! Zion's standard is unfurled
The dawning of a brighter day,
Majestic rises on the world.

Another hymn of the same type, and one of the most popular of the Mormon hymns, was written by W. W. Phelps. It began:

The Spirit of God like a fire is burning
The latter-day glory begins to come forth:
The visions and blessings of old are returning
The angels are coming to visit the earth.

The use of hymns in Mormonism is almost as old as the Church organization itself. One of the first references to music in the Mormon Church occurred about three months after the Church was organized in 1831. Emma Smith, the wife of Joseph, was at that time directed,

. . . to make a selection of sacred hymns, as it shall be given thee, which is pleasing unto me, to be had in my Church, for my soul delighteth in the song of the heart; yea, the song of the righteous is a prayer unto me. And it shall be answered with a blessing upon their heads. Therefore lift up thy heart and rejoice, and cleave unto the covenants which thou hast made.[4]

This meant that hymns should be published and that Joseph's wife should do the selecting.

Edition followed edition of Mormon hymn books both in this country and in Europe.[5] The first English edition, published jointly by Brigham Young, Parley P. Pratt, and John Taylor, while they were on a mission to England, consisted of three thousand copies.[6] An article in the *Millennial Star* of August 15, 1851, lists the different editions in England; the eighth edition in 1851 had the largest output of any, twenty-five thousand copies.[7]

From the first, vocal music was an essential part of Mormon worship. Mrs. B. G. Ferris, wife of the territorial

secretary to Utah in 1853, a woman who gave praise grudg-
ingly to anything Mormon, was favorably impressed by the
singing at religious services.[8] A few years later two Frenchmen travelling across the continent attended religious services in Salt Lake City. One of them wrote:

> The choristers and band belonging to the choir executed a piece
> of one of our greatest masters; and we feel bound to say that the
> Mormons have a feeling for sacred music, that their women sing
> with soul, and that the execution is in no notable degree sur-
> passed by that which is heard either under the roof of Westmins-
> ter, or the frescoes of the Sistine Chapel.[9]

Burton attended a Mormon service in 1860, hoping to hear
some non-religious work performed by the choir. On the
day of his attendance only hymns, however, were sung;
and he was very favorably impressed by the rendition of
these. The Mormons sang "decidedly well," wrote Burton,
in comparison with the singing of the congregations in English country and town chapels where, added Burton, "had
the Psalmist heard his own psalms 'In furious mood, he
would have tore 'em.'"[10] Richardson, an American journalist, attended a service in the bowery at Salt Lake City at
which a melodeon furnished the sole accompaniment, yet
he found the singing admirable.[11] Brigadier General Rusling, who visited Salt Lake City in October, 1866, described
as well as explained the source of this fine singing, when
he wrote: "The singing was strong and emotional, and
swept through the tabernacle a mighty wave of praise. Of
course it lacked culture, but then there were passionate and
glowing hearts back of it, for all sang 'with the spirit' if
not 'with the understanding also.'"[12]

A new faith that has gone through difficulties builds up
a passionate devotion in those who remain firm in their
beliefs. It was this passion which Brigadier General Rus-

ling sensed in the singing at the Tabernacle. On the first evening that Chandless spent in Salt Lake City he wandered to the workshop of a shoemaker, where a few Mormons were accustomed to meet. He returned regularly to this shop and found that at these gatherings

... songs were sung in turn: songs of Sion. The cobbler sang as he worked; his was a stirring air such as would have suited the matchless war-cry, *The Sword of the Lord and Gideon.* The words too were vigorous, part denunciatory, part hopeful: one could almost have fancied the singer one of the stern old Puritans. I recollected one stanza commenced *Tremble Ye Nations,* and the chorus repeated after each denunciation was

> "But Sion shall have peace,
> Israel must increase
> Glory to the Lord of Hosts
> Israel is free".[13]

It was with this same spirit that the Mormons sang their way across the plains to the words of "O California, that's the land for me," or their warriors out on the plains in 1857 fortified themselves with:

> Then let us be on hand,
> By Brigham Young to stand,
> And if our enemies do appear,
> We'll sweep them from the land.[14]

At first there were difficulties for those interested in the musical development of early Utah. Jensen, in his *History of Provo,* tells of an incident in that town which throws light on how the people of Provo gained some of their musical leadership. At one of the religious services in Provo the presiding officer found difficulty in starting a hymn.

Suddenly, William J. Strong, an English convert who had recently arrived in the settlement, announced a hymn and began to sing. Several other converts who were seated with him joined in the singing. So successful were they that the "English brethren and sisters" were asked to sing another hymn. This little incident led to the selection of William J. Strong as Provo's first official chorister, and to the organization of the first chorus.[15]

By 1855, Provo had formed a permanent and competent choir under the direction of another Englishman, James E. Daniels, who retained the position of chorister at the Provo church for thirty-five years. In order to obtain accompaniment for his singers, the leader invented a transposing keyboard, an instrument which, by being properly adjusted, could be made to play in any key desired.[16]

In 1852 the town of Lehi organized its first choir, which early in its career made a place for itself among the inhabitants by following the pleasant English custom of serenading during the Christmas holidays.[17] In the years that followed, the choir took an active part in the life of the city, proving its ability in concerts outside of Lehi, and frequently joining forces with other choirs for coöperative concerts. In Springville, a singing class was organized during the winter of 1854-56 by a Mr. Messenger from the East. For this event "nearly all the people in town, young and old, turned out to be instructed. . . . Great enthusiasm reigned and everybody sang."[18] In 1855, two Frenchmen were forced to camp out one night in the cheerless streets of Cedar City in southern Utah while cold November winds blew across the desert. In order to keep warm they wandered about the village until music in the church attracted their interest; and upon entering the church they were agreeably surprised by the musical exercises, which "were good beyond anything to be expected in such a place."[19]

Among the ephemeral institutions founded in Salt Lake City during the winter of 1854-55 was the Deseret Philharmonic Society. A letter in the *Deseret News* of March 1, 1855, announced the object of this society to be the cultivation of all kinds of music. The writer of the letter went on to say that on the advice of Brigham Young, James Smithers, the leader of the Tabernacle Choir, had been chosen president of the new society and conductor of its music. John M. Jones, who later was to be for a short period leader of the theatre orchestra, was at this time appointed leader in the instrumental department of the new society. The letter in the *Deseret News* continued:

It is needless for me to expatiate on the advantages of such an organization, confined as it is to no band or party, but intended to combine the musical talent of the city, and to promote the love and study of harmony throughout the Territory.

I wish . . . to inform our brethren and sisters preparing to come from Europe and the Eastern states and who feel an interest in the objects of this society, as to what kind of music we are most in want of, so that it may be a little guide to them in their selection, which they can either donate or loan to the society on their arrival here.

We are much in want of the oratories of Handel, Haydn, Mendelssohn, etc.; the masses of Mozart, Haydn, Beethoven, etc., and new works of merit, the whole with full orchestral accompaniments in separate parts, and as much as possible. We also want the best overtures, Simphonies, and dancing music for a full orchestra, together with Quartets, Trios, Duets, Solos, Glees, Songs, etc.

Band, as well as choral music, received attention even during the early days of Mormonism. As the Nauvoo Legion increased in size, it was considered necessary to grace its maneuvers with music from a brass band. The commanding officer, General Joseph Smith, asked for volunteers from the ranks who were able to play musical instruments. From those who volunteered, the Nauvoo Brass Band was formed.[20] Much of the musical lore and tradition of early Mormonism were built about this organization and its members.

Gustavus Hills, who was appointed copyist and arranger

of music for the brass band organization, was evidently a
person of prominence in the musical life of Nauvoo. He
was also chosen professor of music for the proposed University of Nauvoo. In addition to these offices he was head
of a music lyceum in Nauvoo. These are the only details
available concerning his connection with Mormon music.
More is known about the career of William Pitt, who had
the reputation of being the best versed musician in the
band. He was the first of the Englishmen who were to become the musical guides of their fellow Saints. An indication of Pitt's musical interests may be seen in the fact that
he brought with him a large collection of music for band
instruments when he migrated from England to Utah. Pitt,
who played several instruments, had some ability in ar-
ranging the music for small orchestras. For many years
he performed as violinist at the Salt Lake Theatre. James
Smithers, already mentioned as president of the Deseret
Philharmonic Society, played the trombone in the Nauvoo
band. William Cahoon, later a prominent citizen of Salt
Lake City, played a bass drum of his own manufacture.
The band as finally composed at Nauvoo consisted of two
trumpets, two trombones, four clarionets, two French
horns, two piccolos, two key bugles, and a cavalry cornet.
Uniforms were out of the question because of the cost, but
some semblance of unity to the spectator's eye was
achieved by having all the members of the band wear
white trousers.

Years after its formation, when Nauvoo existed in the
Mormon mind only as a bitter memory, the members of
this band were still appearing at gala occasions in Utah.
They provided much of the entertainment during their
first few years in the far West as a band, as variety enter-
tainers, analogous to our present-day vaudeville perform-

ers, and also as the first group to attempt dramatic entertainments in Salt Lake City.

With the Nauvoo Brass Band as a nucleus, an orchestra
of stringed and other musical instruments was formed in
Nauvoo in 1843. Its name, the Quadrille Band, indicates its
function in the community. One of its members stated that
this group played at the first dance allowed by the Prophet.[21] After the exodus from Nauvoo and during the dole-
ful winter at Winter Quarters, the Quadrille Band did its
part in providing cheer for the Saints. It also played in
various settlements in Iowa near the Mormon encampment
for stipulated sums or for the proceeds of a collection.

Several of the members of the Nauvoo Brass Band were
among the first arrivals in the Salt Lake Valley. In time,
all of the members arrived and once more the Nauvoo
Brass Band was entertaining the Mormons on all important
public occasions.[22] A letter sent from Salt Lake City in
May, 1852, and published in the *Millenial Star* of that
year shows that the Nauvoo Brass Band had a competitor
for the public favor by that time. This letter stated that
"Brother Ballo, the celebrated musician has got up a new
instrumental band. Yesterday, being training (of the mil-
itia), they made their first appearance in public, and played
many soul-cheering airs."[23] The following year the two
bands, Ballo's and the Nauvoo Brass Band, combined to
play at the laying of the corner stone for the Salt Lake
Temple.[24] In time the organization which had been started
at Nauvoo went out of existence, and Captain Ballo and
his band became preëminent among Utah bands until the
death of Captain Ballo in 1861.

In 1855, members of Captain Ballo's Band tried to advance interest in instrumental music by building a music
hall in the Fourteenth Ward "for practising music, teaching
classes, or for concerts."[25] When this building was erected,

it was to become the property of the Church, should the band dissolve. Captain Ballo, the leader in this enterprise, had been born in Sicily, in 1805.[26] He came to the United States in 1825 and was for eight years a musican in the United States Army. He at one time played in the West Point Band, which, during the early years of the century, was reputed to be the best in the country.[27] In 1847, he joined the Mormon Church and in 1852 came to Salt Lake City.

Other towns in Utah followed the example of Nauvoo and Salt Lake City, but the growth of musical organizations was slow. There was a lack of instruments and of music sheets—both formidable obstacles to any widespread forming of bands. Springville inhabitants gave evidence of their interest in their local band by paying John Taylor of Provo forty dollars a month to give two band lessons in Springville each week during 1854 and 1855.[28] By the late sixties bands were organized at American Fork, Morgan City, and Ogden City.[29] A band was formed at Lehi from the membership of a fife and drum corps in that town "through which eventually all the male talent in the town passed."[30] Following the organization of the centralized Sunday School Union in 1867, and with that as the source for recruits and as a coördinating factor among young musicians, various musical corps were formed.

The popularity and use of these bands and orchestras in early Utah does not imply that there was present, as yet, any discriminating musical taste in the audiences of Utah. A description of the band's playing for the Independence Day Ball in 1863 at Salt Lake City is probably a true picture of the status of Utah music as compared with music in the eastern United States. A witness to that event wrote:

I will say that I could better understand that immemorial usage which has restricted Saints to the use of the harp, after hearing their performance on other instruments. They played, however, quite as well as the ball-room bands of most Eastern towns no larger than Salt Lake City, if we except those whose population has become somewhat Teutonized; and what they lacked in quality, they made up in quantity. The Mormon principle of devoting to the Church one-tenth of all a man is and has, was fully exemplified by the violins who gave it in the form of elbow, and by the trombones who blew that proportion of their annual increase into the ears of the Saints during the first four contra-dances. The merrymakers enjoyed the music . . . which, after all was the only matter of consequence.[31]

But at the time this description was written a group of men was at work introducing into Salt Lake City a firmer foundation for musical appreciation. But the year 1863 is somewhat ahead of the story.

Closely allied to the Mormon interest in music was their interest in dancing, an interest which goes back to the early days of the Church. The enthusiastic participation of the Mormons in dancing was closely allied to the development of their orchestras, and was also a means of bringing the entire community together.[32] The dance among some groups, such as the Russian peasants or the Spaniards, became a means of making the members realize, at least temporarily, their common unity. To the Mormon people the dance was a means of gaining some enjoyment from life —although at times they engaged in their quadrilles with true frontier, or perhaps Puritancial, seriousness. Thus the Mormons danced quadrilles at Winter Quarters during the winter of 1846 as they prepared for their long journey to the West.[33] As the Mormon Battalion started on its march to the coast, the Mormon camps gave the departing soldiers farewell dances.[34] How paradoxical would such conduct seem to their religious predecessors, John and Charles Wesley! With un-Puritanical levity, dancing contributed its mite to help banish dull care from the Mormon pioneer camp-fires. Once Utah became settled, the Friday evening dance in each village community gained recognition as one of the major events of the week. As with all other aspects of life in Utah, where every ounce of energy counted in converting a barren land into a region of farms, the dance had utilitarian value. Brigham Young realized this value and controlled the dance in the interests of the Church, and the community.

Observers of Salt Lake City life frequently noticed the leadership taken by the Church at the community dances.[35] When the dancers had met, the leading ecclesiastical officer of the district, who as a matter of course was present, offered prayer. After receiving the blessing of the Church, the dancers began; and from the opening strains, gusto and physical vigor drove temporal cares from the minds of the Saints. These Western dancers would have none of the "wishy-washy eastern dances." Quite frequently the strenuous exercises lasted until the small hours of the following morning.

At times there were complaints that the dances were carried to excess, especially to the detriment of lectures or to the neglect of schools.[36] One of the reading, writing, and arithmetic teachers complained that dancing teachers were greatly in demand, and received their pay first, while other teachers had to wait.[37] Orson Pratt made a similar complaint in a sermon preached on February 10, 1856.[38] Once Brigham Young had to forbid the use of the religious edifices in Salt Lake City to the devotees of dancing.[39]

Although the Mormon dance was nothing more than a mélange of American dances, with such innovations as polkas frowned upon, Church authorities made the dance one more factor in binding the Mormon group into a closely knit union of leaders and adherents. The dance was one of the lighter aspects of community life, an aspect which eased the way between the serious religious and material comprehensiveness of the Church's leadership and that employed in the realm of music, drama, and education.[40]

The organizing of instrumental musicians into bands and orchestras for the dances and religious services kept the interest of many Utahans alive until later teachers could improve the quality of their playing. These early groups were also a means of demonstrating to some of the young people the possibilities of music as a means of expression. In Springville Henry Walker and James Orton were responsible for introducing music of a little higher order than had been heard in that community previous to the coming of these men in the early sixties.[41] In the same town the leader of the local choir assisted at concerts with a bass viol which he had made with his own hands. This instrument and a dulcimer made by one of the villagers created much interest among the youths of the settlement. Previous to this a melodeon which the bishop of the district had purchased had been the musical delight of the inhabitants, especally of the young.[42] Each settlement required players for its dances; and since the Salt Lake Theatre was the model, dramatic entertainment in each settlement must have its musical accompaniment too. Another use for musical instruments was seen at the Tabernacle, where instruments assisted the choir in the devotional exercises. Thus there were two channels of interest in musical affairs in Utah during the fifties and early sixties—one in the musical organizations employed at the dances and theatricals, with the local bishop sponsoring the whole entertainment; and another evident in the use of orchestras and bands at the Mormon devotional exercises.

Little information is available concerning that *sine qua non* of musical development—the love and practice of music in the home and among informal groups. There is no record that the regency of the proposed University of Deseret answered the Macedonian request for help in this sphere of music that appeared in the *Deseret News* near the end of 1851: "Why cannot music be introduced into our schools in Utah, and from them reach our domestic circles? Will the REGENCY please to answer?"[43] Chandless noted that during his visit in 1855 it was a matter of general comment that there were but five pianos in the Territory.[44] Remy wrote that during his visit, also in 1855, the violin, an instrument carried across the plains with much more ease than the piano, could be heard on all sides as one passed Salt Lake City homes during an evening.[45]

Once more Chandless gave a picture of home life in this respect, a side of Mormonism which the majority of travellers neglected for the more popular subjects of polygamy and the absolutism of Brigham Young. This observant Englishman was, at the close of the day, accustomed to visit a Mormon family. After the children were lulled to sleep and the economical housekeeper had extinguished the candles, the people talked:

. . . and between times the women would sing hymns with their clear sweet voices. Mormon hymns they were, yet not all devoid of pathos, at least in these evening hours: one, for instance, that spoke of those whom we should never see "till the resurrection morn." Who has not lost some dear one? And who, turning his thoughts homeward, across mountains and prairies, and Atlantic might not fear some loss yet unknown? Walking home on such evenings one could not think the Mormons altogether a filthy, sensual people.[46]

Susa Young Gates, a daughter of Brigham Young, gave a picture of the status of music in the home of the Mormon leader when she wrote:

Music was, from before my remembrance, the constant com-

panion, bore, and comfort of father's family. Himself a natural
musician and a fine bass singer, he early bought musical instruments—pianos, organs, and a beautiful harp—and procured as
competent musical teachers for the children as the country afforded. We inherited almost universally, his taste in this direction, and the old piano in the long parlor was rarely allowed to
rest its weary keys.[47]

From these meagre beginnings a group of English Mormons developed an interest in worthy music among the
Mormon people which has persisted to the present.[48] These
cultivators of musical taste were John Tullidge, George
Edward Percy Careless, David C. Calder, and Charles J.
Thomas. Each one of these became a prominent music
teacher, and together they bore the brunt of the musical
work of early Utah. Ebenezer Beesley, Evan Stephens,
and John J. Daynes may be mentioned as a few of those
who helped carry on work in the same sphere. The musical development of Utah was built around the efforts of
individuals. Hence to a great extent the story follows the
biographies of these men. In some respects these teachers
of music had a promising field in which to work. The Mormon group was fairly homogeneous in its beliefs. By connecting the Church officers with those individuals interested in developing music in the Territory, men like Calder,
Careless, and Thomas could accomplish much more than
they could have done as free lances.

John Tullidge, one of the first to advance the cause of
music in Utah, had been born at Weymouth, Dorsetshire,
England, in 1807.[49] From the age of six, when he sang with
a Methodist choir in his native town, until his death at Salt
Lake City in 1873, he was whole-heartedly devoted to in-
culcating musical appreciation in the minds of those with
whom he came in contact. In his youth he gained some
fame as a tenor singer, eventually going to London, where

he studied harmony and counterpoint under the world-renowned Hamilton. For several years following this training, he toured the English provinces with a glee club. Eventually he settled at York, where he won the position of principal tenor at the York philharmonic concerts, and finally became one of the four conductors of the York "Harmonicus Society." From this position he went to the conductorship of St. Mary's Cathedral Choir in Newport, South Wales.

Upon becoming a member of the Mormon Church in England, John Tullidge enthusiastically began planning methods by which music could aid, to use his own expression, "the work of the great reformation" which Mormonism was to bring to the world. His work, primarily that of a critic and advocate, extended over a period of sixteen important years in the musical life of the Mormon Church.

In a letter to the editor of the *Millennial Star* on February 24, 1857, Tullidge related his varied career as teacher of vocal music to various groups in the United Kingdom. He could now see, he wrote, that "the providential finger, which has hitherto guided me on, is evidently pointing to the reforming and establishing of vocal music in the great Latter-day Saint Church."[50] Out of his previous experience he had evolved a method of teaching sight reading by means of diagrams. He gained quick results by the ease of his method and by eliminating a great deal of theory, and by demanding strict attention from his classes while in session. These methods had been developed by Tullidge after a study of both the Hullah and the Curween systems, which were receiving attention at that time. These systems were convenient methods for teaching musical notation to large classes of workingmen and others who were unable to give the time or pay for individual teachers such as the older methods ordinarily required. Tullidge now hoped to bring his own method into use among the English Mormons, and his plan had received the approbation of Franklin D. Richards while that individual had been president of the European mission.[51]

Evidently by the following year, 1858, the indifference of the Saints to vocal music had made an impression upon him, for he wrote:

> The study of the art of singing does not appear to carry that importance to the minds of the members of our Church which it should do; and that portion of service which ancient Israel considered so necessary to their divine worship, is as yet, in a scientific sense, not fully appreciated by Israel of the last days. They have a great love for singing; and, with a patient and systematic course of training, they would excel the world and I can only ascribe it to our religion, which engenders one of the greatest requisites for the sublime and grand in music, viz., energetic spirit.[52]

In two lengthy letters to the *Millennial Star*, published on February 21, 1857,[53] and on January 2, 1858,[54] Tullidge pointed to the need of a new psalmody among the Latter Day Saints. He felt horrified "at the results which occurred when the members of his religion in casting about for tunes picked out any which happened to be most conveniently at hand."[55] He complained that in some of the adopted airs the religious sense of Mormonism was lost in adaptations from popular, and even from obscene, tunes.[56] At other times, he added, the musical ear was jarred by irregularity of rhythm and by varied accent, brought about in the effort to make the music fit the words.[57] Then also "the 'Mormon' spirit in its freshness and vigor, needs a different style of music to that dolorous, whining, class so incompatible with praise from full and grateful hearts."[58] In order to overcome this difficulty,

Tullidge passed from words to action and, early in 1857, composed and published a *Latter Day Saints' Psalmody* of about forty selections.[59]

Tullidge's efforts in the English mission drew a favorable editorial from the editor of the *Millennial Star*.[60] Tullidge's son, Edward, later prominent in Utah, worked with his father to convince Franklin D. Richards, president of the European mission, of the possibilities that could accrue to Mormonism by the use of music.[61] John Tullidge in one of his letters to the *Millennial Star* enclosed a note from Richards which gave the president's imprimatur to the Tullidges' efforts.

This letter of Richards said in part:

Although an incompetent critic myself, I entertain a very great pleasure in the performance of good music. It is an embellishment of education which helps to subdue and chasten the soul as well as to purify its delights, and I esteem it a most valuable work in the reformation.[62]

The elder Tullidge's interest in music is shown by the musical department he conducted in the *Utah Magazine*. From the time of his arrival in Utah in 1863 until his death ten years later, he was actively engaged in musical work in the home of the Saints. In 1869, after five years residence in Utah, John Tullidge was as keen in his desires as he had been in 1857 and 1858. He wrote detailed articles explaining the various methods of class teaching for vocal music in England and the United States. In these he explained the Hullah and the Curween tonic-sol-fa systems as well as his own. After comparing the systems, Tullidge came to the conclusion that composers in the new systems of notation would not gain much by leaving the old. He thought:

The result would only be, that students of new systems could not understand each other's music, while the students of the old one could read and enjoy music in common all the world over . . . Besides a vocal notation that does not take in instrumental music, must be alone, an imperfect one. The horizontal form would render it impossible to read rapid passages at sight, with instrumental, and even with vocal music there is a difficulty of sight.[63]

Some of the best writing upon musical subjects that appeared in early Utah came from the pen of John Tullidge in 1869, who was musical editor of the *Utah Magazine* at this time. Articles bearing his name described musical affairs in the settlements. Once more he agitated for Zion's own psalmody,[64] endeavoring to show the benefits of congregational singing.[65] Volume III of the *Utah Magazine* explained to the tyro Saints examples of musical terms such as counterpoint, fugue, and canon.[66] In the same volume are articles on the "Life of Handel,"[67] on "Mendelssohn and Jenny Lind,"[68] on a comparison of ancient and modern harmonies,[69] and an extract from *Demorest's Young America* on "Mozart's Fiddle."[70]

The editor of the *Utah Magazine* did his utmost to arouse home composers and received some compositions which it published. The first printing done in Utah with musical type appeared in this publication. The correction of one of C. J. Thomas' compositions (as well as the inadvertent omission of the title "professor") brought an exchange of remarks between that individual and John Tullidge. The compositions submitted for publication led the musical editor to write an article on the necessity of composers being guided by the laws and principles which musicians of the past had evolved. "The light of nature" was not sufficient for a composer: he had to be guided by the rules of musical composition.[71]

John Tullidge, by virtue of his musical reviews and his explanations of the principles and history of music, may be described as the publicity man in the movement that was taking place in the musical life of Salt Lake City. The results of his work were not confined solely to Salt Lake City but were carried from there to the settlements throughout the Territory. Tullidge's time and effort were not entirely absorbed in editorial work and writing. He gave concerts himself and toured various parts of the Territory with his pupils.[72] In Salt Lake City he taught voice and composition. While engaged upon some musical work for the Salt Lake Theatre Orchestra, in which he was employed as arranger of music, he met with an accident which caused his death in 1873. Thus from the time of his conversion in the fifties until the time of his death he was closely connected with the musical life of the Mormons.

Another pioneer in Utah music was Charles J. Thomas, who had been a resident of London, England, when he joined the Mormon Church. His musical experience before he arrived in Utah during 1862 had been broadened by playing at theatres in the English metropolis. His knowledge of theatrical work immediately won for him in his new home the conductorship of the orchestra in the recently erected Salt Lake Theatre; at the same time that he received this conductorship, he succeeded James Smithies as conductor of the Tabernacle Choir. In addition to playing in London theatres, Thomas had gained much of his knowledge of music while travelling between London and Glasgow with an Italian opera company. Thomas raised the musical status of the Tabernacle choir from that of the ordinary country village choir to a much higher level. In 1864, he went on a mission to St. George, in southern Utah, where he continued utilizing his musical knowledge for the benefit of a Utah community.[73]

A third pioneer in Utah music was David C. Calder, an active leader in the community music of early Salt Lake

City. He came from Thurso, Caithness, Scotland, where he had been born on June 18, 1823.[74] He joined the Mormon Church in August, 1840, when Orson Pratt was in charge of the missionary work of Scotland. About the time of the young Scot's conversion to Mormonism, Hullah's system of sight reading of music was receiving much attention. Calder joined one of the classes in this system and later taught Hullah's method in Scotland.

This musical pioneer migrated to Salt Lake City, arriving there in September, 1853. For a number of years he was chief clerk to Brigham Young and connected with a number of Church enterprises such as the *Deseret News* and Zion's Coöperative Mercantile Institute. Tullidge gives this chief clerk of Brigham Young credit for arousing the interest of the Mormon leader in classes for the study of choral music. This seems plausible, considering Calder's interest in music, his experience in group teaching, and his proximity to Brigham Young.

At any rate under the direction of David O. Calder and the patronage of President Brigham Young, two singing classes of two hundred each were organized during 1861 in Salt Lake City.[75] The Curween tonic-sol-fa method was used. This was one of the devices mentioned in a study of Mr. Tullidge's career—a method which was considered simpler than the ordinary notation for teaching classes of amateurs quickly. In December, 1862, Calder organized two more classes of two hundred each.[76] During the year he had also organized the Deseret Musical Association, the purpose of which was "the encouragement and extension of vocal music throughout the State of Deseret."[77] President Brigham Young was chosen head of this organization, "to which," according to the *Deseret News*, "he gave every encouragement."[78] David O. Calder was elected vice-president and did the actual guiding and directing that was necessary.

At the beginning of its career the Deseret Musical Association gave two concerts. For fifty cents "payable in cash or produce" one was offered a program consisting of "anthems, quartettes, trios, duets, songs, readings, pianoforte, harmonion and concertina solos, with choice pieces of music by theatrical orchestra."[79] Selections were made from the opera *The Barber of Seville* and Haydn's *Creation*.[80]

Several days after one of these concerts the *Deseret News* of December 17, 1862, announced that David O. Calder was forming another class in the Curween method of notation. The editor added to the announcement:

We sincerely trust and may confidently premise that Professor Calder's efforts, being pecuniarily uncompensated, will not fail of being suitably prized, and that his classes will be filled to the utmost capacity of the house by the music-loving youth of our city, as also those of riper years, who, with souls "moved by the concord of sweet sounds" have desires to acquire a practical knowledge of the science of vocal music.

The excellency of the Tonic Sol-Fa method, taught by Professor Calder, was briefly illustrated in the opening of the first concert given in the Tabernacle in this city. Its simplicity and adaptability were satisfactorily exhibited to all present.

On July 22, 1863, the editor of the *Deseret News* wrote: "We understand the Deseret Musical Association purposes giving a series of public concerts during the summer. Mr. Calder's classes continue to be a great attraction for the young and we are pleased to learn of their progress in the science of music." The following month the same newspaper announced that there had been printed a program of songs, duets, and glees which were to be sung at a concert early in October. The article also reported that for

the following winter there was planned a concert in which
four hundred juvenile voices would be united. The editor
wisely pointed out the possible immediate and after effects upon youth when it was allowed to take part in this
public exhibition. He wrote of the proposed juvenile concert:

> Their ages [i. e. of the participants] and general education are
> such as to disarm criticism on the assumption of individual pro-
> digies; but the exhibition of musical education in a collective
> capacity cannot fail to be a demonstration.[81]

Tribute was again paid by the newspaper to the manner
in which Calder gave his time and President Young his
patronage to the Deseret Musical Association. The editor
believed it was at President Young's suggestion that the
October concert was to be given during the semi-annual
conference, "as a fitting opportunity for directing the attention of our citizens to the adoption of the system in the
settlements."[82]

Unfortunately for the music lovers of Utah, soon after
this concert a series of deaths in Calder's family—five of
his children dying in an epidemic—and his own ill-health
forced him to surrender his work as teacher of class music
in Salt Lake City.[83] The Musical Association lagged, but the
seed had been planted in fertile ground. Calder, however,
remained close to the musical development of the Territory, for in 1860 he had established the first music store in
Utah. Twenty-four years later its business had increased
twenty-fold.[84]

In partnership with G. E. P. Careless, Calder founded
the *Utah Musical Times,* the first number of which was
published on March 15, 1876. Publication continued for
one year. Although this paper provided a good advertising

medium for the music shop, it went far beyond this purpose in its aims and in its actual accomplishments.

The first number of the *Utah Musical Times* stated that
the editors

> . . . realize the necessity of considering the present musical
> condition of the community so as to direct our labors in the best
> manner possible for the advancement of an art so well calculated
> to add to the pleasures of home, to the amusement of the people,
> and to the worship of God. Much has been done in choirs, and in
> drilling the members in their several parts, but the work of pop-
> ularizing music and bringing it within the reaches of the masses,
> remains to be done. Our people are musically inclined. The
> amount of money spent for organs, pianos, and other musical in-
> struments, and the liberal patronage bestowed by them upon
> musical entertainments gives evidence of the fact.[85]

With this introduction the publishers went to work with
a will to inform the people of Utah concerning musical
affairs in Utah and in the world at large. Articles appeared
concerning Beethoven,[86] the Wagner Festival at Baireuth
in August, 1876, [87] music in the schools of Utah,[88] teaching
music to classes, and choir singing.[89] Several articles were
written warning the people of Utah against fraudulent sel-
lers of cheap pianos.[90] Readers were asked to contribute
musical compositions as well as literary productions.[91] One
reason for publishing the musical compositions of home
authors in the *Utah Musical Times* was to make these compositions available throughout the Territory.[92]

George Edward Percy Careless, Calder's partner in the
music business and in the publication of the *Utah Musical
Times,* was born in London on September 24, 1839.[93] As a
boy he studied music at the Royal Academy of London.
After his apprenticeship, he continued to live in London
and played in orchestras at Exeter Hall, Drury Lane, and
the Crystal Palace. In 1850, he was baptized a member

of the Church but did not migrate to Utah until 1864.
Soon after his arrival in the valley, he was appointed leader
of the theatre orchestra by Brigham Young. He served in
this position for two periods of six years each. The new
leader of the orchestra did not share in the local Salt Lake
belief that quantity and quality were inseparable. Careless immediately began to divorce these two elements in
the orchestra under his charge by reducing its numbers
from twenty to seven players. And, as a further move in
the same direction, he finally prevailed upon Brigham
Young to pay the seven members three dollars a night for
their services. The task of the orchestra leader far away
from musical centres and publishing houses was no easy
one. Besides directing he had to compose the dramatic
and curtain music. Among the musical plays for which
he composed were *Pocahontas, Cinderella, Aladdin,* and
The Crystal Slipper.

"Professor" Careless, a title assigned him in Salt Lake
City, was director of the Tabernacle Choir for fourteen
years; in 1879 he organized an orchestra of his own. The
financial success of his artistic productions speaks well
for the Salt Lake audiences of the period. Perhaps his
greatest single contribution to the musical taste of Salt
Lake City came with the production of the oratorio, *The
Messiah,* in 1875. Mormons and non-Mormons worked
together to make this event a success. E. W. Tullidge's
experienced judgment led him to believe that this concert
marked an event in the history of the city.[94]

In addition to these outstanding exponents of better
music in Utah, there were individuals of lesser stature,
who nevertheless contributed their share to the musical
life of the Territory. Ebenezer Beesley's birth occurred,
it was said, under particularly favorable auspices for his
later musical career. He was born in a room in Oxford-

shire, England, which was used by the local Wesleyans for
choir practice. At the age of nine Beesley was baptized
into the Mormon Church.[95] Ten years later he was on his
way to Utah, where he continued an interest in vocal
music. At the age of twenty-one he was leading the singing
in the Nineteenth Ward Sunday school. From the Sunday
school leadership he went on to more important work.
During a number of years he led the Nineteenth Ward
Choir. After a systematic study of the violin, in 1863 he became a member of the Salt Lake Theatre Orchestra. Probably his greatest contribution to music in the Territory came
from his interest in musical compositions and in his efforts
to have music published. At first he had to copy the music
for Sunday school use by hand. The *Juvenile Instructor,*
established as a Sunday school paper in 1866, helped satisfy the need of the Sunday schools throughout Utah for
more exact and quicker methods of obtaining music sheets.
In addition to the work of overseeing the publication of
song books and a *Latter Day-Saints' Psalmody,* Ebenezer
Beesley found time to conduct singing classes and glee
clubs. In 1880, he achieved the summit of his professional
career by his appointment as director of the Tabernacle
Choir. It is worth noting that upon Director Beesley's re-
tirement from the Salt Lake Tabernacle Choir, he went to
Tooele City, following a personal request from Bishop Atkins of that town for a music teacher.[96]

Wales was a profitable recruiting ground for Mormon
missionaries in the fifties.[97] And it would have been strange
if converts from that home of good singers had not contributed to Mormon music. In 1863, a new brass band from
Cardiff, Wales, under the leadership of George Parkman
appeared in Salt Lake City and serenaded President Brigham Young. The *Deseret News* recorded that "They introduce the novelty in some pieces, of amalgamating the

vocal with the instrumental." After their interesting sere-
nade in Salt Lake City, the same newspaper reported that
these newly converted Welshmen intended to make their
homes in Box Elder County, where many of the Welsh
converts to Mormonism were settling.[98]

From out of that same county came another Welshman,
Evan Stephens, who received his initial training during
President Young's time and was a capable successor to the
leaders who had led the Tabernacle Choir before him. Evan
Stephens had been born in South Wales on June 28,
1854, of Mormon parentage. In 1866, the boy went with
his family to Willard (later Willard City), in Box Elder
County, Utah. There Evan Stephens found time to attend
school and to become interested in the work of the village
choir between intervals of hard manual labor.[99] The leader
of the choir took a liking to the young Welsh lad and per-
suaded him to join the singers. Years later Stephens re-
marked that his discovery of music "was like suddenly
finding oneself deeply in love. The world became a new
creation and rhythm began to manifest itself in everything.
I walked in rhythmic motion to the field and behind the
cows, and music was found everywhere."[100] Shadrach
Jones, the choir basso, continued to inspire the lad with
stories of the leading Welsh musicians. Evan's brother,
John, "who was homesick for his beloved Wales and its
feasts of music, described to the boy the grand chorals
of the old country." Another brother purchased a four-
octave organ, which Evan soon taught himself to play.
Attendance at the Salt Lake conference gave him the
chance to hear the great organ there. During his youth,
much of this music lover's energy went to earning his
living as a farm laborer, as a hod carrier, and as a section
hand on the Utah Northern Railroad. His musical career
was even more varied. Eventually he became leader of

the Willard Choir. At the same time he was organist in the Sunday school, a member of the local glee club, and a performer in dramatics. In addition, he composed music for concert work and the drama, and tried his skill in writing plays for the local players.

In 1879, he received the position of organist at the Logan Temple, and in the following year was enabled to devote his entire time to music. His success in teaching large numbers of young people to sing attracted the attention of the Church authorities. In 1882, he commenced work with the Sunday school children of Salt Lake City, where his success eventually brought him to the leadership of the Tabernacle Choir in Salt Lake City. During the years 1888 and 1889, he organized the Stephens Opera Company, which performed *The Bohemian Girl, Martha,* and *The Daughter of the Regiment.* In 1889, he acted as director for the newly formed Salt Lake Choral Society, which sponsored musical festivals in Salt Lake City for several years. A farewell concert was given him in 1916, after twenty-six years of service as director of the Tabernacle Choir, and after thousands of young people had received the benefits of his love for music and his training in it.[101]

Joseph Daynes was another of the converts from the British Isles who had musical interests. He had sung in an English glee club, before coming to Utah in the sixties. He brought with him his eleven year old son, Joseph John. The father, a bass singer, assisted in various concerts at Salt Lake City. His young son sometimes took part in these concerts, and soon the boy's musical ability attracted attention.[102] Brigham Young suggested to the father that the son be properly trained. The father acted upon the suggestion and when the Tabernacle organ was finished in 1867, young Daynes was appointed organist. For about thirty-three years he occupied this position, at the same time taking a prominent part in the musical work of the Twentieth Ward. He also gained a wide reputation among the Latter Day Saints for the musical compositions he contributed to a *Mormon Psalmody*.[103]

Thomas Cott Griggs, another leader of the Tabernacle Choir, was born in Dover, England on June 19, 1845.[104] In 1856, he came to Boston, Massachusetts, with his mother. While in Boston he had his first acquaintance with music, soon becoming a member of the Mormon band organized at that place. Reaching Utah in 1865, he continued his musical interests by playing in Mark Croxall's band. In the early sixties, while he was working at Fairfield, Utah, a class in vocal training was organized there by B. B. Messenger. When Messenger moved from Fairfield, Griggs, his most apt pupil, became interested in furthering his own musical development as well as that of his fellows. In 1866 he became a member of the Salt Lake Tabernacle Choir; he was once appointed conductor of that choir, but resigned the position in favor of Ebenezer Beesley. Much of his energy and talent were devoted to furthering the interest of Sunday school children in music. His appointment as superintendent of the Sunday schools in Salt Lake Stake from 1891 to 1910 and his membership on the publication committee of the Desert Sunday School Union in 1878 gave him special facilities for carrying out his wishes in this respect.

With Calder, Careless, Thomas, and Tullidge leading the way, musical interest in the Territory developed a strength it had not known before. Calder seems to have had the largest number of pupils, for several hundred passed through his classes. Many of these disciples in turn taught music in Salt Lake City. C. J. Thomas, in addition to his work in the chief city of the Territory, went to southern Utah on a mission, residing at St. George, where he con-

tinued his work in music.[105] The concerts given by these
ambitious men were invariably of high order, if Salt Lake
reviews are admitted as evidence.

John Tullidge's first concert in Salt Lake City on September, 1863, began with the overture to *Tancred* by
Rossini, followed by several selections from the works of
Haydn and an anthem, *Zion's Harp,* sung by a choir. The
programme was closed by the entire chorus singing Haydn's *The Heavens are Telling.* Haydn, Handel, and English
glees occupied prominent places in the programmes of
these men, carrying into Utah the results of their early
musical tastes acquired in England.[106]

Their efforts are further illustrated by a concert given
for John Tullidge in 1868. A choir gave Danby's *Awake,
Aeolian Lyre.* Sir H. R. Bishop's *The Chough and the Crow,*
from the semi-opera of *Guy Mannering,* was given with
instrumental accompaniment. Messrs. Williams, Tullidge,
and Daynes sang the glee, *The Red Cross Knight,* which
selection led the critic in the *Utah Magazine* to write "of the
superiority of English authors over all others in this style
of composition."[107] *The Messiah* and the oratorios of Handel
and Haydn proved to be the most popular pieces for choral
work. One can see how far Utah choral work had pro-
gressed by the music at the July 24 celebration for the
year 1876. The Sunday school children gave six of their
popular songs; then the Union Glee Club sang three pieces;
selections on the organ by Joseph J. Daynes followed. The
climax of the musical programme was reached in the
selections of *Blow, Blow, Thou Winter Wind; Inflammatus*
by Rossini; and a chorus from *The Messiah. Inflammatus,*
which was particularly well executed, "was the crowning
effort of the entire musical performance" and "captivated
the immense audience."[108] Mormon choirs had developed
greatly since the days of 1849.

On February 8, 1865, the work of some of the choirs in
various parts of Utah led the editor of the *Deseret News*
to write an editorial on "Music—Its Culture and Influence" in which he expressed pleasure at the growth of the
old and the founding of new choirs, bands, and orchestras
in the Territory. As evidence of this growth of interest he
commented upon the increase in the quantities of sheet
music and instruments that had been imported. Readers
were reminded that the cost and weight of a cabinet organ
was one-third that of a piano. D. O. Calder said that seven
pianos were freighted from the East in the season of 1864
at an aggregate cost of five thousand six hundred dollars,
while five cabinet organs were freighted across the plains
in the same train at a total cost of one thousand dollars.
The writer continued:

The growing musical taste to which we adverted before, is
shown by the fact that a large number of brass instruments are
being ordered from the East, principally by brethren residing in
settlements south of this valley. The progress of the Deseret
Musical Association under the charge of brother Calder, has
stimulated a spirit of emulation in other places; and the orchestral and other bands of this and some other cities have induced
a laudable rivalry which cannot fail to be beneficial to the progress of music in our midst. Viewing it as a branch of useful and
pleasing education, and as tending to develop faculties bestowed
for noble and holy purposes, we wish to see it encouraged, and
feel happy in noting the advancement already made.[109]

The Lehi, Provo, and Spanish Fork Choirs were gaining
reputations among the inhabitants of Utah for their work
during the sixties.[110] John Tullidge was favorably impressed with the work and sight-reading ability of the
choir at American Fork.[111] He found that Bishop Harrington of that place was a lover of good melodies and harmonies and not only stimulated the [Tullidge writes "his"]
band and choir by sanctioning the study of music, but also

attended their rehearsals. Even the owner of the small music store in the village, who was also the leader of the choir, expressed himself as satisfied with the patronage he was receiving.[112]

The tonic-sol-fa method of class teaching sponsored by D. O. Calder was given a trial by some of these choirs. During the winter of 1865-66, Springville had a class of seventy-five in the new method under the direction of a newcomer to that town from England.[113] In December, 1867, D. O. Calder advertised in the *Deseret News* that he would organize a class in both the old and the new methods of notation "for the purpose of training Day and Sunday School teachers, leaders of choirs, and others who desire to qualify themselves in teaching and conducting classes and choirs."[114]

By 1869, the *Utah Magazine* recorded that class teaching had been discontinued in Salt Lake City, but that it was being carried on in the various settlements south of Salt Lake by John Tullidge and C. J. Thomas.[115] Neither of these men was an enthusiastic advocate of the new system and little mention of it was found thereafter either in Salt Lake City or in the settlements.

The use of the tonic-sol-fa method proved to be of as little permanence among the Utahans as did the use of the Deseret alphabet. One succumbed to the older systems of musical notation as the other did to the alphabet in common usage among the Gentiles.

Before 1876 there were scattered items published in Salt Lake papers denoting an interest in music throughout the wards of Salt Lake City and in the settlements spread over the Territory. But the publication of the *Utah Musical Times* shows evidence of a widespread interest in music. In 1876, the editors reported a concert on February 1 by the Fifteenth Ward Choir; on February 17, the Seventh

Ward Choir gave a concert; on the 21st of the month, the Nineteenth Ward Literary Institute gave a musical and dramatic entertainment. On the same date the Sunday School Union gave a concert at the Salt Lake Theatre under the direction of C. J. Thomas.[116] The following month concerts were reported by the Sixth Ward, the Thirteenth Ward, the Nineteenth Ward—"for the benefit of E. Beesley"—the Twentieth Ward; and favorable comment was gained by Major A. S. Kennicott for his concert at the Presbyterian Church.[117] Each month there was a similar display of interest by the amateurs of the city, who performed at these concerts. In June, a series of Sunday school concerts in the Sixth Ward led the editors of the *Utah Musical Times* to wish that the singers have accompanists and that those who planned the concerts would have shorter and better programmes.[118]

Items in the *Utah Musical Times* showed that in 1876 the settlements were not lacking in an interest for things musical. A letter from Kaysville, dated February 6, 1876, announced a concert for the following month by J. D. Montgomery's singing classes. The writer added, "Our worthy bishop gives his hearty support to all institutions which tend to elevate the mind and benefit the people of his diocese."[119] Ten days later a writer reported a Sunday school concert at Heber City.[120] In the same number of the magazine the advancement of music in Plain City was noted by the work of a choir of thirty members with George Bramwell, Jr., as organist.[121] The brother of this organist, also prominent in the choir work at Plain City, later gained a reputation for his work in training bands and choirs in Utah and Idaho.[122] In April, 1876, the Willard City music lovers led by Evan Stephens announced that they planned an entertainment in which much of the music was composed by the musicians in their own city.[123]

There is little evidence as to what was presented at these concerts. Probably much of it was of a type that would entertain or amuse the people.[124] But usually an attempt was made to give one of the so-called classical pieces. The *Utah Musical Times* took the people of Salt Lake City to task in October, 1876, because of their neglect of the Vienna Ladies' Orchestra, which played to small audiences at the theatre for three evenings.[125] Two months later the editors were praising the same people for their attendance at two concerts given by the German military band under the direction of Carl Beck at the theatre.[126] This leads one to believe that the managers of the concerts knew what they were doing when they gave their audiences pieces that would amuse them. Too many classical pieces in their concerts would have received a reception similar to that of the Vienna Ladies' Orchestra.

In 1869, the visit of the Murphy and Mack's Minstrels to Salt Lake City was followed by an editorial in the *Utah Magazine* on the treatment of the home orchestra. The editor

. . . noticed that Murphy and Mack's band received encores for many pieces of clap-trap, while we allowed, at the re-opening of our Theatre, the very effective rendition of Rossini's overture to *Semiramide*, which is so beautiful in its development of rare and choice subjects, notwithstanding its faithful interpretation by the members of our Orchestra, to pass without a single clap, and without a single expression of approbation for the care bestowed by the performers in rendering effective this fine and telling composition.[127]

The following month the somewhat musically unregenerate Salt Lakers partially retrieved themselves in the eyes of the editor of the *Utah Magazine* by an enthusiastic reception of Mozart's *Figaro*.[128] Teachers, editorials, and the encouragement of music by the Church authorities could further the development of music in Utah, but actual appreciation was a matter of time as well.

Once Salt Lake City became accessible by railroad, musical stars and organizations from outside the Territory began performing with some regularity at the Salt Lake Theatre. In November, 1868, when the transcontinental railroad had reached Ogden, Madame Parepa Rosa appeared at the Salt Lake Theatre, the forerunner of many more to come. Scenes from *Il Trovatore* and *Don Pasquale* were given with Orson Pratt, Junior, teacher of harmony and counterpoint in the city, at the piano. George E. P. Careless and the Theatre Orchestra again had a chance to display their ability.[129]

In the following June, Salt Lake City had its first complete grand operas given by a travelling company, The Howson Opera, Burlesque and Comedy Troupe. Offenbach's *The Grand Duchess, Tromb-Al-Ca-Zar,* and *Pierette; Der Freischutz* and *Aladdin* were performed in their entirety; there was also given a burlesque scene from *Il Trovatore.* About a month later Geraldine Warden followed in a series of operatic concerts. Utah, by this time, was in the musical current of the rest of the United States. Here, as in the theatre, the railroad brought a much more strongly organized culture which submerged the slowly maturing one of Utah. The time from 1849 to 1869 was too short a period to allow a distinctive Mormon culture to develop. The connections which the Mormons had hoped to sever in 1847 were reappearing in a different, subtle, and more enduring form after 1869.

Easy communications with the Gentile world effectively prevented any distinctive development of Mormon songs. Although the group resentments, tribulations, and religious beliefs were expressed in their songs, the Mormon hymns never reached the status of the folk song. Like old wine, folk songs need time to. make them mellow and rich; and the Mormon songs did not have the time requisite for this growth. The years from 1847 to 1869 did not give the older Mormons time to throw off their non-Mormon thoughts and memories before a new generation of Mormons had been placed in contact with the Gentiles who came to Utah in the wake of the railroad after 1869. The intermingling of Mormons and Gentiles took place more rapidly in Salt Lake City than in the settlements, but Salt Lake City set the fashion for the remainder of the Territory. Even the smaller settlements were constantly receiving additions of immigrants from outside of Utah, and quite frequently the Utah settlers were kept in contact with the outer world by means of the Mormon practice of sending missionaries out into the world to convert the Gentiles.

Of more importance than the time element in the growth of a group folk song—although the time element is important here also—is a flexibility in the words of the folk song. Word and verses are added as the singers feel that these are more expressive than are the old words. But the Mormon hymns lacked this flexibility.

In the early days of the faith, the Church leaders hastened to publish Mormon hymn books. Often in their eagerness to publish hymns the Mormon composers borrowed tunes from the Gentile world, much to the disgust of at least one of their musicians, John Tullidge. Frequently the *Millennial Star* printed hymns in its regular monthly issues. It was these hymns that the Mormons sang. The appearance of the hymns arranged in long symmetrical printed columns seemed to bring about a finality which discouraged composers of additional verses. Thus from the start there was a definite and complete rigidity in their hymns both original and borrowed which discouraged group improvisations of their songs.

What part did the authorities of the Church perform in developing the musical life of Utah? John Tullidge, after a tour of the settlements in 1869, noticed that wherever he found a music-loving bishop he invariably found a creditable choir, and in many instances a good band, too.[130] Again, one may see the power of the Mormon bishop in Utah life. As especially worthy of note, Tullidge recalled Lorenzo Snow's love of "pure music" and that leader's influence on the Brigham City choir.[131] Johnson speaks of the care which Bishop Johnson, of Springville, gave to the music of his community.[132] Bishop Harrington, of American Fork;[133] Bishop Atkins, of Tooele;[134] and James E. Daniels, High Counsellor in the Utah Stake of Zion, who for thirty-five years was choir-master at Provo,[135] were some of the individuals closely connected with the Church who took an interest in the music of their respective communities.

Encouragement came also from the guiding spirit of Mormon activity during 1847-77, Brigham Young. C. J. Thomas publicly thanked Young for his support.[136] G. E. P. Careless and John Daynes also received marks of Young's favor,[137] and Calder was closely connected with him.[138] Beesley, Stephens, and Griggs received places of prominence in the Church because of their ability in inspiring a love of music in others.[139]

A writer in *Harper's Monthly*, in 1884, wrote after a visit to Utah:

The Salt Lakers are also very diligent musicians. From the great organ in the Tabernacle down to a jew's harp, everybody handles some sort of musical instrument, or sings, and the music shops of the city seem about as brisk as any places on the street. You will hear singing all the time, and in all localities. This, has been encouraged by the Church, as has been the dramatic life of the people.[140]

With some allowance for journalistic exaggeration this article may indicate the status of musical affairs in Utah at the close of Brigham Young's leadership.

To all Mormons the great organ of the Tabernacle was a source of pride. This instrument has an interesting history which illustrates some of the difficulties in early Utah. By 1865, the large Tabernacle had been finished, and the Church authorities decided to build an organ for the services. Specimens of wood were brought in for examination from various parts of Utah. A variety of white pine, found near Parowan and in the Pine Valley, three hundred miles south of Salt Lake City, fulfilled the requirements. This pine had a fine grain; it was also comparatively free from gum and pitch, and without knots. It could be obtained in the requisite lengths and quantity, a necessary consideration, for some of the large pipes of the organ required thousands of feet of timber. Trained mechanics in Salt Lake City went to work on the lumber, and, a few years after the Tabernacle itself was finished, the organ was furnishing music for the services held there.[141]

G. A. Sala, an English traveller, wrote of this organ and its case:

The organ itself like the majority of the things structural among the Mormons, [is] intensely ugly,— indeed if anything of an artistic, or aesthetic nature entered into their religious culture, Mormonism, I take it would soon become as harmlessly effete as Johanna Southcotianism or Walker-Separatism has become in London. For a couple of thousand dollars or so, the organ pipes might have been placed in a tasteful case; but the tasteless designer has reared at the angles of his instrument monstrous fasces of pipes surmounted by squat cupolas, so that they resemble nothing half so much as hundred ton guns "sot on end" as a Down-Easter would say.[142]

Sala's comment shows a lack of penetration concerning the difficulties which were experienced by the pioneers in even doing as much as building an organ. Perhaps the organ was not artistically encased, but it would have been a difficult problem for the pioneer country to obtain the necessary "few thousand dollars" to build the organ themselves. Considerations of its beauty could be left to future generations with, perhaps, more leisure and wealth. And there also was the feeling in a new country that an organ, or whatever else was to be constructed, should be completed and ready for use in as short a time as possible.

There are some rather interesting stories connected with the development of music in early Utah, as witness the request of an individual in Provo addressed to Calder and Careless, music dealers in Salt Lake City, whether they would take rags and paper in exchange for a cabinet organ.[143] An indication of one bishop's willingness to assist the singing in his community may be seen in an item published in the *Millennial Star* during 1870. Bishop Hughes of Mendon, Cache County, wrote to the *Deseret News* on April 3, 1870, offering ten acres of the best land in the settlement, to a "good basso, tenore, alto, and soprano, who were good members of society, and good readers of music, and would settle at Mendon and attend meeting regularly."[144]

William Minturn, an English traveller, was fortunate enough to be in Salt Lake City in 1875, when the class directed by G. E. P. Careless sang *The Messiah*. After witnessing this performance, the traveller made an observation that penetrated beyond the ordinary view of Mormonism when he wrote:

This [giving of musicales] is a great move, and one cannot help but think that if there is something wrong in this society, it will

be eradicated by the elevation of the general taste of the people,—
and what elevates the taste as does music.[145]

By 1877, music had received recognition as a necessary
and integrated feature of Utah life. Credit for this achievement may be placed to several accounts. In the first place,
indistinct as it is, the warp and the woof of musical taste is
woven out of old-world musical tradition. The back-
grounds of Thomas, Careless, and Tullidge illustrate this.
Credit also must be given these individuals for their work
and sacrifices against obstacles which, at times, seemed
insurmountable. Credit must also be given to the Church,
and in particular to the support of Brigham Young—a
support which was absolutely necessary for the success of
any enterprise in Utah during 1847-77.

CHAPTER VIII

AND CROWN THY GOOD WITH BROTHERHOOD

Upon reaching Utah, the Mormons had to conquer a forbidding wilderness. This wild environment strengthened the Church's power in many respects. The Church was the centre of the Mormon's life—economically, spiritually, and socially. The Mormons had had a strong *esprit de corps* in Kirtland, Independence, and Nauvoo. But in spite of hopes and plans, these centres were not as yet destined to be the Mormon heaven on earth. In Utah, however, the Church leaders had certain strategic advantages in planning their campaign for a Mormon Zion. In Utah the centralized water locations, the valleys between the mountains, and the method of group colonization emphasized the community rather than the individual. The gregarious Mormon frequently had meetings with his fellowmen which the ordinary frontiersman had only intermittently during logrollings, revival meetings, election days, and court trials. Even in 1877 Utah was predominantly a rural region. But the dweller in Salt Lake City had the advantage of being nearer to the centre of the Church's cultural development than one living in Kanab on the southern border, or Willard City in the northwest corner of the Territory. The possibilities for the development of the drama and music and for the giving of lectures in the outlying settlements depended upon the interests of the bishop in charge of the community. If the bishop was willing to take the lead, there was the further question of who was able to take part in these developments. If the people were sufficiently interested to take part, the Church leadership had partially achieved its object by giving them its approbation. But the rural brethren in the settlements interested in the arts must have envied the urbanites who lived in the chief town of the Territory.

As soon as the first group of Saints reached the present-day site of Salt Lake City, Brigham Young announced how the land was to be apportioned in the New Zion. Central locations were reserved for public buildings. Then the Church leaders received the next best locations. After these were determined, the remainder of the Saints drew lots. The leaders agreed that the city should be divided into blocks or squares of ten acres, and that lots should be an acre and a quarter, and that the sidewalks should be twenty feet wide, and that the streets should be eight rods wide.[1] Later on Brigham Young urged the planting of shade trees on the streets of Salt Lake City. These trees with the surplus water continuously running through the gutters give the Mormon metropolis the appearance of an oasis in the Utah desert. And for those who like symmetry and regularity in the streets of a city, Salt Lake City is perfection itself.

To both ruralite and urbanite there was but little doubt that the Mormon Church was the most powerful organization in Utah. Until the late sixties, it seemed to be the only strongly organized and omnipresent institution in the Territory. To this "self-evident" truth there was an added corollary, that is, that the most powerful individual in the Mormon Church until the time of his death in 1877 was Brigham Young. Therefore, his attitude towards the development of any cultural activities in Utah has been emphasized.

Under Young's leadership the Church's attitude towards

the development of communal activities in Utah was on the whole favorable and, where applied, was paternalistic. Orson Pratt, in a talk given at the Salt Lake Tabernacle on October 15, 1854, presented the Church's stand when he said:

> The Lord is gathering his Saints into this valley in order to instruct them how to be happy; that is the ultimate object and aim He has in view. He desires us to be well instructed, and to have the straight and narrow path laid out plain before us, showing us, from time to time, what steps are necessary to be taken, that will lead to the greatest amount of happiness; and if we follow them and continue in the path, we shall find that our light will grow brighter and brighter, our happiness greater and greater, and our joys will become more and more intense, until, in the eternal world we shall be swallowed up, as it were, with a fullness of joy—a fullness of happiness.[2]

What kind of individual were it who was struggling against the dryness of Utah and against the devils of this world under the great seal of the Mormon Church? The majority were similar to the frontiersmen who went out from western New York and our northern states before 1840. From 1840 on, there was a large sprinkling of immigrants from northern Europe and the British Isles. Comments by visitors to Utah are, however, interesting enough to be repeated. Such travelers were continusly seeking for expressions of ignorance or of intelligence among the Mormons with whom they rubbed elbows. As usual with impressions received from viewing people in crowds, the observer frequently saw only what he was seeking. Robert Bartholomew, an assistant surgeon in the United States Army in 1858, described the people of Utah as wearing "an expression, which may be styled the Mormon expression and style: an expression compounded of sensuality, cunning, suspicion, and a smirking self-conceit."[3] R. L.

Price, in *The Two Americas,* described the men as thick and brutish.[4] Richardson was impressed by the lack of self-reliance, breadth, and thought in the faces of a Mormon congregation.[5] Brigadier General Rusling considered the people more intelligent looking than he had been led to expect.[6] Ludlow was not impressed by the faces of some Mormon women he saw at work preparing the Salt Lake Theatre for a ball, but he spoke of the improvement of even polygamous Utah in the scale of civilization over "a Staffordshire potter's hovel, or of a den in the mining districts of England."[7] Any complete view of early Mormonism must take Ludlow's point of view into account.

The health of the Mormon people became one of the concerns of the Church leaders. Joseph Smith's pronouncements on this topic were gathered and published as the *Word of Wisdom,* a standard work for the faithful Mormon. This work lists wine, strong drinks, and tobacco as unhealthy for human beings.[8] To some Mormons the listing of hot drinks means the condemnation of coffee and tea.[9] Brigham Young's sermons are replete with advice to the Saints in this world in regard to moderation in the use of diet, dress, and exercise.[10]

Much of the actual work in developing a Zion was undertaken by English converts. Philip Margetts, John T. Caine, and Mrs. Woodmansee, prominent in the early days of the drama in Utah, had been natives of England. William C. Dunbar and James T. Ferguson had come to Utah from Scotland. Englishmen ruled the field of music in early Utah; William Pitt, John Tullidge, G. E. P. Careless, C. J. Thomas, and E. Beesley were among those who received their musical training in England. David O. Calder was a native of Scotland, as was R. L. Campbell, who was interested in the development of education in Utah. Evan Stephens, leaving Wales with his family early in life, came to an environment in Willard City where the Welsh tradition of song was carried on by numerous Welsh settlers.

There are, of course, additional factors that mirror the cultural interests of Utah as a whole during the period from 1847 to 1877. Women played a part, but usually a minor part, in certain aspects of community life. Women acted in the theatres, sang in the choirs, and worked as school teachers. After 1867 they attended the university, a continuation of their practice and privilege of attending the parents' school of the early fifties. All places of leadership, however, were reserved for men. The Mormon Church was managed by men, and the leadership in developing a culture was assumed almost entirely by the male members of the Church.

In specific fields of group activity the Church applied pressure, enthusiasm, and support in varying degrees. The development of education in Utah was neglected by the leaders of the Mormon Church, but this neglect had mitigating circumstances in the lack of wealth in the Territory. With true Western optimism, the Mormons founded their university soon after the first Mormons reached Nauvoo. They did the same soon after settling the Salt Lake Valley. For years, however, actual development of a wide-spread system of schools was neglected, not that the Mormons were hostile to the idea of learning; no one group was interested in doing the spade work. Schools were an easy thing to put off for future consideration. There was no organized drive in this field similar to that in economic coöperation, the theatre, or in music. People could be happy without a thorough education. Two facts of importance affected education in Utah after the railroad arrived in the Territory. First, there was an increase of wealth; secondly, there was the coming of the mission schools of the Baptists, Presbyterians, and other sects. This

latter factor aroused the Mormons to action. At the same
time the increasing wealth of Utah gave the Mormons more
means with which to work. Mormons such as Karl Maeser,
Dr. J. R. Park, and R. L. Campbell were leaders in the
move for better educational facilities in Utah. In this respect the Church was not the leader.

The Church, however, did take a prominent part in developing the theatre, especially in Salt Lake City. The Salt
Lake Theatre was a source of pleasure to the actors and to
the audience. It was also an inspiration to the various
towns scattered up and down the valleys of Utah. Few
individuals would have dared to assume the financial risk
of an enterprise of this sort in the Utah of 1862; the Church,
with the ability and resources of the community at its call,
gave the theatre a position of prominence and a community support that made for its success. Even as late as 1875,
when the Salt Lake Theatre was managed by individuals
and was failing, Brigham Young took over the management; and, again having the advantage of this close connection with the Church, the Salt Lake Theatre once more
prospered.[11]

In the field of music the Mormon Church also took the
lead. Brigham Young was not whole-heartedly enthusiastic concerning this feature of community life. But the
leaders in musical affairs, such as Calder and Thomas, tell
of Young's encouragement. Not especially interested in
this development and detailed work himself, the Mormon
leader passed this work on to others. And once those interested were given free reign and support in their musical
work, they developed among the Mormons a taste and
widespread interest in music that has lasted until the present day.[12] The coming of the railroad did not affect this
development, as it did the drama in Utah. Consequently
the musical development undertaken by the Mormon

Church, because of its comparative permanence and its widespread use by individuals in Utah, amply repaid the efforts of Thomas, Careless, Tullidge, and Calder. If one were selecting any field of culture development that had a success greater than that of any other, music would be the field selected.

There was another motive that appeared in the development of a community life in Utah which must be considered. Was the Church, in taking over the agencies of culture in Utah, acting strictly from disinterested motives? Were the debating societies and the theatre absorbed by the Church, not because of any inherent love of culture, but because the leaders wanted to control every agency that might be a possible opponent of the faith? This factor was also present. The societies organized in 1854-55 and during the late sixties did not need financial backing to succeed. Yet the Church soon absorbed these organized channels of social communication. The Church evidently thought that it could manage the societies better than could individuals. The groups were possible points for heresy to arise and for questionings to gain vogue; therefore the Church absorbed the growing societies by its own organizations of the Deseret Theological Institute and the young people's mutual improvement associations. The desire to secure the happiness of the people was mixed with the desire to control all of Utah life.

The Church's control brings up another question which is easier to ask than it is to answer. Did the Church's absorption of these literary, dramatic, and debating societies hinder or further Utah's cultural development? The question cannot be answered directly. It is the age-old question of individualism versus paternal collectivism. To some individuals, as to John Hyde, Jr., the restrictions of group leadership must have been severely irksome. Few frontier communities, however, advanced as far as did many Mormon communities in facilities, meagre though they were, for enjoying a life that was hard enough in many respects.

An editorial in the dedicatory number of the *Utah Magazine* asserted "that as a community, we back Art and Science with a force unheard of in the world before."[13] Such boastfulness must be heavily discounted. But to the vast majority of the Mormons the social leadership of the Church was a welcome relief from their difficult lives, both in Europe and in Utah. Although the Church did not succeed in its efforts to build an indigenous culture, it did bring glimpses of happiness into lives that, without such leadership, would have been even more barren than they were. Even if the millennium on earth was not achieved, many Mormons were confident that the Church was pointing the way.

NOTES

NOTES

CHAPTER I.
AMERICA THE BEAUTIFUL. MORMONISM

[1] Quoted by Phillips Russell, Emerson, The Wisest American (New York, 1929). 193-194.

[2] Ibid., 195.

[3] I. W. Riley, The Founder of Mormonism, 70 (New York, 1902, also London, 1903.)

[4] For anti-Mormon versions of Joseph Smith's character see W. A. Linn, The Story of the Mormons (New York, 1902) or I. W. Riley, The Founder of Mormonism; a somewhat popular account from this same point of view is H. M. Beardsley, Joseph Smith and His Mormon Empire (New York, 1931).

The Mormon version of Joseph Smith's early days may be found in E. W. Tullidge's, History of Salt Lake City (Salt Lake City, 1886); O. F. Whitney's, History of Utah, 4 volumes, (Salt Lake City, 1892-3). The most recent addition to the literature on this subject is J. H. Evans, Joseph Smith (New York, 1933). The work of H. H. Bancroft, History of Utah (San Francisco, 1890) in general follows this version.

[5] A copy of the charge made against the Mormons by the Missourians of this period may be found in A History of the Church, Joseph and Heman Smith (Lamoni, Iowa, 1917), 312-315.

[6] Latter Day Saints' Biographical Encyclopedia, 9.

[7] For diaries and experiences of men who participated in these events see Autobiography of James S. Brown; Sergeant Daniel Tyler, A Concise History of the Mormon Battalion in the Mexican War (1881); and F. A. Golder, The March of the Mormon Battalion (New York, 1928).

[8] Catholic Church in Utah, 263.

CHAPTER II
MAY GOD THY GOLD REFINE
MORMON ECONOMIC COOPERATION

[1] The subject of Mormon coöperation in the economic sphere has been treated by J. H. Warner, Social Coöperation Among the Mormons (Johns Hopkins University Studies, VI, 1888); Hamilton Gardner, "Coöperation Among the Mormons," Quarterly Journal of Economics, XXXI, 1917. Also in such general works as C. H. Brough's, Irrigation in Utah and E. E. Ericksen's The Psychological and Ethical Aspects of Mormon Group Life. Three magazine articles concerned mainly with the later developments of Mormon economic coöperation, but helpful even for the earlier development are: one by C. B. Spahr in the Outlook, February 3, 1900; another by Professor

Richard T. Ely in *Harper's Magazine* for April, 1903; and a third by Glen Miller in *World's Work*, for December, 1902.

[2] R. T. Ely, *Harper's Magazine*, CVL, (April, 1903), 668.

[3] For examples of this willingness see *Autobiography of James S. Brown*, 129, 392, 407, 447, 449-452, 478; *Latter Day Saints' Biographical Encyclopedia, passim;* Stenhouse, *Rocky Mountain Saints*, 568-574; Ann Eliza Webb, *Life in Mormon Bondage*, 131-134.

[4] Talbot, *My People of the Plains*, 218.

[5] Tullidge, *Salt Lake City*, i, 647, quotes from *Journal of Heber C. Kimball*.

[6] Tullidge, *Salt Lake City*, ii, 7.

[7] Bancroft, *op. cit.*, 409. In 1852 the Mormon Church in Ireland claimed 245 people. On April 17, 1840, the Scotch branch had three elders and twenty-one members; April, 1841, 368 members; and by the close of 1853 more than three thousand. At the close of 1852 the Wales branch claimed five thousand members. For an individual account of missionary work in British Isles see autobiography of James S. Brown, *Life of a Pioneer*, 418-434.

[8] Bancroft, *op. cit.*, 409. *Mormon Handbook*, 51. *House Executive Documents*, 4 Cong. 2 Sess., I, 601. *The Autobiography of Parley Pratt* and the *Biography of John Taylor* show the experience of some of these missionaries. In Remy and Brenchley, *A Journey to Great Lake Valley*, II, 198, Remy reports of Mormon successes among the inhabitants of Sandwich Islands. James S. Brown, in *Life of a Pioneer*, tells of his experience as a Mormon missionary to the Sandwich Islands.

[9] *Millennial Star*, XLI, 692-3; *Deseret News*, July 19, 1865.

[10] Bancroft, *op. cit.*, 406.

[11] Stenhouse, *Rocky Mountain Saints*, 202. Cf. Bancroft, *op. cit.*, 406.

[12] Remy in his work gives a total of 30,000 immigrants up to 1859, figures thought too high by Burton. Remy, *op. cit.*, II, 211; Stenhouse, *op. cit.*, 575 Bancroft, *op. cit., passim*, for emigration.

[13] Bancroft, *op. cit.*, 431.

[14] Coman, *The Economic Beginnings of the Far West*, II, 182.

[15] Tullidge, *Salt Lake City*, i, 649.

[16] Burton, *City of the Saints*, 296. The Women's Relief Societies of Utah gave part of their money to this fund. See *Woman's Exponent*, I, *passim*.

[17] J. R. Young, *Memoirs*, 286.

[18] Dickens, *Uncommercial Traveller*, 230. For similar conditions at the New York port of embarkation, see the New York *World*, July 10, 1860, page 5.

[19] Henry Mayhew, *The Mormons or Latter Day Saints* (London, 1851).

[20] S. C. Johnson, *Emigration from the United Kingdom to North America*, (London, 1913), 107, *et seq*.

[21] Stenhouse, *Rocky Mountain Saints*, 578, 579 and Tullidge, *Salt Lake*

City, i, 654. *Autobiography of James S. Brown*, 434.

22 Nearly all the Mormon immigrants went to Salt Lake City and were distributed from there.

23 Coman, *op. cit.*, II, 184.

24 *Ibid.*, II, 184. For reception of an immigrant train, on August 29, 1859, see *Autobiography of James S. Brown*, 404: "[When Brigham Young] . . . was told the condition of the [immigrant] company, he sent word to Bishop Edward Hunter to have the tithing yard cleared for the cattle, to have cooked food for all who needed it, and to have the company camp in Union Square."

25 *Cf.* Bancroft, *op. cit.*, 305, 316. *Autobiography of James S. Brown*, 457, 466: "Volunteers were asked to settle in Arizona, those thinking it better to wait, were reminded of the passage in the *Doctrine and Covenants*: 'He that waiteth to be commanded in all things is a slothful servant.'"

26 Webb, *The Real Mormonism*, 141-143. *Deseret News*, March 19, 1856. For Mormon colonization in Canada see L. Thwaite and R. P. Porter, *Alberta*, 229-233 and *Index to Canada and Its Provinces*. Charles W. Kindrick (United States Consul at Cuidad Juarez, Mexico) has an article "The Mormons in Mexico," *Review of Reviews*, June, 1899.

27 *Book of Doctrine and Covenants*, Sec. 42; 32-34; 65; 61; 4-5. The basis of Mormon doctrine may be found in this work. The references are from the edition of 1891.

28 *Ibid.*, Sec. 51: 1-3.

29 *Ibid.*, Sec. 42: 20-54.

30 Isaac Morley and John Corrill had formerly been connected with Rigdon's communistic scheme at Kirtland. The new members were Oliver Cowdery, W. W. Phelps, Sidney Gilbert, and John Whitmer. This revelation may be found in *Doctrine and Covenants*, Sec. 57.

31 *Doctrine and Covenants*, Sec. 82:12.

32 *Doctrine and Covenants*, Sec. 119. For further details on the United Order see Bancroft, *op. cit.*, 359, note 18. The idea keeps constantly recurring in Mormon thought, and at times in Mormon practice.

33 Quoted by Bancroft, 351. Note 12.

34 Greeley, *Overland Journey to California*, 213-14.

35 Linn, *op. cit.*, 573, note 1. Bancroft, 351, note 15.

36 *Op. cit.*, XII:36; *Cf. Ibid*, VIII:202; VIII:345; XIV:89.

37 Ericksen, *op. cit.*, 68.

38 *Rocky Mountain Saints*, 665.

39 *Journal of Discourses*, XVI: 111; XV: 163-164; VIII: 345.

40 Tithing of the Church in 1914 was $1,887,920—*Eighty-Fifth Annual Report*. In 1917 $21,691,489—*Eighty-Eighth Annual Report*. There was expended for ward and stake purchases—$925,270; for Church schools and seminaries—$893,000. *Report of Ninety-second Annual Conference*, (1922), 8.

[41] *Op. cit.*, 24. *Cf. Tullidge's Quarterly Magazine*, I, i, 16, "It was in 1868 that the Apostles made their first attempt to establish the Order of Enoch though, ever and anon, it had been talked of for years at Conference times under the name of 'Consecrations.' " "Consecration," according to the revelations of 1831, meant the surrender of one's surplus property to the Church.

[42] *Tullidge's Quarterly Magazine*, II, ii, 311.

[43] Erickson, *op. cit.*, 51. This, of course, was not in strict accordance with the retention of individual property which Joseph Smith advocated.

[44] *Tullidge's Quarterly Magazine*, I, iiii, 557-563; an article by Bishop Liljenquist who had charge of the Hyrum United Order.

[45] Johnson, *op. cit.*, 83.

[46] J. R. Young, *Memoirs*, 225, 226.

[47] *Ibid.*, 250-1. The author on page 226 of his *Memoirs* writes: "each family had their separate home, which was sacred to the family, subject strictly to the parents' government and disicipline." It is to be remembered that all property was turned over to the bishop and then he returned to each family what was needed by them—their "stewardship" or "inheritance." *Cf. Supra*, 24 and 25, and *Latter Day Saints' Biographical Encyclopedia*, 467-477, for statements of Joseph Wright, who participated in another branch of the United Order.

[48] McClintock, *Mormon Settlements in Arizona*, 131. Also see Letter from Lorenzo Snow to Bishop Lunt in *Tullidge's Quarterly Magazine*, II, iii, 401-2.

[49] McClintock, *op. cit.*, 131. Letter from Lorenzo Snow to President F. D. Richards, in *Tullidge's Quarterly Magazine*, II, 404. *Cf. Gazetter of Utah and Salt Lake Directory*, (1874), 55. E. R. S. Smith, *Biography of Lorenzo Snow*, 302-306.

[50] *Tullidge's Quarterly Magazine*, II, 403.

[51] Coman, *op. cit.*, II, 180.

[52] Webb, *The Real Mormonism*, 132.

[53] *Ibid.*, 132. Several times before 1869 *The Deseret News* had to discontinue publication because of lack of paper, as from August 19 to November 15, 1851.

[54] L. E. Young, *The Founding of Utah*, 196; *History of the Young Ladies' Mutual Improvement Association*, 24-25. About 1870 Zina D. Huntington Young, a wife of Brigham Young, was sent upon a mission to establish silk culture in Utah. "She fed and took care of millions of worms" and "lived to see the silk industry fostered and made comparatively successful through legislative enactment." *Cf.* Governor Emery's message to the Territory of Utah on January 14, 1878 (page 14) in which he says ". . . it has now been demonstrated by actual experiment that our climate and soil are admirably adapted to the mulberry tree and the production of silk." He recommended also the industry to the Legislature's favor. Also an article on "Silk

Culture" in *The Contributor* II, 115-116. Letter of Brigham Young to Albert Carrington, January, 1869, *Millennial Star*, 100-101.

[55] Webb, *op. cit.*, 131.

[56] *Ibid*, 131.

[57] Johnson, *op. cit.*, 37; Stenhouse, *Op. cit.*, 345-6.

[58] Johnson, *op. cit.*, 75. Reminiscences of Mary E. L. Neff in *Memorial to Elizabeth Claridge McCune*, 75: "In the summer of 1867 Miss Elizabeth Parks, Miss Elizabeth Ann Claridge, Miss Hetty Grace, and myself were called by the Ecclesiastical authorities of the [Nephi] ward to study telegraphy. Our teacher, Wm. A. C. Bryan, had been called in the autumn of 1866 by President Brigham Young to study telegraphy under Professor Cowles."

[59] Webb, *op. cit.*, 134, and Warner in *John Hopkins University Studies*, VI; also *Deseret News*, May 27, 1868.

[60] Warner, *op. cit.*, 430. *Tullidge's Quarterly Magazine*, I, 387 gives the constitution and by-laws of the institution which came out of this suggestion.

[61] Warner, *op. cit.*, 432, quotes letter of J. Brainerd Thrall of Salt Lake City. Johnson, *History of Springville, Utah*, 79. A correspondent in *Utah Magazine*, III, 525, wrote a letter from San Pete, dated December 5, 1869 ". . . the bishop announced today, in public, that henceforward they will sell no goods to those not having any goods in the cooperative store." And this store had forced all other stores in the town out of business.

[62] Ericksen, *op. cit.*, 53. *Cf.* Hannah Cornaby, *Autobiography and Poems*, 57, for the attitude of a Mormon who favored the United Order. See letters from Utah in *Millennial Star*, XXX and XXXI for 1868 and 1869 for illustrations of Mormon emphasis upon coöperative stores during those years. *Ibid.*, XXXI, "Reports of Thirty-Ninth Semi-Annual Conference at Salt Lake City", 715, 731, 747, 763.

[63] Gardner, *Quarterly Journal of Economics*, XXXIII, 489 ff. C. B. Spahr, *Outlook*, February 3, 1900; and Ericksen, *op. cit.*, part 3, *passim*.

[64] *Op. cit.*, I, 365.

[65] *Land of Sunshine*, 259, October, 1901. An article "Mormonism" by Lorenzo Snow written while he was President of the Church.

CHAPTER III

CONFIRM THY SOUL IN SELF CONTROL

THE FUNCTION OF INTELLIGENCE

[1] I. Woodbridge Riley's, *The Founder of Mormonism* is a study in the environmental influences—laying stress upon the psychopathic—that went into Joseph Smith's religion. The biographies of Joseph Smith written by the Mormon writers, J. H. Evans, George Q. Cannon, and E. W. Tullidge hold to the theory that Joseph Smith received his revelations from a divine source, that earthly influences were so secondary as to be negligible. *Cf.* J. A. Widtsoe's, *Joseph Smith as a Scientist* (Salt Lake City, 1908) for an at-

tempt to show by inductive reasoning that Joseph Smith was divinely guided.

[2] *Doctrine and Covenants*, 132:20.

[3] *Journal of Discourses*, I, 334, (Brigham Young).

[4] *Ibid.*, VII, 160; Lorenzo Snow, *Land of Sunshine*, October, 1901, 257; *Millennial Star*, XIV, 385.

[5] *Doctrine and Covenants*, 99:36.

[6] *Ibid.*, 131:6.

[7] J. A. Widtsoe, *Joseph Smith as a Scientist*, 137-138.

[8] *Cf.* N. L. Nelson's, *Scientific Aspects of Mormonism*, *passim*.

[9] *Doctrine and Covenants*, 88:118. See also 88:78 and 79.

[10] *Journal of Discourses*, XII, 158-159.

[11] *Doctrine and Covenants*, 130:18.

[12] *Ibid.*, 130:19.

[13] Sermon by Brigham Young (delivered August 31, 1862) published in *Deseret News* of October 22, 1862.

[14] "Circular of Chancellor of University of Nauvoo," *Times and Seasons*, III, 631. For same in respect to University of Deseret see *Millennial Star*, XII, 294-296.

[15] *Millennial Star*, XXI, 281; XXX, 252.

[16] Reported in *Deseret News*, July 26, 1850. Gunnison, *History of the Mormons*, 81. Lieutenant Gunnison was in the region of Salt Lake City at the time Phelps made this speech, July 24, 1850. He gives Phelps' ideas as those of the Church.

[17] Bancroft, *op. cit.*, 108.

[18] *Journal of Discourses*, XIX, 46; VI, 99; VIII, 6. Gunnison, *History of the Mormons*, 81. *Deseret News*, October 22, 1862; February 25, 1863.

[19] At the Tabernacle, March 19, 1854. *Journal of Discourses*, III, 105-106.

[20] *Journal of Discourses*, XII, 158-159; XVII, 515. *Millennial Star*, XIV, 51; XXVII, 323-326.

[21] *Journal of Discourses*, II, 246. Burton relates that while he was visiting Salt Lake City Orson Pratt was suspected of relying too much upon education by books rather than by inspiration from on high. *City of the Saints*, 353. *Cf.* Remy and Brenchley, *A Journey to Great Salt Lake City*, II, 175-176.

[22] *Millennial Star*, XXI, 647.

[23] *Ibid.*, XXI, 648.

[24] *Ibid.*, XI, 645-647. The writer of this article refused to accept authority in 1869, and was cut-off from the Church. *Cf.* Bancroft, *op. cit.*, 647-649.

[25] Hyde, *Mormonism*, 123.

[26] Werner, *Brigham Young*, 144, quotes from *Brigham Young's Journal*, August 20, 1842.

[27] *Latter Day Saints' Biographical Encyclopedia*, 127.

28 *Ibid.*, 126-127; *General Catalogue Dartmouth College* (1769-1910), 247.

29 Bancroft, *op. cit.*, 775.

30 *Biography and Family Record of Lorenzo Snow*, 3-6.

31 *Latter Day Saints' Biographical Encyclopedia*, 723-24; *General Alumni Catalogue, University of Pennsylvania* (1917), 591.

32 *Latter Day Saints' Biographical Encyclopedia*, 144.

33 *Ibid.*, 337-339; *General Catalogue Union College*, (1797-1804), 25.

34 J. C. Bennett, William E. McLellin, and Sampson Arvard were some of these doctors. *Cf.* Bancroft, *op. cit.*, *index* for these names. Willard Richards, second counsellor to President Brigham Young from 1847-1854, practiced medicine in Boston before he joined the Church. *Latter Day Saints' Biographical Encyclopedia*, 53.

35 Total population of Utah (1870) 86,786. *Ninth Census of United States* (1870), 328 and 335. The Mormon population of Utah in *ibid.*, 556 is 85,350.

36 *Latter Day Saints' Biographical Encyclopedia, passim.*

37 *Ibid.*, 8, 34, 62.

38 B. H. Roberts, *Life of John Taylor*, 23.

39 M. F. Cowley, *History of Life and Labors of Wilford Woodruff*, 21.

40 *Autobiography of Parley P. Pratt*, 100.

41 *Millennial Star*, XXX, 17-18. See *Journal of Discourses*, VIII, 9.

CHAPTER IV
GOD MEND THY EVERY FLAW
EDUCATION

1 E. P. Cubberly, *Public Education in the United States*, (Cambridge, Mass., 1919), 118-154.

2 There is a copy of this constitution in the Harvard College Library.

3 *Utah Acts, etc.*, (1855), 59-61.

4 *Ibid.*, 287-289.

5 44 Cong., 1 Sess., *House Ex. Doc.*, IV, ii, 459.

6 *Ibid.*, IV, ii, 459.

7 *Ibid.*, IV, ii, 459.

8 Published in *Woman's Exponent*, (December, 1873), II, 103.

9 44 Cong., 2 Sess., *House Ex. Doc.*, IV, ii, 459.

10 *Ibid.*, IV, ii, 459-460.

11 *Journals, Legislative Assembly of Utah Territory* (1860-61), 15. This publication will hereafter be referred to as *Journals*.

12 *Ibid.*, (1862-63), XVI.

13 *Journals*, (1869), 14-15 for Acting Governor Higgins' "Message." Governor Woods' "Message" is in *ibid.*, (1872), 19.

14 *Ibid.*, (1876), 28-29.

15 Italicized in *Journals*.

16 *Times and Seasons*, II, 284.

17 Others on the Board were Samuel H. Smith, Charles C. Rich, John T.

Barnett, Wilson Law, John P. Greene, Vinson Knight, Isaac Galland, Elias Higbee, Robert D. Foster, James Adams, Samuel Bennett, Ebenezer Robinson, John Snider, George Miller, and Zenos M. Knight, *Ibid.*, III, 631.

[18] *Ibid.*, III, 631.

[19] B. H. Roberts, *The Rise and Fall of Nauvoo*, 85.

[20] General James Arlington Bennet was the other recipient of the degree of LL.D. at this time (April 22, 1842), *Journal of Church History*, XV, 278. (Published by the Reorganized Church of Jesus Christ of Latter Day Saints.) This "General" was a lawyer who gave his address as Arlington House, Long Island, New York, Linn, *The Mormons*, 253, note 1.

[21] *Millennial Star*, XII, 294-296.

[22] *Ibid.*, XII, 244; *Journals*, (1851-52), 102.

[23] R. L. Campbell to S. W. Richards in *Millennial Star*, XIV, 508.

[24] *Journals*, (1851-52), 153.

[25] *Cf.* Bancroft, *op. cit.*, 234, note 9.

[26] *Journals* (1869), 177; *ibid.*, (1872), 19; *Woman's Exponent*, II, 21; *Utah Magazine*, III, 399.

[27] *General Catalogue of College of New Jersey*, (1741-1896), 77; Also *Deseret News*, April 11, 1860.

[28] *Deseret News*, April 11, 1860.

[29] *Ibid.*, April 11, 1860.

[30] *Ibid.*, February 22, 1860.

[31] "Governor's Message," *Journals*, (1860-61), 15; Burton, *City of the Saints*, 425.

[32] *Deseret News*, April 18, 1860.

[33] *Salt Lake City Directory*, (1869), 73.

[34] *Doctrine and Covenants*, 55:4.

[35] Whitney, *Life of Heber C. Kimball*, 83; *cf. Times and Seasons*, V, 754, 755.

[36] *Times and Seasons*, III, 631, 653.

[37] *Latter Day Saints' Biographical Encyclopedia*, 774; Bancroft, *op. cit.*, 596, note 60; *Ibid.*, 324, note 10, quotes *Utah Sketches* (*MS.*), 172; Whitney, *History of Utah*, IV, 325-26.

[38] Gardner, *History of Lehi*, 95.

[39] *Exploration and Survey of Valley of Great Salt Lake*, 143.

[40] Remy and Brenchley, *op. cit.*, 177-178.

[41] *Cf.* Bancroft, *op. cit.*, 708; Jensen, *Provo*, 398.

[42] Bancroft, *op. cit.*, 318, note 45. Johnson, *History of Springville, Utah* 2-6.

[43] Letter written by G. A. Smith in *Millennial Star*, XIV, 669.

[44] Bancroft, *op. cit.*, 313, note 24.

[45] *Ibid.*, 324, note 10.

[46] *Millennial Star*, XIV, 491.

47 Quoted by *Millennial Star*, XXII, 348.

48 Joshua Williams to Albert Carrington, December 2, 1869, in *Millennial Star*, XXXII, 42. In 1862 there were six schools at Provo, *ibid.*, XXIV, 236. In 1863 the Pinto settlement had twelve houses and one school, *ibid.*, XXV, 452. In 1864, the four-year-old settlement of Plain City had sixty families and a school of sixty students, *ibid.*, XXVI, 236. For other places see *ibid.*, XXIV, 283-284; XXXII, 302, 303; XXXIII, 62, 303; *Deseret News*, March 11, 1863, and September 14, 1864; *Journal Legislative Assembly*, (Utah, 1860-61), 79.

49 Remy and Brenchley, *A Journey to Great Salt Lake City*, II, 176. The Paris (first) edition of this work was published in 1860.

50 *Cf.* Hyde, *Mormonism*, (New York, 1857), 122-124 with Remy and Brenchley, II, 176-179.

51 Remy and Brenchley, *op. cit.*, II, 204-205.

52 Burton, *op, cit.*, 423-424.

53 *Sinners and Saints*, 188-189.

54 Remy and Brenchley, *op. cit.*, II, 180.

55 Hyde, *op. cit.*, 119. Hyde, an apostate Mormon, was desirous of proving all evil of the Mormons; therefore, his statements must be treated with caution. However, on this point, the Church leaders confirmed his accusations.

56 L. E. Young, *Chief Episodes in the History of Utah*, 44.

57 Hannah Cornaby, *Autobiography and Poems*, 37, 38.

58 "Report Territorial Superintendent of Schools" in *Journals*, (1862-63), 75.

59 *Journals*, (1869), 176.

60 *Loc. cit.*, XIII, 106.

61 *Millennial Star*, XII, 244.

62 *Deseret News*, April 13, 1854.

63 Copies of this alphabet are printed in Remy and Brenchley, *op. cit.*, II, 185; Burton, *op. cit.*, 420; Bancroft, *op. cit.*, 713; and *Deseret News*, April 11, 1860, which also has an article in the type.

64 *Acts Legislative Assembly*, (1885), 110-11; *Millennial Star*, XVII, 251.

65 *Utah School Report*, (1876), 4, reads: "The Superintendent takes great pleasure in seconding the efforts of Brigham Young and the Board of Regents of the University of Deseret in the introduction of the Deseret Alphabet." See also, *ibid.*, (1869), 1-2; *Journals* (1869), 180; and *Millennial Star*, XVIII, 331; XXI, 289; XXIX, 77; XXX, 157, 190; XXXI, 29.

66 Bancroft, *op. cit.*, 714.

67 Hyde, *Mormonism*, 120. The author claimed that these schools met with little response during his residence in Utah, that is from 1853 to 1855.

68 *Millennial Star*, XIV, 200-201, 419.

69 *Deseret News*, February 21, 1852; *Journal of Discourses*, III, 293.

70 *Deseret News*, December 5, 1860.

71 *Ibid.*, December 7, 1859.

72 *Ibid.*, March 11, 1863.

73 *Ibid.*, March 11, 1863. *Cf.* Cowley, *Wilford Woodruff*, 423.

74 *Journal of Discourses*, III, 293-296.

75 *Deseret News*, March 27, 1861; E. R. S. Smith, *Lorenzo Snow Biography*, 251-259. For evening schools, see *Deseret News*, December 28, 1854, and December 5 and 12, 1860.

76 *Jubilee History of Sunday Schools*, 13; see *Latter Day Saints' Biograpical Encyclopedia*, 705, for the life of Richard Ballantyne, who was the first Sunday school teacher in Utah and prominent in that Church Sunday school work for many years; Cornaby, *Autobiography and Poems*, 37.

77 *Jubile History of Sunday Schools*, 15.

78 *Ibid.*, 28.

79 *Times and Seasons*, II, 722.

80 *Millennial Star*, XV, 204.

81 *Ibid.*, XV, 374, 375, 503, 564, 596, 647.

82 *Ibid.*, XV, 468.

83 *Ibid.*, XV, 564, 566.

84 *Doctrine and Covenants:* Section 88; also 1-74.

85 *Autobiography of Parley P. Pratt*, 100.

86 *Millennial Star*, XXX, 90; *Cf. Journal of Discourses*, XII, 158-159.

87 *Millennial Star*, XXX, 156.

88 *Ibid.*, XXX, 157.

89 *Ibid.*, XXX, 411.

90 *Ibid.*, XXX, 190.

91 *Ibid.*, XXX, 331.

92 *Ibid.*, XXXII, 378; *Ibid.*, XXX, 412; "The School of the Prophets [at Provo] meet once a week," May 20, 1868. For Ogden see *ibid.*, XXXI, 101.

93 *Journals*, (1852), 170. This figure was largely incomplete owing to the unorganized state of the Territory. The auditors stated that all payments and receipts had been made through the tithing office because of lack of money. *Ibid.*, 172.

94 *Ibid.*, (1861), 19.

95 *Ibid.*, (1869), 20.

96 *Ibid.*, (1876), 35.

97 *Ibid.*, (1876), 36.

98 *Seventh Census*, (1850), xxxiii.

99 *Population of the United States in 1860 . . . Eighth Census*, iv.

100 *Ninth Census, . . .Compendium*, 8.

101 *Tenth Census*, (1880), I, 3.

102 *Ibid.*, (1880), VII, 3.

103 *Ibid.*, (1880), VII, 4—estimated.

104 *Ibid.*, (1880), VII, 17.

105 *Journals*, (1851-2), 171.

106 *Ibid.*, (1851-52), 171.

107 *Ibid.*, (1860-61), 18.

108 *Ibid.*, (1869), 21, 22.

109 *Ibid.*, (1876), 38. In this same year of 1874, the auditor's report showed appropriations paid to Deseret University totalled $13,070.87.

110 *Report Utah Commission to Secretary of Interior*, (1887), 10. Bancroft, *op. cit.*, 707; D. S. Tuttle, *Reminiscences of a Missionary Bishop*, (New York, 1906), 102-103; Noble, *Sermon at South Church*, (Boston, 1885), 18; Stenhouse, *Rocky Mountain Saints*, 704.

111 *Report Utah Commission*, etc., (1887), 10; *Catholic Church in Utah*, 289-290.

112 *Report Utah Commission*, etc., (1887), 10.

113 *Ibid.*, (1887), 10.

114 Until 1880 the Mormons used their meeting-houses for public school purposes. Thus, taxes for school repairs, etc., were used to the Mormon advantage. After 1880 taxes could not be collected if these buildings were recorded as Church property. *Cf.* Bancroft, *op. cit.*, 708-709.

115 *Journal of Discourses*, XII, 31-32.

116 *Ibid.*, XII, 31.

117 *Ibid.*, XII, 32.

118 *Journal of Discourses*, XII, 376.

119 Hyde, *Mormonism*, 115-120.

120 *Journal of Discourses*, XII, 377.

121 *Ibid.*, XII, 138-139. Also see summary of speech by Daniel H. Wells at opening of University of Deseret (December 2, 1869) in *Millennial Star*, XXX, 18-19.

122 *Deseret News*, December 30, 1867, advertised that writing and arithmetic would be taught at the University. *Millennial Star*, XXX, 19, 27-28.

123 *Millennial Star*, XXX, 17.

124 *Ibid.*, XXX, 19.

125 *Ibid.*, XXX, 19. *Latter Day Saints' Biographical Encyclopedia*, 773-774.

126 Ollivant, *A Breeze from Salt Lake*, 70-71. Ollivant, an Englishman, spent a few days in Salt Lake City in June, 1870. He visited some of the common schools and the university.

127 Tullidge, *Salt Lake City*, (Appendix), 22.

128 *Latter Day Saints' Biographical Encyclopedia*, 785.

129 *Millennial Star*, XXXIV, 11, and Ollivant, *op. cit.*, 70-71.

130 XXXIV, 11, 28.

131 *Ibid.*, XXXII, 379.

132 *Biennial Report of Territorial Superintendent of Common Schools*, (1874-75), 18.

133 A copy of the Deed of Trust is in *Utah Genealogical Magazine*, XVII, 3.

134 *Cf.* Jensen, *Provo*, 348.

135 *Ibid.*, (1872), 19.

136 *Journals*, (1869), 177; *ibid.*, (1872), 187, 188.

137 *Journal of Discourses*, XVIII, 357.

138 J. F. Rusling, *The Great West*, etc., 193; *The Young Women's Journal*, (Salt Lake City, 1890), I, 163; Baskin, *Reminiscences of Early Utah*, 203.

139 Cubberly, *Public Education in the United States*, 131.

140 *Ibid.*, 139.

CHAPTER V
AND EVERY GAIN DIVINE
VARIOUS GROUP INFLUENCES

1 Bancroft, *op. cit.*, 109, note 53, states that the publication of the *Times and Seasons* began November, 1839.

2 *Times and Seasons*, IV.

3 *Ibid.*, IV, 208.

4 *Ibid.*, IV, 208.

5 *Millennial Star*, I, 1.

6 *Ibid.*, I, 100, 216.

7 *Ibid.*, I, 156-158.

8 *Ibid.*, IX, 367.

9 *Ibid.*, VIII, 126.

10 *Ibid.*, XXVIII, 148, 165.

11 *Ibid.*, XXVIII, 392.

12 From August 19, 1851 to the following November 19 and again during 1864 the *Deseret News* was discontinued because of the scarcity of paper.

13 Tullidge, *History of Salt Lake City*, Appendix, 14.

14 Stenhouse, *Rocky Mountain Saints*, 630.

15 *Millennial Star*, XXI, 647 (October 8, 1859).

16 The personal statements of Godbe, Harrison, Kelsey, Lawrence, and E. W. Tullidge concerning their versions of the struggle with Young at the time it occurred may be found in *Tullidge's Quarterly Magazine*, I, 14-85. Stenhouse in his *Rocky Mountain Saints*, 622-645, gives his version of the affair. For a brief summary of the Church attitude see Bancroft, *op. cit.*, 645-646. For the attitude of the Church authorities see *Journal of Discourses*, XIII, 53, 179, 334.

17 *Tullidge's Quarterly Magazine*, I, 18-20.

18 *Ibid.*, I. 31.

19 *Utah Magazine*, III, 410.

20 *Ibid.*, III, 390.

21 Stenhouse, *Op. cit.*, 213, 629. Bancroft, *op. cit.*, 645-646.

22 *Utah Magazine*, III, 282.

23 *Ibid.*, III, 8, 26, 42, 57, 72, 105, 121, 153, 185, 201, 234, 249, 266, 312, 322.

24 *Ibid.*, III. Each issue from May 8 to October 1869, contained a character: Jesus, Charlemagne, and Alfred were some of the characters treated.

25 *Ibid.*, III, 422.

26 *Ibid.*, III, 408-409.

27 *Ibid.*, III, 295.

28 *Ibid.*, III, 12.

29 *Tullidge's Quarterly Magazine*, I, 65.

30 *Millennial Star*, XII, 244, 274, 296. *Cf. ibid.*, XIII, 14.

31 *Ibid.*, XIV, 20.

32 Hyde, *Mormonism*, 129.

33 Chandless, *A Visit to Salt Lake City*, 243-244.

34 *City of the Saints*, 286.

35 J. M. Sjodahl, *Utah Genealogical Magazine*, XII, 72.

36 *The Deseret News*, August 17, 1864, published an article on new books of English and American publishers, an oasis in an otherwise barren period of book news in Utah.

37 *Poems by E. R. Snow*, I, 142, 161, 162, 170.

38 *Times and Seasons*, V, 762-763.

39 Section 14 of *"Act Creating Territory of Utah,"* passed September 9, 1850, *Utah Acts, etc.*, (1855), 118-119.

40 *Millennial Star*, XIV, 322.

41 *Utah Acts, etc.*, (1885), 177-178.

42 *Journals*, (1863-64), 78-79; *Cf. ibid.*, (1860-61), 91-92; *ibid.*, (1861-62), 40.

43 Chandless, *op. cit.*, 243-244.

44 *Cf.* Remy and Brenchley, *op. cit.*, II, 188, and Burton, *City of the Saints*, 235-236, 419, in which the reading facilities of Salt Lake City are discussed. Remy's observations are not always his own, however.

45 Bancroft, *op. cit.*, 585.

46 *Deseret News*, August 20, 1862.

47 *Loc. cit.*

48 R. L. Campbell to F. D. Richards (January 7, 1856), *Millennial Star* XVIII, 332: "The Seventies have framed a constitution for a library."

49 *Loc. cit.*

50 Gardner, *Lehi*, 101.

51 *Deseret News*, June 15, 1864.

52 *Woman's Exponent*, II, 164.

53 *Improvement Era*, *passim*; *Utah Musical Times*, I, 189; *Woman's Exponent*, 77; Gardner, *Lehi*, 104.

54 *Journals* (1863-64), 115-116, report the passing of an "act incorporating Seventies' Library."

55 *Deseret News*, December 26, 1867; *Utah Magazine*, I, 91, 103, 139; *Salt Lake City Directory*, (1869), 73.

56 *Who's Who in the Lyceum*, (Philadelphia, 1906), 19; I. W. Riley, *Joseph Smith*, 153.

57 L. E. Young, *Utah, Genealogical Magazine*, V, 107.

58 *Deseret News,* February 21, 1852.

59 *Life of a Pioneer,* 126.

60 *Millennial Star,* XIV, 200-201.

61 *Deseret News,* November 5, 1862.

62 *Ibid.,* December 10, 1862. Other lectures are discussed in *ibid.,* February 4, 1863.

63 *Ibid.,* March 2, 1864. See editorial *ibid.,* December 2, 1863 discussing reopening lecture course.

64 *Ibid.,* December 26, 1867.

65 *Utah Magazine,* I, 91.

66 *Millennial Star,* XXXIII, 171. See also *ibid.,* XXXIII, 172; XXXIV, 16; *Salt Lake City Directory,* (1869), 13.

67 James S. Brown, *Life of a Pioneer,* 309.

68 *Deseret News,* December 7, 1859. Isaac Higbee's letter in *Deseret News,* February 2, 1852, indicates there was a lyceum in Provo in 1852.

69 *Ibid.,* March 11, 1863; *ibid.,* February 25, 1863, summarizes a lecture on "Navigation" given at Provo by a former sailor.

70 *Ibid.,* February 25, 1863.

71 *Deseret News,* March 16, 1854. *Millennial Star,* XXXIII, 159, discusses lectures at Willard City. *Deseret Evening News,* January 5, 1877 discusses proposed lectures at Meadow, Millard County.

72 Remy and Brenchley, *op. cit.,* II, 183.

73 *Deseret News,* December 2, 1863.

74 Bancroft, *op. cit.,* 636, note 90.

75 *Latter Day Saints' Biographical Encyclopedia,* 188.

76 *Jubilee History of Sunday Schools,* 14; West, *Life of Franklin D. Richards,* 175. If missionary work led to doubt, few of the doubters have expressed their doubts as has J. F. Gibbs in his *Lights and Shadows of Mormonism,* (Salt Lake City, 1909.)

77 *Journal of Discourses,* I, 46, 66, 198.

78 *Ibid.,* I, 160, 204, 209.

79 *Ibid.,* I, 209.

80 *Ibid.,* I, 53; XIII, 37, 183, 197.

81 *Ibid.,* XIII, 310, 356.

82 *Ibid.,* XIII, 124.

83 *Ibid.,* V, 79. The speaker told of a journey from San Bernardino to Great Salt Lake City.

84 *Ibid.,* V. 221. The Sunday afternoon service took the place of a morning service with the Mormons.

85 Cowley, *Wilford Woodruff,* 361; Hyde, *Mormonism,* 128-129.

86 Hyde, *op. cit.,* 128; *Deseret News,* July 11, 1855, February 13, 1856.

87 Hyde, *op cit.,* 129. Hyde was a member of this organization.

88 E. R. S. Smith, *Biography and Family Record of Lorenzo Snow,* 251-60.

[89] *Deseret News*, October 3, 1855; *ibid.*, August 27, 1856.

[90] Cowley, *op. cit.*, 364.

[91] *Loc. cit.*, March 14, 1855.

[92] Hyde, *op. cit.*, 129.

[93] *Millenial Star*, XVII, 515.

[94] *Ibid.*, XVII, 520-521.

[95] Hyde, *op. cit.*, 128. See also *Improvement Era, II*, 746.

[96] *Deseret News*, April 23, 1856. See also Cowley, *Wilford Woodruff*, 402-403.

[97] *Deseret News*, October 13, 1858.

[98] *Utah Gazetteer and Directory*, (1884), 48.

[99] The first number was published January 11, 1868.

[100] *Cf.* chapter on "Education". The University opened as a commercial school in 1867. Dr. Park introduced the classical course in 1869.

[101] West, *F. D. Richards*, 179-181.

[102] *Improvement Era*, XXVIII, 713-714; *Woman's Exponent*, II, 61; *Millennial Star*, XXXIII, 140.

[103] Johnson, *op. cit.*, 75.

[104] Junius F. Wells in *Improvement Era*, XXVIII, 715.

[105] *Ibid.*, XXVIII, 715.

[106] *Ibid.*, XXVIII, 715; Jensen, *Provo*, 222-223; Johnson *op. cit.*, 77; Gardner, *Lehi*, 104.

[107] Johnson, *op. cit.*, 77; *Improvement Era*, XXVIII, 715.

[108] *Improvement Era*, XXVIII, 713, 715.

[109] *Ibid.*, XXVIII, 1023-1024.

[110] See G. W. James, *Utah, The Land of the Blossoming Rose*, (Boston, 1922), 149; C. B. Spahr in *Outlook*, February 3, 1900; R. Ely, "Economic Aspects of Mormonism," *Harper's Magazine*, (April, 1903), CVI, 675; Nelson, *Escalante*, 30.

[111] *Tullidge's Quarterly Magazine*, I, 214.

[112] *Ibid.*, I, 214.

[113] *Ibid.*, I, 216.

[114] *Deseret News*, August 5, 1863; *Tullidge's Quarterly Magazine*, I, 215.

[115] *Millennial Star*, XII, 246.

[116] Remy and Brenchley, *op. cit.*, II, 188. *Deseret News*, October 3, 1855, contains a letter to Brigham Young describing a wonderful image sent him from the Sandwich Islands.

[117] *Deseret News*, October 13, 1858.

[118] *Utah Magazine*, (March 7, 1869), I, 103.

[119] I. W. Ayers, *Life in the Wilds of America*, 245-246; *Gazeteer of Utah and Salt Lake City*, (1874), 178; *Millennial Star*, XXXIII, 402; *Woman's Exponent*, I, 172.

[120] *Millenial Star*, XXXIII, 303, copied from the *Deseret News*.

[121] *Sinners and Saints*, 222.

[122] Linn, *The Story of the Mormons*, 118-119.

[123] Evans, *Joseph Smith*, 264.

[124] *Woman's Exponent*, 28:13, December, 1899, page 78; Bancroft, *op. cit.*, 726-727.

[125] *Relief Society Magazine*, 2:2, (February 1915), 55.

[126] Werner, *Brigham Young*, 333.

[127] *Ibid*, 337.

[128] *Cf.* *Discourses of Brigham Young*, (Editor J. A. Widtsoe, Salt Lake City, 1925), *Chapter* XVIII.

[129] Gates and Widtsoe, *The Life Story of Brigham Young*, 306.

CHAPTER VI
THINE ALABASTER CITIES GLEAM
THEATRE

[1] Beard, *Rise of American Civilization*, I, 795.

[2] *Cf.* Schouler, *History of the United States*, (1894 edition), IV, 16 and Rhodes, *History of the United States*, II, 547. Joseph Jefferson in his *Autobiography*, 29-30, tells of the disastrous effects upon a dramatic troupe of which he was a member when they ran into a religious revival at Springfield, Illinois. J. F. Daly, *Life of Augustin Daly*, 14, shows that this distaste was not caused solely by religious beliefs, writing of the period about 1848, the author says: "The dread of contamination from too close association with things theatrical, which my mother [the author was a brother of Augustin Daly], in common with many other good people, felt in those days was excusable for more than one reason. In every theatre there was an upper tier with a bar, where strong drinks were supplied and (in some houses) where the profligate of both sexes resorted."

[3] *The Contributor*, I, 136; J. S. Lindsay, *The Mormons and the Theatre*, 8. John S. Lindsay played as a member of the Salt Lake Dramatic Company for a greater part of its existence.

[4] O. F. Whitney, *History of Utah*, II, 34. The author is the son of H. K. Whitney, one of the founders of the Deseret Dramatic Association and a player in the Social Hall at Salt Lake City.

[5] Other members of this early dramatic company were Robert Campbell, Robert T. Burton, George D. Grant, Edmund Ellsworth, Henry Margetts, Edward Martin, William Glover, William Clayton, Miss Orum, Miss Judd, and Miss Mary Badlam. Lindsay, *op. cit.*, 8; and Pyper, *Romance of an Old Playhouse*, 40.

[6] H. G. Whitney, *Drama in Utah*, 5.

[7] The bowery also meant a structure covered with boughs and limbs of trees used for religious meetings in the summer. Pyper, *op. cit.*, 40.

[8] Pyper, *op. cit.*, 45; *Cf. Latter Day Saints' Biographical Encyclopedia*, I,

672, (incorrectly numbered 688), for Bishop Raleigh's autobiographical statement.

9 Tullidge, *History of Salt Lake City*, 884.

10 *Ibid.*, 884.

11 *Deseret News*, January 22, 1853.

12 Pyper, *op. cit.*, 50.

13 Ferris, *The Mormons at Home*, 149; Burton, *The City of the Saints*, 229, writes concerning Salt Lake City: "Sir E. L. Bulwer will perhaps be pleased to hear that the "Lady of Lyons" excited more furore here than in Europe."

14 Tullidge, *op. cit.*, 738; Lindsay, *op. cit.*, 13.

15 Pyper, *op. cit.*, 54. W. C. Dunbar was evidently in Salt Lake City in June, 1858, for he sang "O Ye Mountains High" at the conference between the United States Commissioners and the Mormon authorities at that time. Tullidge, *op. cit.*, 214; *Latter Day Saints' Biographical Encyclopedia*, 728.

16 Lindsay, *op. cit.*, 15-17.

17 Pyper, *op. cit.*, 73.

18 Jensen, *History of Provo*, 398.

19 *Ibid.*, 400. The Cluff family prominent in the affairs of the Church were also prominent in the organization of this association.

20 *Ibid.*, 401.

21 Gardner, *History of Lehi*, 96.

22 *Ibid.*, 96-97.

23 E. R. S. Smith, *Biography and Family Record of Lorenzo Snow*, 268.

24 *Ibid.*, 268-269.

25 *Ibid.*, 270.

26 Lindsay, *op. cit.*, 22, 23. Lindsay was not a member of the Mechanics' Dramatic Association nor was he present when this speech was made, but he was acquainted with men who were present and had an intimate knowledge of the dramatics in Utah of this period.

27 Tullidge, *History of Salt Lake City*, 740.

28 Pyper, *op. cit.*, 75, quotes from a speech made by Hiram B. Clawson on March 20, 1907. Those interested in dramatics at Provo also received material aid from the government sale at Camp Floyd; *Latter Day Saints' Biographical Encyclopedia*, 729.

29 *Romance of an Old Playhouse*, 78.

30 Bancroft, *History of Utah*, 415; Cf. Burton, *op. cit.*, 297, and Mayhew, *The Mormons*, 251.

31 Pyper, *op. cit.*, 277, 279.

32 Whitney, *Drama in Utah*, 7.

33 Cf. *Deseret News* and *Journal of Discourse* for 1862.

34 Justin McCarthy, "Brigham Young," *Galaxy*, Feb. 1870. Rev. H. R. Jones, *San Francisco and Back*, 125.

[35] Sheepshanks, *A Bishop in the Rough,* 121.

[36] Bowles, *Across the Continent,* 103.

[37] F. H. Ludlow, *Heart of the Continent,* 370-371.

[38] Thus Justin McCarthy, *Galaxy,* and Reverend H. A. Jones, *San Francisco and Back,* who came on the railroad were unfavorably impressed by the Salt Lake Theatre. Mrs. Ferris (*Utah and the Mormons,* 307) felt the same way in 1853 when she observed Mormon theatrical life and its headquarters.

[39] *Cf.* F. T. Townshend, *Ten Thousand Miles of Travel, Sport, and Adventure,* 197; J. F. Rusling, *The Great West, etc.,* 178-179; Bowles, *op. cit.,* 103, Sheepshanks, *op. cit.,* 121.

[40] Pyper, *op. cit.,* 94.

[41] *Ibid.,* 105.

[42] *Deseret News,* June 29, 1864.

[43] Pyper, *op. cit.,* 113-119.

[44] *Ibid.,* 147; Tullidge, *History of Salt Lake City,* 751.

[45] Pyper, *op. cit.,* 148-149.

[46] *Ibid.,* 151.

[47] A. H. Quinn, *History of American Drama from the beginning to the Civil War,* 387 (New York, 1923), Mr. Quinn attributes this change in theatrical production to the influence of Dion Boucicault's work as manager.

[48] *Deseret News,* August 6, 1862.

[49] *Ibid.,* August 6, 1862.

[50] *Ibid.,* August 26, 1863. The Thespian Association was an organization of young actors from Salt Lake City. *Cf. Deseret News,* June 3, 1863.

[51] *Deseret News,* March 11, 1863.

[52] *Ibid.,* February 25, 1863.

[53] February 25, 1863.

[54] *Deseret News,* February 16, 1865 for Nephi, also see *Memorial to Elizabeth Claridge McCune,* 16; *Deseret News,* December 28, 1864, for item from Mount Pleasant; *ibid.,* March 15, 1865 for Beaver; *ibid.,* August 17, 1864 contains a report of the Saint George Dramatic Association; *ibid.,* April 1, 1863, for Logan; Jensen, *History of Provo,* refers to a lack of interest in the drama at Provo for several years prior to 1877, in which year, John C. Graham, a former member of the Salt Lake Stock Company came to Provo and brought about a revival of interest; Lever, *History of San Pete and Emory Counties,* 91, 398; Bancroft, *History of Utah,* 704, note 52, writes that in the period about 1880, Parowan had the second largest theatre in Utah, one with a seating capacity of about 800; a letter in *Utah Musical Times,* I, 14 (dated February 12, 1876), from Payson states: "We have a local theatrical company which performs occasionally."

[55] This speech may be found in the *Journal of Discourses,* IX, 242-245.

[56] *Ibid.,* IX, 242.

[57] *Ibid.,* IX, 243.

[58] *Cf.,* Appendix, *Heaven on Earth,* 232-233.

[59] *Ibid.,* 233.

[60] *Ibid.,* 234.

[61] *Ibid.,* 232.

[62] *Ibid.,* 234.

[63] *Ibid.,* 234.

[64] *Journal of Discourses,* IX, 242.

[65] *Ibid.,* VIII, 128-129.

[66] Lindsay and Pyper in their works and Tullidge's *History of Salt Lake City,* contain lists of the plays given during this period. The *Deseret News* frequently makes comments upon the performances.

[67] Rusling, *The Great West,* etc., 178-179.

[68] *San Fransisco and Back,* 125.

[69] *Mormons at Home,* 149-150.

[70] Chandless, *A Visit to Salt Lake,* etc., 224.

[71] *Loc. cit.*

[72] Sheepshanks, *A Bishop in the Rough,* 118.

[73] Alfred Lambourne, *A Play-House,* 16-17. For some reminiscences of the opening night of the Salt Lake Theatre, see Pyper, *op. cit.,* 274-281.

[74] Dixon, *New America,* I, 202-204.

[75] Pyper, *op. cit.,* 160; *ibid.,* 66, Mrs. Lillian Tuckett Freeze, a daughter of the Mrs. Tuckett who left for the Camp Floyd theatre wrote to Mr. Pyper concerning her mother, "When President Brigham was asking for talent to amuse and instruct the pioneer people, he called on Mrs. Tuckett to accept a mission for two years to perform in The Bowery and later in the Social Hall."

[76] *Op. cit.,* 289.

[77] Lindsay, *op. cit.,* 64-69; Ferris, *Utah and the Mormons,* 306.

[78] Lindsay, *op. cit.,* 64-69.

[79] *Journal of Discourses,* IX, 245.

[80] Lindsay, *op. cit.,* 25.

[81] *Journal of Discourses,* IX, 245.

[82] Pyper, *op. cit., passim.*

[83] J. M. Jensen, *Provo,* 399. This play was performed January or February, 1854. In 1854 William W. Cluff was called on a mission to the Sandwich Islands, *Latter Day Saints' Biographical Encyclopedia,* 340.

[84] Tullidge, *History of Salt Lake City,* 754.

[85] *Ibid.,* 752.

[86] *History of Salt Lake City,* 751.

[87] *Loc. cit.*

[88] *Deseret News,* March 20, 1861 shows the same schedule for the year previous to the opening of the new theatre. Pyper, *op. cit.,* 100-104 gives

a list of the plays and dates upon which they were preformed at the Salt
Lake Theatre during 1862 and 1863.

[89] Lindsay, *op. cit.*, 35.

[90] Pyper, *op. cit.*, 172.

[91] *Ibid.*, 184.

[92] Bowles, *Across the Continent*, 104, (Letter X), 5. *Cf.* Werner, *op. cit.*, 461-462.

[93] Pyper, *op. cit.*, 330.

[94] *Ibid.*, 331; Lindsay, *op. cit.*, 143.

[95] *Woman's Exponent*, II, 61 (September 15, 1873) tells of sale of Theatre by Brigham Young.

[96] Pyper, *op. cit.*, 332.

CHAPTER VII
O BEAUTIFUL FOR PILGRIMS' FEET
MUSIC

[1] L. C. Elson, *History of American Music*, (Revised by Arthur Elson, New York, 1925), 1.

[2] Joseph Smith "was somewhat partial to the Methodists." *Latter Day Saints' Biographical Encyclopedia*, 1. Joseph Young, on whose judgment, Brigham Young, relied in religious matters had been a Methodist preacher; *cf.* Werner, *Brigham Young*, 14. John Taylor, the third president of the Church, had been a Methodist preacher before his conversion to Mormonism.

[3] *Millennial Star*, XIX, 116; XX, 12.

[4] *Doctrine and Covenants*, Sec. 24:3, (dated July, 1830).

[5] The Harvard College Library has copies of an American edition published at Bellows Falls in 1844, another at the same place the following year. Also a Boston edition of 1843.

[6] Tullidge, *History of Salt Lake City, Apendix*, ii, 8.

[7] *Loc. cit.*, XIII, 240.

[8] *Utah and the Mormons*, 286-287.

[9] Remy and Brenchley, *A Journey to Great Salt Lake City*, II, 181.

[10] *City of the Saints*, 259.

[11] *Beyond the Mississippi*, 357.

[12] *The Great West and Pacific Coast*, 168-169.

[13] Chandless, *op. cit.*, 132.

[14] Johnson, *History of Springville, Utah*, 60; Stenhouse, *Rocky Mountain Saints*, 369-372.

[15] *Op. cit.*, 391.

[16] *Latter Day Saints' Biographical Encyclopedia*, 498.

[17] Gardner, *Lehi*, 101.

[18] Johnson, *op. cit.*, 26.

[19] Remy and Brenchley, *op. cit.*, II, 374-375.

[20] *The Contributor*, I, 134.

21 *Ibid.*, I, 135.

22 *Ibid.*, I, 136.

23 *Millennial Star*, XIV, 508.

24 Lindsay, *Mormons and the Theatre*, 13.

25 *Deseret News*, June 27, 1855.

26 *Ibid.*, June 12, 1861, for details of Ballo's life.

27 Elson, *History of American Music*, 42, note 1.

28 Johnson, *History of Springville*, Utah, 26.

29 *Salt Lake Tribune*, February 14, 1926. Tullidge, *History of Northern Utah and Southern Idaho*, 109. For organization of a band at Nephi, see autobiographical article by H. F. McCune in *Utah Genealogical and Historical Magazine*, XVII, 157.

30 Gardner, *Lehi*, 105-106.

31 Ludlow, *Heart of the Continent*, 366.

32 *The Contributor*, I, 135; *Utah Genealogical Magazine*, XVII, 164; *Land of Sunshine*, 258, (October, 1901).

33 *William Clayton's Journal*, 70, 71, 116.

34 F. A. Golder, *March of the Mormon Battalion*, (New York, 1928), 123-124.

35 Remy and Brenchley, *op. cit.*, II, 181; Dixon, *New America*, I, 198-199; Burton, *op. cit.*, 280.

36 *Journal of Discourses*, I, 113; VI, 149.

37 Hyde, *Mormonism*, 119-120. The author was in Utah during 1853 and 1855.

38 *Journal of Discourses*, III, 293-294.

39 *Ibid.*, IX, 194-195.

40 The editor of the *Times and Seasons*, V, 459 (March 1, 1844) answered a query whether or not dancing was permitted by referring to instances where dancing is allowed in the Bible. II Samuel, VI: 13 and 14; Exodus, XV: 18, etc.

41 Johnson, *History of Springville, Utah*, 60.

42 *Ibid.*, 60.

43 *Deseret News*, December 27, 1851.

44 *Op. cit.*, 246.

45 *Op. cit.*, II, 181.

46 Chandless, *op. cit.*, 238.

47 *North American Review*, (March, 1890), CL, 346.

48 *Cf. The Contributor*, XII, 154.

49 The material for John Tullidge's biography is gathered from a letter of his, autobiographical in character, published in *Millennial Star*, XIX, 170-172.

50 *Loc. cit.*, XIX, 171.

51 *Millennial Star*, XIX, 172.

[52] *Ibid.,* XX, 12.

[53] *Ibid.,* XIX, 116, 117.

[54] *Ibid.,* XX, 11–12.

[55] *Ibid.,* XIX, 116.

[56] *Ibid.,* XX, 11.

[57] *Ibid.,* XIX, 116.

[58] *Ibid.,* XX, 12.

[59] *Ibid.,* XX, 10, 11–12.

[60] *Ibid.,* XX, 10.

[60] *Ibid.,* XIX, 172.

[62] *Ibid., XIX,* 172.

[63] *Utah Magazine,* I, 303.

[64] *Ibid.,* III, 39.

[65] *Ibid.,* III, 22.

[66] *Ibid.,* III, 107.

[67] *Ibid.,* III, 40, 96.

[68] *Ibid.,* III, 275.

[69] *Ibid.,* III, 171.

[70] *Ibid.,* III, 147.

[71] *Ibid.,* III, 392.

[72] *Ibid.,* III, 7.

[73] The biographical material concerning Charles J. Thomas' life has been taken from Tullidge, *History of Salt Lake City,* 772 and Pyper, *Romance of an Old Playhouse,* 137–138.

[74] *Latter Day Saints' Biographical Encyclopedia,* 773–774; *Tullidge's Quarterly Magazine,* I, 221–228.

[75] *Tullidge's Quarterly Magazine,* I, 222.

[76] *Ibid.,* I, 222. *Deseret News,* December 17, 1862.

[77] *Deseret News,* March 18, 1863.

[78] *Ibid.,* September 30, 1863.

[79] Advertisement in *Deseret News,* November 26, 1862.

[80] L. E. Young, *Salt Lake Tabernacle,* 11–12. A comment upon this concert without giving the programme may be seen in *Deseret News,* December 17, 1862.

[81] *Deseret News,* September 30, 1863.

[82] *Ibid.,* September 30, 1863.

[83] *Tullidge's Quarterly Magazine,* I, 222.

[84] *Latter Day Saints' Biographical Encyclopedia,* 774.

[85] *Utah Musical Times,* I, 6.

[86] *Ibid.,* I, 3, 19, 35, 187.

[87] *Ibid.,* I, 107.

[88] *Ibid.,* 105.

[89] *Ibid.,* I, 23, 38, 55, 71.

90 *Ibid.*, I, 6, 22, 87.

91 *Ibid.*, I, 137.

92 *Ibid.*, I, 185, and *passim.*

93 The biographical material for G. E. P. Careless' life is drawn from *Latter Day Saints' Biographical Encyclopedia*, 738-739; Pyper, *Romance of an Old Playhouse*, 140-141.

94 Tullidge, *History of Salt Lake City*, 777. This book contains a review of the concert.

95 The material for this biography is drawn from *Latter Day Saints' Biographical Encyclopedia*, 739-740.

96 *Ibid.*, 740.

97 *Millennial Star*, IV, 203; VII, 63; XV, 78.

98 *Deseret News*, October 7, 1863.

99 The material for Evan Stephen's biography is drawn from *Latter Day Saints' Biographical Encyclopedia*, 740-746.

100 Pamphlet under title *Music* in Salt Lake City Free Public Library, from *Utah Educational Review*, 138 (no volume number). *Cf. Latter Day Saints' Biographical Encyclopedia*, 742.

101 *Salt Lake Herald*, August 28, 1916.

102 The material for this biography appears in the *Latter Day Saints' Biographical Encyclopedia*, 746-747; Tullidge, *History of Salt Lake City*, 781.

103 Published in 1889.

104 *Latter Day Saints' Biographical Encyclopedia*, 711-713.

105 Tullidge, *History of Salt Lake City*, 772.

106 *Tullidge's Quarterly Magazine*, I, 220.

107 *Utah Magazine*, I, 150.

108 *Ibid.*, I, 88.

109 *Deseret News*, February 8, 1865.

110 *Ibid.*, July 1, 1863; Hannah Cornaby, *Autobiography*, 44.

111 *Utah Magazine*, III, 279.

112 *Ibid.*, III, 279.

113 Johnson, *History of Springville, Utah*, 72.

114 *Deseret Evening News*, December 20, 1867.

115 *Loc. Cit.*, III, 7.

116 *Utah Musical Times*, I, 12.

117 *Ibid.*, I, 29, 30.

118 *Ibid.*, I, 17.

119 *Ibid.*, I, 13.

120 *Ibid.*, I, 14.

121 *Ibid.*, I, 13.

122 *Latter Day Saints' Biographical Encyclopedia*, 771.

123 *Utah Musical Times*, I, 44. Letter concerning musical affairs in Grantsville, *Ibid.*, I, 190; Nephi., I, 13; Levan, Juab County, *Millennial Star*, XXXIII, 286; Fountain Green, *Ibid.*, XXXIII, 189.

[124] *Deseret News*, February 22, 1865; July 3, 1863; *Utah Musical Times*, I, 29.

[125] *Utah Musical Times*, I, 18.

[126] *Ibid.*, I, 156.

[127] *Utah Magazine*, III, 314-315.

[128] *Ibid.*, III, 347.

[129] Pyper, *op. cit.*, 307.

[130] *Utah Magazine*, III, 427.

[131] *Ibid.*, III, 427.

[132] Johnson, *History of Springville, Utah*, 26, 37.

[133] *Utah Magazine*, III, 279.

[134] *Latter Day Saints' Biographical Encyclopedia*, 546, 740.

[135] *Ibid.*, 498.

[136] *Deseret News*, August 5, 1863.

[137] Pyper, *Romance of an Old Playhouse*, 139-140.

[138] He was chief clerk to Brigham Young from 1857 to 1867.

[139] *Latter Day Saints' Biographical Encyclopedia*, 712, 740, 744, 745.

[140] *Harper's Monthly Magazine*, (August, 1885), LXIX, 398.

[141] L. E. Young, *Salt Lake Tabernacle*, 17.

[142] G. A. Sala, *America Revisited*, 523.

[143] *Utah Musical Times*, I, 118 (October 15, 1876).

[144] *Millennial Star*, XXXII, 302.

[145] *Travels West*, 141.

CHAPTER VIII
AND CROWN THY GOOD WITH BROTHERHOOD

[1] Bancroft, *History of Utah*, 264, 285, 286.

[2] *Journal of Discourses*, II, 237. See also a speech by Brigham Young on the same subject in *ibid.*, XIV, 103.

[3] *Senate Executive Documents*, (36 Cong. 1 Sess.), XIII, 302.

[4] *Op. cit.*, 260.

[5] *Beyond the Mississippi*, 357.

[6] *The Great West*, etc., 180-181.

[7] *Heart of the Continent*, 338. Cf. Fountain, *Un Francais en Amérique*, 133-134; Murphy, *Rambles in North Western America*, 237; Pine, *Beyond the West*, 230; Gunnison, *The Mormons*, 75; and Remÿ and Brenchley, *op. cit.*, II, 361.

[8] *Doctrine and Covenants*, Section 89.

[9] Harris and Butt, *The Fruits of Mormonism*, 13.

[10] Widstoe, *Discourses of Brigham Young*, Chap. XVI.

[11] Pyper, *Romance of an Old Playhouse*, 332.

[12] Lorenzo Snow wrote in the *Land of Sunshine*, (October, 1901), 258: "The universal love of music among the Latter Day Saints, and Utah's phenominal progress in the art, vocally and instrumentally, may be regarded as one of the remarkable achievements of our religion."

[13] *Utah Magazine*, I, 6.

APPENDIX

APPENDIX

APPENDIX

The Views of Brigham Young on Theatres
and Theatrical Performances
Taken from the Deseret News, January 11, 1865

For various reasons, I have felt to make public my views respecting Theatres and theatrical performances. It is well known that we have a theatre in our city which has been erected for the purpose of representing the drama and portraying upon the stage in mimic form, such representations of human life, and character and the world around us as would instruct and please those who might frequent it to spend an evening. I recognize in the Theatre an institution that under judicious guidance, can be used with happy effects for the benefit of the people. There are wants of our common nature which he, who would seek the happiness and enjoyment of his fellow beings, and to govern them properly, would not do wisely to ignore. One of these is the desire for and necessity for recreation. Bigots and sectarians may scout the idea of such a desire of our nature needing gratification—they may denounce its indulgence as something improper and highly reprehensible, especially under, as they would say, the higher law of the gospel; but despite all these reasonings, and the repression which is not unfrequently practiced to carry them into effect, the great fact still remains unaltered, that man is so constituted that in order to enjoy perfect health and a happy existence, he would have recreation and relaxation—he should have the opportunity occasionally afforded unto him of unbending and dismissing from his mind those cares of business, which, if, continually indulged in, might, as he is now constituted, prove oppressive to him.

If the people cannot gratify this desire or want legitimately, and in accordance with the recognized usages of society, with which they may be associated, many will seek its gratification illegitimately, and in violation of, and in opposition to, those usages. In this way many persons are driven into open opposition to the views of society, or if not into open opposition, they are frequently by doing that in secret which the fear of the disfavor of their fellows would defer them from doing openly. Thus, through a misconception of man's wants and the will of Deity respecting him, thousands of persons in the world are led into sin and indulge in reckless practices, who, if they were properly trained might become useful and honored members of society.

With the light which has been revealed unto us, as Latter-day Saints, respecting the will of our God concerning man and also respecting man's own organization and nature, we cannot blindly shut our eyes and pass these things by as matters of no importance. It is the duty and privilege of the Priesthood to teach the people what is right upon these points, and how they can enjoy innocent amusements without sinning, and also point out unto them any and every danger which may menace them in this direction. It is their privilege to take the initiative in all these matters, not holding themselves aloof from the people over whom they are appointed teachers and shepherds, but joining with them in their recreations and restraining them by their example, influence and presence everything that is improper or that would have an evil tendency.

And it has been with these views that I have encouraged the representation of plays among us. We found ourselves here in the midst of these mountains. Our history gives to the world our reasons for being here. When we reached here we were far removed from civilization (so called) and were thrown upon our own resources. We have had to form our own society, and to depend upon ourselves for our own amusements. The Theatre in this city has been built for the sole purpose of furnishing recreation and amusement for the citizens of Salt Lake City and this territory.

In erecting it this object was especially kept in view. Neither the Theatre itself nor the representation upon its boards were intended for any other purpose. It was desirable that a suitable place might be provided where the laboring classes—those whose bodies and brains were weary with toil and close application to business—could enjoy a few hours occasionally, in innocent amusement. Such a place this Theatre was intended to be—a place in every respect suitable for Saints to visit, and where good thoughts would be inspired and where nothing would be seen or heard that would shock the feelings of the most chaste and delicate man, woman, and child—a place in fact where holy angels could be, and where the Spirit of God would reign, and its influence be felt by every person who should enter it. With us the Theatre should be kept as pure, and as completely free from everything that could defile it, as our home sanctuaries. No impropriety of language or gesture, nothing wicked, or that would be likely to lead to wickedness, should ever be permitted there or countenanced in the least; but the actors should be pure in heart —men and women who, in all their representations, would use proper language. All such expressions as "I swear," or "by Heavens," and the name of the Deity, and every other sacred word, should be carefully omitted in plays, and other words be substituted in their stead. The distortion of the muscles of the face and body, and everything that would not produce pleasurable emotions in the minds of the audience should also be studiously avoided upon the stage. Such unnatural contortion and ranting and raving, are painful to witness, and are not true to nature, and afford no correct idea of the characters represented; for it is not to be supposed, for a moment, that persons in real life would be such exaggerations of everything human.

On this account, I have ever felt a strong repugnance to the employment of men and women upon our stage who have been in the habit of following the customs or common habits of the civilized world, and, also, to the representation of plays in which murder and the exhibition of the evil passions and the display of villainy form a prominent part. The representation of plays of this character do not convey pleasure, life, or animation to those who witness them, especially to the youthful mind; but have a directly opposite effect, and arouse such feelings which should never be called into being—a sense of gratification at the sight of murder and the execution of revenge.

In having our brethren and sisters act upon the stage, I have had in view their development in native refinement and grace, and in those qualities which would improve themselves and give zest to their performances and have an elevating and pleasurable effect upon their audiences. If with a theatre conducted upon this plan and developing the talent which we have in our midst, there is not sufficient attraction for our citizens then the object for which the theatre was erected has not been accomplished. It is plain that with our knowledge and clearly-defined views upon this subject we cannot take any other course than this and be justified. We cannot descend to the level of the wicked world, and copy after their fashion, and escape sin. When our actors perform in that spirit which they should ever have, their performances will always be pleasing and interesting to true Latter-day Saints, and their acting will be attractive to every well-disposed man and woman of correct taste. It is true that if their performances were to be measured by the standard of acting in the world, they might not bear close criticism; but is that standard a correct one? Is it not possible for our performers to develop a taste which shall be peculiar to us and be in conformity with views respecting the stage and its influences? We know that there are plays, which are not objectionable when put on the stage in some communities, that would be unsuitable for representation here. The moral sense of our community would be shocked by witnessing the performances of certain classes of plays; and if such were persistently put upon the boards, either the people should discontinue attendance, or they would gradually become demoralized. A style of acting, also, that in other places would meet with commendation and applause should not experience such a reception here.

The addresses of our Elders to the people, when judged by the world's standard, are not accepted as specimens of oratory; yet they have an effect upon the hearts of the people which the most finished oratory, unaccompanied by the Spirit which pervades and attends them, fails to have. So also with our efforts to instruct, please, and amuse one another by means of the stage, and in all our other social amusements and pleasures; though we may not conform to the standard of the world, it is our privilege, nevertheless, to have that spirit with us that will cause light and peace and joy and a feeling of satisfaction to fill our bosoms; and the honest stranger when he joins with us in our recreations, and witnesses the performances of our actors, will be so pleased with the Spirit, which he will feel, that he will not stop to notice the faults or to criticise unfavorably the acting. This has been the case in the past, and it will continue to be so, if we act according to our knowledge.

                                                    Brigham Young

BIBLIOGRAPHY

SELECTED BIBLIOGRAPHY

A. Books on Utah by Travellers and by Residents

Ayer, I. W., *Life in the Wilds of America and Wonders of the West.* Grand Rapids, Michigan, 1880.

Bailey, Mrs. F. A., *My Summer in a Mormon Village,* Boston, 1889.

Ballantine, Mr. Serjeant, *The Old World and the New,* London, 1884.

Barneby, W. H., *Life and Labour in the Far, Far West,* New York, 1884.

Barnes, Demas, *From the Atlantic to the Pacific, Overland* (A series of letters), New York, 1866.

Baskin, R. N., *Reminiscences of Early Utah,* Salt Lake City, 1914.

Beadle, J. H., *Life in Utah,* Philadelphia, 1870.

Bertrand, L. A., *Mémoires d'un Mormon,* Paris, 1862.

Blake, Mary E., *On the Wing,* Boston, 1883.

Boddam-Whetham, J. W., *Western Wandering,* London, 1874.

Bowles, Samuel, *Across the Continent,* New York, 1869.

Burton, R. F.,*The City of the Saints and Across the Rocky Mountains to California,* New York, 1862.

Carlton, A. B., *The Wonderlands of the Wild West,* Salt Lake City, 1891.

Carvalho, S. N., *Incidents of Travel and Adventure in the Far West,* New York, 1858.

Chandless, William, *A Visit to Salt Lake and a Residence in the Mormon Settlements at Utah,* London, 1857.

Codman, John, *The Mormon Country, A Summer with the Latter Day Saints,* New York, 1874.

De Leon, Edwin, *Thirty Years of My Life on Three Continents,* 2 v. London, 1890.

Dixon, W. H., *New America,* 2 v. London, 1867.

Eytinge, Rose, *Memories of Rose Eytinge,* New York, 1905.

Ferris, Benjamin G., *Utah and the Mormons*, New York, 1854.

Ferris, Mrs. B. G., (Wife of late U. S. Secretary for Utah), *The Mormons at Home*. (A series of letters, 1852-3), New York, 1856.

Goodard, Frederick B., *Where to Emigrate and Why*, New York, 1869.

Goodwin, C. C., *As I Remember Them*, Salt Lake City, 1913.

Greeley, Horace, *Overland Journey to California*, New York, 1860.

Greenwood, Grace, (Mrs. S. J. Lippincott), *New Life in New Lands*, New York, 1873.

Gunnison, Lieutenant J. W., *The Mormons or Latter-Day Saints in the Valley of the Great Lake*, Philadelphia, 1852.

Humson, W. L., *From the Atlantic Surf to the Golden Gate*, Hartford, 1869.

Huret, Jules, *En Amérique*, Paris, 1905.

Hyde, John, Jr., *Mormonism, Its Leaders and Designs*, New York, 1857.

Ingersoll, Ernest, *Crest of the Continent*, Chicago, 1885.

Jones, Rev. Harry A., Prebendary of St. Paul's, *San Francisco and Back*, 3rd ed., London, (n. d.).

Kane, Thomas L., *The Mormons, a Discourse Made Before Historical Society of Pennsylvania*, March 26, 1850, Philadelphia, 1850.

Kelly, W. Esq. J. P., *An Excursion to California Over the Prairies, Rocky Mountains, and Great Sierra Nevada*, 2 v. London, 1851.

Lindsay, John S., *Mormons and the Theatre*, Salt Lake, 1905.

Ludlow, F. H., *Heart of the Continent*, New York, 1870.

McClure, A. K., *3000 Miles Through the Rocky Mountains*, Philadelphia, 1869.

Marshall, W. G., *Through America or Nine Months in the United States*, London, 1882.

Minturn, William, *Travels West*, London, 1877.

Murphy, J. W., *Rambles in North Western America*, London, 1877.

Ollivant, J. R., *A Breeze from the Salt Lake*, London, 1871.

Pine, G. W., *Beyond the West*, Utica, New York, 1871.

Price, R. L., *The Two Americas*, Philadelphia, 1877.

Rae, W. F., *Westward by Rail*, London, 1870.

Remy, Jules and Brenchley, Julius, *A Journey to Great Salt Lake City*, 2v., London, 1861.

Richardson, A. D., *Beyond the Mississippi*, Hartford, 1867.

Robinson, Phil., *Sinners and Saints*, London, 1883.

Rusling, James F., *The Great West and the Pacific Coast*, New York, 1877.

Ruxton, G. F., *Life in the Far West*, New York, 1859.

Sala, G. A., *America Revisited*, London, 1886.

Sheepshanks, John, Bishop of Norwich, *A Bishop in the Rough*, edited by Rev. D. Wallace Duthie, London, 1909.

Stansbury, Howard, *Expedition and Survey of the Valley of Great Salt Lake of Utah*, Philadelphia, 1852.

Stenhouse, T. B. H., *Rocky Mountain Saints*, New York, 1873.

Stenhouse, Mrs. T. B. H., *A Lady's Life Among the Mormons*, New York, 1872.

Toponce, Alexander, *Reminiscences of Alexander Toponce, Pioneer*, Salt Lake City, 1923.

Toutain, Paul, *Un Francais en Amérique*, Paris, 1876.

Townshend, F. Trench, *Ten Thousand Miles of Travel, Sport, and Adventure*, London, 1869.

Turenne, Le Comte Louis De, *Quartorze Mois dans l'Amérique du Nord, (1875-1876)*, 2 v. Paris, 1879.

B. Magazines and Newspapers

The Contributor, Vols. I-XVII, Salt Lake City, 1880-1896.

Deseret News, Great Salt Lake City and Salt Lake City, 1850-1877.

Journal of History, Vols. I-XVIII, Published by Reorganized Church of Jesus Christ of Latter Day Saints, Independence, Missouri, 1908-1925.

Juvenile Instructor, Vols. I-XLI, Salt Lake City, 1866-1906.

Millennial Star, Vols. I-XL, Liverpool and London, 1840-1880.

Times and Seasons, Vols. I-VI, Nauvoo, Illinois, 1840-1846.

Tullidge's Quarterly Magazine, Vols, I-III, Salt Lake City, 1880-

1885.

The Utah Magazine, Vols. I-III, Salt Lake City, 1868-1869.

Utah Musical Magazine, Vol. I, Salt Lake City, March, 1876-February, 1877.

Woman's Exponent, Vols. I-V, Salt Lake City, January 15, 1873-May 15, 1877.

C. Artices In Other Magazines

Browne, Albert G., "The Utah Expedition," *Atlantic Monthly,* III, (May, 1859) *et. seq.*

Cannon, George Q., "Utah and Its People," *North American Review,* CXXXII, (May, 1881).

Davis, Mrs. Sam P., "Early Theatrical Attractions in Carson (Nevada)," *Nevada State Historical Papers,* IV, (Reno, 1924).

Gates, Susa Young, "Family Life Among the Mormons," *North American Review* CL, (Jan., June, 1890), 339-350.

Gardner, Hamilton, "Coöperation Among the Mormons," *Quarterly Journal of Economics,* XXXI, 1917.

"Communism Among the Mormons," *Quarterly Journal of Economics,* XXXVII, 1922.

McCarthy, Justin, "Brigham Young," *Galaxy,* (February, 1870).

Naisbitt, Henry W., "Polysophical and Mutual," *Improvement Era,* Vol. II, 741-747, (1896-1899).

Snow, Lorenzo, "Mormonism," *Land of Sunshine,* (October, 1901).

Tullidge, E. W., "The Reformation in Utah," *Harper's Magazine,* (1871).

Wells, Junius F., "Historical Sketch of the Y. M. M. I. A.," *Improvement Era,* XXVIII, (June, 1925).

D. United States Government Publications

Seventh Census of the United States, (1850), Government Printing Office, Washington, 1853.

Population of the United States in 1860, Compiled from Eighth Census, Joseph C. Kennedy. Government Printing Office, Washington, 1864.

Compendium of Ninth Census, (1870), Government Printing Office, Washington, 1872.

Tenth Census of the United States, 47 Congress, 2 Session. *House Miscellaneous Documents*. 42, XIII.

"Education," *Report of the Secretary of the Interior*, (1871-1872), 42 Congress, 2 Session, II. *House Executive Documents*, II, part 2.

"Education," *Report of the Secretary of the Interior*, (1876-1877), 44 Congress, 2 Session, *House Executive Documents*, IV, part 2.

E. Territorial Publications

Acts, Resolutions, and Memorials Passed at the Several Annual Sessions of the Legislative Assembly of the Territory of Utah [*Also contains Constitution of the Provisional State of Deseret, the Deseret Laws, and the Organic Act of Utah.*] *1851-52*, Salt Lake City, 1855.

Biennial Report of Territorial Superintendent of Common Schools, 1874-1875, Salt Lake City, (n. d.)

Journals of the House of Representatives, Council and Joint Sessions of the Legislative Assembly of Utah, (1851-1877), Salt Lake City.

Utah School Reports, (1867, 1869, and 1871), Salt Lake City.

F. Autobiographies and Journals

Brown, J. S., *Life of a Pioneer*, Salt Lake City, 1900.

Burnett, Peter H., *Recollections and Opinions of an Old Pioneer*, New York, 1880.

Clayton, William, *Journal*, Salt Lake City, 1921.

Cornaby, Hannah, *Autobiography and Poems*, Salt Lake City, 1881.

Egan, Howard, *Pioneering in the West*, Richmond, Utah, 1917.

Golden, F. A., (in collaboration with T. A. Bailey and J. L. Smith), *The March of the Mormon Battalion to California: Taken from the Journal of Henry Standage*, New York, 1928.

Harris, Sarah H., (Wife of Broughton D. Harris, Secretary and Treasurer of Utah, 1851), *An Unwritten Chapter of Salt Lake*, New York, 1901.

Hemenway, Charles W., *Memoirs of My Day In and Out of Mormondom*, Salt Lake City, 1887.

Lee, John D., *Journals* (1846-47 and 1859), edited by Charles Kelley, Salt Lake City, 1938.

Lee, John D., *Mormonism Unveiled*, St. Louis, Missouri, 1881.

Little, James O., *From Kirtland to Salt Lake City*, Salt Lake City, 1890.

Pratt, Parley Parker, *Autobiography*, Chicago, 1874.

Reynolds, John, *My Own Times*, Belleville, Illinois, 1855.

Tyler, Daniel, *A Concise History of the Mormon Battalion in the Mexican War*, Salt Lake City, 1881.

Young, Ann Eliza, *Life in Mormon Bondage*, Philadelphia, 1908.

Young, John R., *Memories of John R. Young, Utah Pioneer* (1847), Salt Lake City, Utah, 1920.

G. Official Works of Church of Jesus Christ of Latter Day Saints

The Book of Doctrine and Covenants, Salt Lake City, 1891.

Discourses of Brigham Young, Selected and arranged by John A. Widtsoe, Salt Lake City, 1926.

Journal of Discourses, by Brigham Young, His Two Counsellors, the Twelve Apostles, and Others, 25 v. London and Liverpool, 1854-1855.

History of the Church of Jesus Christ of Latter Day Saints—History of Joseph Smith, the Prophet, by Himself. An introduction and notes by B. H. Roberts, Salt Lake City, 1902.

Pearl of Great Price, Joseph Smith. Selections from the revelations, translations, and narrations of Joseph Smith, Salt Lake City, 1891.

H. Biographies

Beardsley, H. M., *Joseph Smith and His Mormon Empire*, New York, 1931.

Cowley, M. F., ed., *History of Life and Labors of Wilford Woodruff*, Salt Lake City, 1909.

Evans, J. H., *Joseph Smith*, New York, 1933;

Charles Coulson Rich, New York, 1936.

Gates, Susa Young and Leah D. Widtsoe, *Brigham Young,* New York, 1930.

Gates, Susa Young, *Memorial to Elizabeth Claridge McCune,* Salt Lake City, 1924.

Jensen, Andrew, *Latter Day Saints' Biographical Encyclopedia,* Salt Lake City, 1901.

Nibley, Preston, *Brigham Young,* Salt Lake City, 1936.

Riegel, O. W., *Crown of Glory, The Life of James J. Strang,* New Haven, 1935 (See also for a life of Strang and his experiences, Quaife, M. J., *The Kingdom of St. James,* New Haven, 1930).

Riley, I. Woodbridge, *The Founder of Mormonism, A Psychological Study of Joseph Smith, Jr.,* London, 1903.

Roberts, B. H., *Life of John Taylor,* Salt Lake City, 1892.

Smith, Mrs. E. R., *Biography, Lorenzo Snow,* Salt Lake City, 1884.

Stanley, Reva, *The Archer of Paradise, A Biography of Parley P. Pratt,* Caldwell, Idaho, 1937.

Tanner, J. M., *Biographical Sketch of J. R. Murdock,* Salt Lake City, 1909.

Tullidge, E. W., *Brigham Young,* New York, 1876.

Werner, M. R., *Brigham Young,* New York, 1925.

West, T. L. R., *Richards, F. D.,* Salt Lake City, 1924.

Whitney, O. F., *Life of H. C. Kimball,* Salt Lake City, 1888.

Widtsoe, Leah, (see Susa Young Gates).

I. Other Works

Allen, E. J., *The Second United Order Among the Mormons,* New York, 1936.

Arbaugh, G. B., *Revelation in Mormonism,* Chicago, 1932.

Bancroft, H. H., *History of Utah, 1840-1887,* San Francisco, 1890.

Beard, C. A. and Mrs. M. R., *The Rise of American Civilization,* 2 v. New York, 1927.

Brough, C. H., *Irrigation in Utah,* Baltimore, 1898.

Creer, L. H., *Utah and the Nation,* Seattle, 1929.

Coman, Katherine, *Economic Beginnings of the Far West,* 2 v. New York, 1912.

Driggs, B. W., *History of Teton Valley, Idaho*, Caldwell, Idaho, 1926.

Ericksen, E. E., *The Psychological and Ethical Aspects of Mormon Group Life*, Chicago, 1922.

Fohlin, E., *Utah—Past and Present*, Salt Lake City, 1908.

Gardner, H., *History of Lehi* (Utah), Salt Lake City, 1913.

Gates, Susa Y., *History Young Ladies' Mutual Improvement Association*, Salt Lake City, 1911.

Geddes, J. A., *The United Order Among the Mormons* (Missouri phase), Salt Lake City, 1924.

Harris, F. S. and Butt, N. I., *The Fruits of Mormonism*, New York, 1925.

Hinds, W. A., *American Communities* (revised edition), Chicago, 1902.

Jensen, J. M., *History of Provo*, (Utah), published by author, 1924.

Johnson, D. C., *A Brief History of Springville, Utah, from its First Settlement, September 18, 1850, to September 18, 1900.*

Jubilee History of Latter-Day Saints' Sunday-School (1849-1899), Salt Lake City, 1900.

Kauffman, Ruth and Reginald W., *Latter-Day Saints*, London, 1912.

Lambourne, Alfred, *A Play-House*, Salt Lake City, 1914.

Lever, W. H., *History of San Pete and Emery Counties*, Ogden, 1898.

Linn, Alexander W., *The Story of the Mormons*, New York, 1902.

McClintock, J. H., *The Mormon Settlements in Arizona*, Phoenix, Arizona, 1921.

Midgeley, Joshua H., *United Order, Its Practical Accomplishments Outlined*, Salt Lake City, no date given.

Nelson, Lowry, *Escalante, A Study in Social Origins*, Provo, 1930.

Pyper, George D., *The Romance of an Old Playhouse*, Salt Lake City, 1928.

Quaife, M. J., *The Kingdom of St. James*, New Haven, 1930, (covers same ground as O. W. Riegel's, *Crown of Glory*, cf. bibliography on biographies).

Tullidge, E. W., *Northern Utah and Southern Idaho*, Salt Lake City, 1889.

Warner, J. H., *Social Cooperation Among the Mormons (Johns Hopkins University Studies*, VI) Baltimore, 1888.

Webb, R. C., *The Real Mormonism*, New York, 1916.

Whitney, C. F., *Mormon Activities*, Salt Lake City, 1913.

Young, Levi E., *Chief Episodes in the History of Utah*, Chicago, 1912.

The Founding of Utah, New York, 1923.

Zion's Cooperative Mercantile Institution, Copy of Agreement, Order, Certificate of Incorporation and By-Laws, Salt Lake City, 1870.

INDEX

Abelard, 78.
Acadia, New York, 12.
Adams, George J., 130, 132.
Africa, 126.
Alberta, Canada, 37.
Alpine, Utah, 82.
America, 11.
American Fork, Utah, attendance at
    Theological School, 82; band, 164;
    choir, 185.
Anti-Brighamite, 15.
Anti-Masonic feeling, 12.
Apostles, Twelve; authority and
    duties, 27; 55, 85, 115.
Arizona, 37, 112.
Artists, 122-125.
Bishop Atkins of Tooele, 180, 191.
Australia, 150.

Ballo's Band, Captain, 163, 164.
Bancroft, H. H., quoted, 55, 76, 105.
Bands, in early days, 161-165; use at
    services, 167; Parkman's Brass
    Band, 180; Croxall's, 183; in Utah
    and Idaho, 187; bishop's influence
    on, 191.
Baptists, 55, 199.
Barlow, James M., 132-133.
Bartholomew, Robert, 197.
Batavia, New York, 12.
Beck, Carl, 188.
Beesley, E., benefit performance, 187;
    place in church, 191; from England,
    198.
Beethoven, 161.
Bellerive, C. L., 86.
Bennett, James Gordon, 64-65.
Bennett, John C., 64.
Bernhisel, Doctor John M., 55, 105.
Bible, God's law, 52; as textbook,
    74; advocated as textbook, 84-87;
    mentioned, 102; justified use of
    music, 156.
Big Cottonwood Canyon, 132.
Book of Doctrine and Covenants,
    better economic order, 44; guide to
    Mormon theology, 51; as textbook,
    74; advocated as textbook, 84-87;

familiarity of Mormons with, 103.
Book of Mormon, origins, 14-15;
    printed at Nauvoo, 16; published
    in England, 31; presented to Queen
    Victoria, 31; God's law, 52; and
    educated people, 54; as textbook,
    74; in Deseret alphabet, 75; re-
    ferred to, 79; advocated as text-
    book, 84, 87; "The Three Witness-
    es." 93; mentioned, 102; character-
    ized, 103.
Boston, Massachusetts, 11, 138, 141,
    183.
Bowles, Samuel, editor of Springfield
    Republican, 138, 153-154.
Box Elder County, Utah, 181.
Bramwell, George, Jr., 187.
Brigham City, Utah, coöperative
    branch, 43-44; United Order, 47;
    Lorenzo Snow's work at, 55; the-
    atricals, 134-135; Lorenzo Snow in,
    143; choir at. 191.
Brook Farm, 11.
Brown, James S., 108, 109.
Bryce Canyon, 123.
Bull, Joseph, 95.
Bulwer-Lytton, 101, 132.
Burgess, William, 133.
Burton, Richard F., Mormon educa-
    tion, 71; on education, 89; book-
    stalls in Salt Lake City, 103; read-
    ing rooms. 105; attends Mormon
    service, 158.

Cahoon, William, 162.
Caine, John T., called to mission
    field, 132-133; on cost of theatre,
    137; manages theatre, 154; English
    convert. 198.
Calder, D. O., volunteers to teach
    music, 78; teaches commercial sub-
    jects, 86; edits *Deseret News*, 96;
    cultivator of musical taste, 169;
    biography, 174-178; importance in
    music, 183; on freighting costs, 185;
    organizing classes, 186; connection
    with Young, 191; request to, 193;
    native of Scotland, 198; Young's